旅游管理专业应用型本科规划教材

新编旅游交际英语

（第二版）

徐琰 编著

清华大学出版社

北京

内 容 简 介

《新编旅游交际英语（第二版）》以"吃、住、游、购、娱"一条龙的涉外旅游服务为教学内容的整体设计思路，突出训练学生在旅游服务方面的实践能力和跨文化交际能力。

本教材内容简明扼要，图文并茂，强调导学，有的放矢，不仅介绍了涉外旅游服务的常规实务和技巧，还紧密结合情景教学法，按类别编排独特的旅游文化资源，重点介绍中国最著名的自然和文化景观，如湖泊、园林、石窟、庙宇、佛塔、名山、皇宫、皇陵、博物馆和古镇等，同时也穿插介绍中西餐饮、工艺品、绘画、书法、丝绸、茶、戏剧、桑拿、按摩、针灸、武术等多角度文化和艺术内容，以典型代表为例，使学生能见微知著，融会贯通，举一反三，学以致用。此外，为适应出境旅游的需求，本教材还简要介绍了境外旅游服务，以点带面，同时倡导绿色环保旅游，促进国民文化素质的提高。

本教材既可以作为各类院校旅游或旅游管理和英语专业的基础教材、公共选修课教材，以及涉外旅游服务的培训教材，也可以作为旅游英语爱好者的兴趣读物。

本教材是 2013 年浙江省教育科学规划课题的一个重点项目成果，项目编号为 SB144。

图书在版编目（CIP）数据

新编旅游交际英语/徐琰编著．—2 版．—北京：清华大学出版社，2021.3（2024.7重印）
旅游管理专业应用型本科规划教材
ISBN 978-7-302-57580-1

Ⅰ．①新… Ⅱ．①徐… Ⅲ．①旅游−英语−口语−高等学校−教材 Ⅳ．①F59

中国版本图书馆CIP数据核字（2021）第028817号

责任编辑：邓 婷
封面设计：刘 超
版式设计：楠竹文化
责任校对：马军令
责任印制：刘海龙

出版发行：清华大学出版社
    网 址：https://www.tup.com.cn，https://www.wqxuetang.com
    地 址：北京清华大学学研大厦 A 座 邮 编：100084
    社 总 机：010-83470000 邮 购：010-62786544
    投稿与读者服务：010-62776969，c-service@tup.tsinghua.edu.cn
    质量反馈：010-62772015，zhiliang@tup.tsinghua.edu.cn
    课件下载：https://www.tup.com.cn，010-62788951-223
印 装 者：三河市君旺印务有限公司
经 销：全国新华书店
开 本：185mm×260mm 印 张：16.75 字 数：658 千字
版 次：2015 年 8 月第 1 版 2021 年 5 月第 2 版 印 次：2024 年 7 月第 4 次印刷
定 价：49.80 元

产品编号：082217-01

第二版前言

随着中国旅游业的不断发展和经济的全面增速，中国的入境旅游人次逐年上升，但与世界其他旅游大国（如法国、美国和意大利等国）相比，中国入境游在国际上的竞争力还是稍逊一筹，仍有极大的提升空间。

为了吸引更多的境外游客，中国各地特别是一些重点旅游城市和地区一直以来都在积极地探索文化旅游业，创新旅游模式，开发新的旅游产品，持续优化旅游环境。因此，为了更好地介绍日新月异的旅游基础设施和旅游产品，优化教学内容，与时俱进，我们对 2015 年 8 月出版的《新编旅游交际英语》一书进行了修订，主要体现在以下几个方面。

（1）照片全面更新，图文并茂，呈现更加直观、形象的旅游信息。

（2）更新了一些旅游数据和信息，旅游交际内容更加符合现今旅游市场的接待要求。

（3）全面梳理和更新每个单元的教学内容，力求语言更加地道、自然。

本教材依然以情景和话题为交际主线，设计多种菜单式教学模块，供不同的涉外旅游服务从业人员、涉外接待人员或旅游英语爱好者根据实际需求进行自由选择。

每个单元由预备练习（Warm-up）、教学内容（Part A/B/C）、旅游服务用语列表（Part D：Language Checklist）以及语言实训（Part E：English in Use）几个部分组成。预备练习注重导学；语言实训对重点教学内容温故而知新，重在情景模拟、问题解决，强调交际，便于学以致用；旅游服务用语列表针对正文中所涉及的重点内容、旅游景点专有名词和术语以及重难点词汇做了系统的罗列和提炼，同时还提供了大量配有中文翻译的实用句型语料，使读者一目了然，易于模仿，举一反三，快速掌握旅游交际英语技能，丰富中国传统旅游文化知识。

（4）充分利用互联网数字化多媒体技术提供学习支持服务：增加全书中所有对话以及独白的录音，并印有二维码供学习者随时扫码，学习模仿；所有语言实训练习答案也以二维码形式呈现，方便学生下载；在清华大学网络教育平台为教师提供主要内容的配套PPT，方便其备课和教学使用。

笔者全面负责教材中的教学活动设计和教学内容的修订工作；中国美术学院英语副教授兼英语导游任汶参与其中第三单元和第四单元的修订工作；现旅居德国的美国语言专家、欧洲著名英语教师培训师 Linda Gallasch 博士担任语言顾问，审阅全稿；象山假日皇冠酒店餐饮总监 Robbie Kelder 担任西方美食顾问。教材中部分照片由笔者拍摄，中国传媒大学学生常量提供故宫照片两张，浙江开放大学姚宗顺提供西湖照片两张，杭州蝶来望湖酒店公关部鲍淑君提供酒店照片四张，其余照片均来自摄图网。授予肖像权的有徐可歆、袁野、任汶、赵雯婷、李善政夫妇、Werner Hutterer 夫妇、Jan Hutterer、Robbie Kielder、Samuel Pfaff 教授及其家人。浙江开放大学杨堤负责录音合成和剪辑工作。

此外，为了真正体现跨文化旅游交际英语的特色，录制音频时，在杭州市旅游协会和杭州市金牌导游联合工作室何亭的热心引荐和大力支持下，我们诚邀一些杭州市金牌英语导游及资深英语导游本色出演。同时，我们也特邀国内外语言专家以及国外餐饮总监、资深领队、国外职业配音师等国际友人表演各类角色。具体名单如下：

中方录制人员：澳大利亚昆士兰大学策略传播专业研究生徐可歆，浙江开放大学副教授兼英语导游徐琰，杭州市金牌英语导游金东昇、李德煜和张杰，美国瓦尔普莱索大学孔子学院（Confucius Institute at Valparaiso University）中方院长及旅游翻译专家刘建刚（博士）教授，上海远通总经理（原杭州市优秀英语导游）孙旭东，浙江育英职业技术学院副教授兼英语导游葛秀华，中国政法大学外事接待处常乐，北京外国语学院毕业生童爱云，原浙江省中国旅行社集团有限公司出境领队土枭虬。

外方录制人员：美国语言专家 Linda Gallasch 博士、象山假日皇冠酒店餐饮总监 Robbie Kelder、德国基尔霍夫咨询股份有限公司（Die Kirchhoff Consult AG）资深咨询师 Jan Hutterer、德国石荷州成人教育协会原会长及资深境外游学领队 Werner Hutterer 及其夫人 Christel、英国开放大学学习技术和交际专家 Agnes Kululska Hulme 教授、美国资深教师兼教材编著者和教师培训师 Vicki Hollett、杭州汉普森英语培训机构英国籍老师豆豆、美国职业配音师 Mathew Paul Pietri 和 Uzair Mir、加拿大职业配音师 Carol Harris 和 Maliha Khalid、突尼斯职业配音师 Hanna Thaalbi、澳大利亚职业配音师 Spyro Kouvaras。

鉴于中国旅游业的持续发展，旅游基础设施日新月异，旅游产品层出不穷，相关的一些旅游数据和旅游产品信息需要不断地更新。但是万变不离其宗，中国的旅游文化精髓是不变的，一些基本的语言交际内核也是不变的。希望广大学习者可以灵活运用教材中的语言文化素材和交际模式，有的放矢，推陈出新，提高跨文化交际能力，成功地将具有中国特色的旅游文化推广至全世界。

最后，衷心感谢所有参与本教材修订工作的嘉宾，也特别感谢清华大学出版社编辑团队的大力帮助和辛勤付出。由于水平有限，书中若有疏漏之处，敬请各位读者指正。

徐 琰

2020 年 12 月

第一版前言

《新编旅游交际英语》旨在培养学生在从事接待、导游、领队、酒店服务和管理等涉外旅游服务时综合应用英语语言的交际能力，突出训练其旅游服务的实践能力，以达到从事一般旅游业或涉外接待活动所需的跨文化交际水平，并能通过旅游服务行业平台，结合地域旅游文化特色，简明扼要地把中国的名胜古迹和博大精深的文化介绍给国外游客或外宾，以提升地域旅游产品在国外的知名度，从而加快中国旅游走向国际的步伐。

《新编旅游交际英语》对"吃、住、游、购、娱"一条龙的涉外商务交际旅游服务进行了整体设计。本书的教学内容着重于如何提高中国旅游从业人员或涉外接待人员对外宾的服务质量和跨文化交际能力，既针对旅游服务行业的特点和各类学生的实际语言水平，化繁为简，主要介绍涉外旅游服务的常规实务，又兼顾学员高层次的学习需求，紧密结合情景教学和文化灌输，基于地域性的旅游文化资源，全方位介绍具有中国特色的旅游文化。前者指的是与涉外接待、导游、领队、酒店服务和管理人员等有关的一般旅游服务工作流程，后者指的是基于浙江特别是杭州的各种旅游文化资源，按类编排，简要介绍中国最著名的自然和文化景观（湖泊、园林、石窟、庙宇、佛塔、名山、皇宫、皇陵、孔庙、博物馆和古镇等），同时也穿插介绍主要的中西式菜肴和宴会特点、工艺品、绘画、书法、丝绸、茶、戏剧、桑拿、按摩、针灸、武术和民间排舞等文化内容。为了进一步拓展学生的知识面，本书最后还增加了境外旅游服务的内容，希望能借此抛砖引玉，以点带面，以应对日益增多的境外旅游服务需求。更为重要的是，本书还积极倡导文明旅游，注重环保，希望大家做有责任心的旅游者，以提高中国游客的整体素质。

本书图文并茂，以情景和话题为交际主线，设计多种菜单式教学模块，供不同的涉外旅游服务从业人员、涉外接待人员或旅游英语爱好者根据实际需求进行自由选择。每个模块均设有课前教学启动的问题或练习，以及强调情景模拟和注重解决问题的任务驱动型或功能化的课后练习，强调交际，注重导学。此外，本书还附有参考答案，适合自学。

本书分五大教学模块，共十三个单元：接送服务（第一、二单元：接站服务和陪同送客）；酒店和餐饮服务（第三至第六单元：酒店服务、餐馆服务、中式菜肴和宴会服务）；文化景观介绍（第七至第九单元：湖泊、园林和石窟，庙宇、佛塔和名山，皇宫、皇陵和孔庙）；购物、休闲娱乐服务（第十至第十二单元：礼品购物、休闲娱乐和养生活动）；境外旅游服务（第十三单元：西方主要旅游名胜和休闲娱乐活动）。

由于本书是按菜单式教学模块编排，具体教学中，教师可根据学生的实际水平和兴趣爱好选择教学内容并依此进行考核。例如，偏好导游工作的学习者可着重选学"接送服务""酒店和餐饮服务""文化景观介绍""购物、休闲娱乐服务""境外旅游服务"等一系列导游服务内容。但为了教学内容的连贯性，模块一中的第二单元"陪同送客"可放在最后教学。对意向从事酒店餐饮服务的学习者来说，模块三"酒店和餐饮服务"则是必学内容，也是重点考核内容。

本书编写人员的具体分工如下：主编徐琰，负责全书的教学设计和统稿工作，编写了第一、三、七、八、九和十一单元；副主编夏倩，协助统稿工作，编写了第十、十二和十三单元；姬莹编写了第六单元，胡旭霞编写了第五单元，王爱编写了第二单元，王雁君编写了第四单元。

在本书的编写过程中，许多朋友给予了很大的帮助并提出了宝贵的修改意见，如加拿大英属哥伦比亚大学（University of British Columbia）教授及独立制片人 Karin Lee 和其家人，特别是 Naya Tsang、德国职业领队 Werner Hutterer 夫妇、中国计量学院陈红博士和浙江广播电视大学李更春博士等。另外，陈仕云编辑为本书做了大量的工作。本书作者在此一并表示衷心的感谢。

由于作者水平有限，虽然竭尽全力，在数百页文字中仍无法穷尽广博的中国旅游文化内容，同时难免会产生一些缺失错漏，恳请各位读者、教师同仁不吝赐教和指正。

编　者

2015 年 4 月

目　录

模块三　文化景观介绍

模块四 购物、休闲娱乐服务

模块五 境外旅游服务

参考文献/253

Contents

Module I Pick-up and Drop-off Service

Module II Hotel and Restaurant Services

Module III   Introduction to Cultural Sites

Module IV   Services for Shopping, Leisure and Entertainment Activities

Module V   Outbound Travel Service

Module I
Pick-up and Drop-off Service

Unit 1　Meeting the Guests

Warm-up

1. Do you know the six ancient capital cities in China? Match the names with the pictures. Work with your partner and compare answers.

1) _____　　2) _____　　3) _____

4) _____　　5) _____　　6) _____

2. How can you be sure you are meeting the right tourist group at the airport?
3. What points should be included in your welcome talk? Make a list of ideas and compare with another student.

Part A　Meeting the Tourists and Business Guests

Dialogue 1

Situation: *Chen Yan, a tour guide from Hangzhou CTS (Hangzhou China Travel Service), meets Joe Simpson, the tour leader of an American tour group, at Xiaoshan International Airport (萧山国际机场) one evening.*

Questions for comprehension and discussion:

★ What does Chen Yan say to Joe Simpson first?

★ How do they introduce themselves and greet each other?

★ What does she confirm after the greeting?

★ How does she greet the group?

Chen Yan: Excuse me, are you Mr Joe Simpson from the Pacific Travel Agency?

Joe Simpson: Yes, I am.

Chen Yan: Great! Glad to meet you, Mr Simpson. I'm your local guide Chen Yan. Chen is my surname.

Joe Simpson: Hello, Ms Chen. Glad to meet you, too. You can just call me Joe. We're sorry that the flight was delayed. Have you been waiting for a long time?

Chen Yan: Not too long, just about ten minutes. Well, just call me Chen Yan, which is the Chinese way.

Joe Simpson: OK, Chen Yan.

Chen Yan: Right. Well, is everyone in your group here now?

Joe Simpson: Yes, they are.

Chen Yan: There are 16 people in your group, is that right?

Joe Simpson: Yes, exactly, including me.

Chen Yan: Hello, good evening, everyone. Welcome to Hangzhou. I hope you had a pleasant flight. Do you have all your luggage? Shall we go straight to the hotel now? Our coach is in the parking lot. This way, please.

Dialogue 2

Situation: *Li Binhong, a tour guide from Hangzhou CITS (China International Travel Service, 杭州国际旅行社), meets Emily Jason, the tour leader of a Canadian group, at Xiaoshan International Airport one afternoon.*

Questions for comprehension and discussion:

★ Who is Li Binhong supposed to meet?

★ Does she meet the right person?

★ How do they introduce themselves and greet each other?

★ What does she confirm after the greeting?

★ What would you do to avoid picking up a wrong group if you were the guide?

Li Binhong: Excuse me, madam, are you from Canada?

Emily Jason: Yes, I am. Are you the tour guide from Hangzhou CITS?

Li Binhong: Yes. I'm Li Binhong. Li is my family name, and Binhong is my first name. You may call me Binhong if you like. I also have an English name, Susan. Either of the names will do.

Emily Jason: I'll try your Chinese name, Binhong. Is that right?

Li Binhong: Yes, good. So you must be Ms Lina Woods.

Emily Jason: Oh no, I'm sorry. Lina Woods became sick just before we left for China.

Li Binhong: Oh, I'm sorry to hear that.

Emily Jason: That's all right. I'm replacing her as the tour leader for this group. I'm Emily Jason. Nice to meet you, you can call me Emily.

Li Binhong: Nice to meet you too, Emily.

Emily Jason: I'm sorry we didn't have time to tell you about the tour leader replacement. As you know, the time was really tight, and there was little time left due to the **emergency** (紧急突发事件).

Li Binhong: Oh, don't worry about it! I understand. It's an emergency, isn't it? I'll let our director know the change as soon as possible.

Emily Jason: Thank you.

Li Binhong: You're welcome. So is this your group?

Emily Jason: Yes, it is. We have 12 people plus me.

Li Binhong: Good. Hello and good afternoon, everyone! Welcome to Hangzhou. Are you ready to leave now? Follow me, please.

Dialogue 3

Situation: *Jin Bing works for a textile company in China. Jin Bing is meeting an American visitor Ken Kailer at the railway station. He waits for him and holds up a large name card.*

Questions for comprehension and discussion:

★ What is Ken's concern?

★ If you were Jin Bing, what would you do then?

Ken Kailer: Hello, I'm the one you are looking for. My name is Ken Kailer.

Jin Bing: Oh, hi, Mr Kailer. Glad to meet you. I'm Jin Bing from Junying Textile Company (俊英纺织品公司). Jin is my surname. You can call me Jin Bing as my colleagues do.

Ken Kailer: Fine, Jin Bing, nice to meet you too. By the way, you can call me Ken. Now where are we heading?

Jin Bing: Since you've just arrived, shall we first go directly to your hotel so that you can put your luggage in the room, and then go to our company to meet our general manager Mr Wang? He's looking forward to seeing you soon. But he is in a meeting now and won't be free until 3:30 this afternoon.

Ken Kailer: Good. How long will it take us to go to the hotel then? Do we have enough time?

Jin Bing: It's 1:30 now. The hotel is not far away from here, only 30 minutes by car from the station. Our company is near the hotel, just ten minutes walk away.

Ken Kailer: Perfect.

Jin Bing: Let's go then. Our driver is waiting for us outside.

Part B   A Welcome Talk

Situation: *After getting on the coach, the tour guide Chen Yan gives a welcome talk to the tourists.*

Questions for comprehension and discussion:

★ How does Chen Yan greet and welcome the tourists on the coach?

★ What does she say when the coach starts to leave for the hotel?

★ What does she say to the tourists on the way to the hotel?

★ What does she say when the coach is near the hotel?

★ If you were Chen Yan, what would you say to the tourists?

Hello, ladies and gentlemen, good evening! I'm Chen Yan, your local guide from Hangzhou China Travel Service, and this is our driver, Mr Li Yihua. Mr Li is a very responsible driver with over 15 years of driving experience. We're glad to meet you all here in Hangzhou. Now on behalf of Hangzhou China Travel Service (Hangzhou CTS), I'd like to extend a warm welcome to you all. Welcome to Hangzhou, the paradise city in China with three fascinating **world heritage sites** (世界遗产地) which we're very proud of. Do you know what they are? First is the **West Lake Cultural Landscape of Hangzhou** (杭州西湖文化景观), the second is the **Grand Canal** (大运河), and the third is **Liangzhu Culture** (良渚文化). Besides, our city successfully held the **G20 Summit** (20 国峰会) in 2016 and will hold the **19th Asian Games** (第 19 届亚运会) in 2022. It's also one of the most livable cities in China. So you see, you're in the right place now, aren't you?

As Confucius, a great ancient thinker and educator, once said, "Isn't it delightful to have friends coming from afar? " Mr Li and I will do our best to make your trip here pleasant and memorable. If you have any suggestions or problems, please feel free to let us know, for we're always at your service. My mobile phone number is 19537843511, and the plate number of our coach is A4528. I hope you'll note them down and keep them in mind during your visit here.

It's now 20:30 Beijing standard time. Make sure to reset your watch. We're on the way southwest to our hotel, **Deefly Lakeview Hotel** (蝶来望湖宾馆), a very modern hotel at an ideal location in the downtown area, only a one-minute walk to West Lake. The coach ride to your hotel will take about 50 minutes. I'd like to take this opportunity to talk about our city.

Hangzhou, the capital city of Zhejiang Province in the south of the **Yangtze River Delta** (长江三角洲), is not only the political, economic and cultural center of the province but also a well-known tourist city. As it is located in the lower reaches of the Qiantang River or Qianjiang (钱塘江/钱江) approximately 180 kilometers southwest of Shanghai — an easy train ride away, it's known as the "back garden of Shanghai" by most Chinese people. It's also the southern **end** (终点站) of the 1,794 km-long **Beijing-Hangzhou Grand Canal** (京杭大运河), one of the two greatest man-made projects in ancient China (the other is the Great Wall as you most likely know).

Like many other cities in China, Hangzhou has been developing into a big city. The city proper covers 8,000 square kilometers with a population of over 8 million in 2019. In other words, it's 10 times larger than New York city but with nearly the same population. **The metropolitan area** (大杭州) is even larger. It includes not only 10 **boroughs** (行政区) but 1 city at county level and 2 counties as well with a total area of 16,596 square kilometers and over 10 million people.

However, broadly speaking, central Hangzhou is divided into four areas in terms of Qiantang River, the Grand Canal and **Xixi Wetland** (西溪湿地) as well as West Lake. That's the **CBD of Qianjiang (Qiangtang River) New Town** (钱江新城核心区) along Qiantang River in the east; the canal area in the north along the Grand Canal including the downtown area; the world-renowned West Lake Cultural Landscape around West Lake in the south; the Xixi Wetland Area in the west including the **Town of Future Science and Technology** (未来科技城) and the world famous **Alibaba Group** (阿里巴巴集团).

Hangzhou lies in a sub-tropical zone with four distinctive seasons. The yearly average temperature is about 17 degrees Celsius with the highest around 40 degrees in summer and the lowest about 6 degrees below zero in winter. But nowadays, due to global warming and extreme weather, the weather here in Hangzhou can sometimes be a little strange.

Located at about 30° north latitude, Hangzhou enjoys a favorable climate, fertile land and rich resources. The 30° north latitude in the world runs through some world wonders such as the **Great Pyramid** (金字塔) in Egypt, ancient **Maya** (玛雅) region, **Himalaya Mountains** (喜马拉雅山), and some great rivers like the **Nile** (尼罗河), the **Mississippi River** (密西西比河), the Changjiang River or Yangtze River in China, etc. Hangzhou has been renowned as "the home of silk and tea" and is considered to be a "paradise for tourists".

Well, do you know how the name of this city Hangzhou came into being? In ancient times, much of the area of Hangzhou was covered with water. People needed boats to go from one place to another. According to **legend** (传说), **Yu the Great** (大禹) once came here. Yu was the founder of the first dynasty of China, the **Xia Dynasty** (夏朝, 2070 – 1600 BC). He successfully **harnessed** (治理) China's river system and controlled the floods. Hence Hangzhou's original name, **Yu Hang** (禹杭), meaning "a land where Yu's boat landed". A Temple has been dedicated to Yu the Great, and his tomb was built in Shaoxing, a city not far from Hangzhou.

Historically speaking, the area of Hangzhou is one of the **cradles of Chinese civilization** (华夏文明发祥地) especially with its prosperous **Liangzhu Culture** (良渚文化) **dating back** (回溯) over 5,000 years. During that period, jade carving and silk production were already popular there, as China was the first producer of silk in the world.

The city of Hangzhou has a history of over 2,200 years; that is, its recorded history can be **traced back to** (追溯到) the Qin Dynasty (221 – 206 BC), as it was first built as Qiantang

County and was named after the river as Qiantang in 221 BC. Hangzhou did not take its present name, which means a land **accessible** (可进入的) only by boat, until 589 in the Sui Dynasty.

During the Sui Dynasty (581－618), major construction on the southern section of the Grand Canal was carried out, turning it into a prosperous commercial city then. The Grand Canal, which eventually linked Hangzhou to Beijing, was noted as one of the world's longest **artificial waterways** (人工河道) forming one of the country's most important **economic arteries** (经济动脉).

Hangzhou has been regarded as one of China's six ancient capitals, because it served as the capital of both the powerful **Wuyue Kingdom** (吴越国) in the 10th century and the Southern Song Dynasty (1127–1279). A **Venetian merchant** (威尼斯商人), **Marco Polo** (马可·波罗, 1254–1324) visited Hangzhou in around 1280 and wrote that it was "without doubt the finest and noblest city in the world". He was also **fascinated** (着迷) by the **luxurious** (华丽的) silk available in the city at that time.

Hangzhou silk was not only chosen as a **tribute** (贡品) to the imperial rulers but also exported overseas. Marco Polo's description of Hangzhou made both the city and the silk well-known worldwide. Just imagine, some 800 years ago, how these beautiful silks, fine soft **satins** (绸缎) and fantastic **brocades** (锦缎) were carried to European countries via the famous **Silk Road** (丝绸之路) and caught the fancy of westerners.

OK, that was a brief history of Hangzhou. Now very soon we'll come to the largest river in

this province. Please look to the front and you'll be able to see a big bridge over the Qiantang River. Presently there are 10 bridges over the river, it's the third one. It's 5,700 meters long and was completed in 1997. The river is known for its **spectacular** (壮观的) **tidal bore** (潮涌). During the Mid-autumn Festival every year, it attracts thousands of people from near and far including tourists, who come to view this **awesome** (令人惊叹的) natural phenomenon and experience the **mighty** (强大的) power of nature. The waves surge from the sea into the river going upstream all the way to the end of the lower reaches of the river.

Now, let's look to the right. You can have a good view of modern Hangzhou skyline dominated by the skyscrapers. That's the CBD of Qianjiang New Town featuring the **iconic architecture** (标志性建筑) such as the golden globe-like Hangzhou International Convention Center (HICC, 杭州国际会议中心), the **crescent-like** (新月) Hangzhou Grand Theater (HGT, 杭州大剧院), Hangzhou Civic Center (HCC, 杭州市民中

心), Zhejiang Fortune and Finance Center (浙江财富金融中心) as well as the so-called **City Balcony** (城市阳台) which extends 322 meters long and about 80 meters wide over the river. The International Convention Center resembles the rising sun, and the Grand Theatre looks like **a curved moon** (一弯月亮), the **imposing** (壮观的) **architectural complex** (建筑群), designed by the world famous **Uruguayan architect** (乌拉圭建筑师) Carlos Ott (卡洛斯·奥特), symbolizing the past and future of our city, **manifesting** (表明) the new **era of Qiangjiang** (钱江时代) in contrast to the **epoch of West Lake** (西湖时代).

Now we have entered the downtown area, the Uptown borough (上城区) in particular. It's home to the **remains** (遗址) of **imperial palace of the Southern Song Dynasty** (南宋皇城). This is **Jiefang Road** (解放路) running from east directly to West Lake. It's one of the busiest streets, offering great shopping, dining and comfortable hotels. You can also see some metro stations. Up to now, 6 metro lines have already been used in the city. By the way, in order to meet the needs of the 19th Asian Games, a **backbone network** (主干网络) of **urban rail transit** (城市轨道交通) with a total length of 516 km will have been completed including 10 metro lines, one express line and two intercity lines by 2022. It's estimated that more metro lines, express lines or intercity lines will be planned as the entire city continues to grow.

Well, we are about to enter the **West Lake Tunnel** (西湖隧道). It's over 1,300 meters long and was completed in 2003. That means we are approaching West Lake soon. West Lake and its surrounding hills make up the **West Lake Cultural Landscape of Hangzhou** (西湖文化景观)  which has been on the list of **UNESCO World Heritage Sites** (联合国教科文组织世界遗产地) since 2011. It covers an area of over 33 square kilometers featuring fascinating scenery, dozens of **renowned** (著名的) temples and pagodas as well as 3 famous **causeways** (堤) and 3 **artificial islands** (人工岛). I bet you can't wait, right?

Our hotel is quite near now, just about five minutes away. If you're a night-life lover, you can take a walk down the pedestrian streets nearby or along the lake after checking in. If we had arrived a bit earlier, you might have the chance to enjoy the fascinating **musical fountain** (音乐喷泉) on West Lake about 800 meters away. Anyway, you won't miss it tomorrow evening. It starts at 7 pm and 8 pm every evening and lasts for 15 minutes.

Since we'll be having a boat tour of West Lake at 9:30 tomorrow morning, we'll meet in the hotel lobby at 9:00 tomorrow. And shall we set the

morning call for 7:30 am? Great, so let's meet at 9:00 am tomorrow in the lobby. And we do hope you'll have a very pleasant stay here in Hangzhou. Here is our hotel. Please double check your baggage and follow me.

Part C Tips on Giving a Welcome Talk

Questions for comprehension and discussion:

★ Brainstorm any tips on how to give a welcome talk.

★ On the way to the hotel, what may most of the tourists expect to hear?

★ What do you think a welcome talk should be like?

On the way to the hotel, most of the tourists will be quite excited to hear about the new place, and expect to be told about what they will see. Therefore, a welcome talk made by a tour guide is very important. It should be warm, thoughtful and exciting.

In the welcome talk, as a tour guide, you should first extend a warm welcome to the tourists who have arrived. Your guests will be very happy and feel at home to hear the warmest greeting from you, their local guide in a strange country. Second, you should introduce yourself, the driver and the tour operator for whom you work. In the meantime, you should assure the tourists that your team will do your best to offer them satisfactory service. Then you should tell them about the location and the facilities of the hotel. After arriving at a new place, most tourists would like to know exactly where they are, and what their hotel will be like. After that, if time **permits** (允许), you should give a brief introduction to the city or town, such as the population, climate, customs and history. Although many tourists have already read some information about the tourist destinations before the tour, they would still like to learn more specific information from the local guide. Interesting facts and information are always welcome. Last but not least, you should wish the tourists a good time during their stay, and confirm the following day's activities as well as the meeting time and place. Besides, you should also remind the tourists to reset their watches according to the local time, remember the plate number of the coach and your phone number as well.

In short, you should remember the following elements when giving a good welcome talk:

☆ extend a warm welcome to the tourists;

☆ introduce your team on behalf of the tour operator;

☆ inform the tourists of the local time, offering your contact number;

☆ give a brief introduction to the city, town or the place;

☆ confirm the meeting time and place for the next day's activities;

☆ offer them best wishes for a pleasant trip.

Part D   Language Checklist

A. Vocabulary

tour operator 旅行社 travel agency/service 旅行社 CTS (China Travel Service)/ CITS (China International Travel Service)中国旅行社/中国国际旅行社	scenic spot 景点 tourist attraction 旅游胜地 holiday resort 度假胜地 historic site 历史古迹 national nature reserve 国家自然保护区 borough/administrative region 行政区域	ancient capital 古都 metropolis/megacity 大都市 metropolitan area 大都市区
Liangzhu Culture 良渚文化 cradles of Chinese civilization 华夏文明发祥地 Silk Road/Route 丝绸之路	Beijing-Hangzhou Grand Canal 京杭大运河 Yangtze River Delta 长江三角洲 Qiantang Tidal Bore 钱塘潮	date back/trace back 回溯 be traced back to 可追溯到
legend 传说 Yu the Great 大禹，夏禹	Marco Polo 马可·波罗 Venetian merchant 威尼斯商人	tribute 贡品

B. Key Patterns

Inquiring About Identity 询问身份	• Excuse me, are you Mr Joe Simpson from the Pacific Travel Agency? • Excuse me, are you the tour leader of the group?
Introducing Yourself and Others 自我介绍和团队介绍	• May I introduce myself? • First, let me introduce myself. My name is…/I'm …, you can just call me… • I'm your local guide Fang Lin from China International Travel Service. • I'd like to introduce our driver, Mr Li Bing. He has been working as a professional driver for at least 10 years. • May we introduce ourselves? This is our driver, Mr Chen. He's a responsible driver with over 15 years of driving experience.
Greetings 问候	• Nice/Pleased to meet you./I'm pleased to meet you all. • It's great to meet all of you here today.
Welcoming 欢迎	• On behalf of …, I'd like to extend a warm welcome to all of you. • I am glad to welcome you all! • Welcome to Beijing/Shanghai/Hangzhou/…
Adjusting the Time 调整当地时间	• It's 14:20 Beijing standard time. Please reset your watch. • Make sure/Remember to reset your watch. 请调整一下时间。 • You may reset your watch./You may adjust the time. 你们可以调整一下时间。
Introductory Remarks 介绍城镇概况的引语	• First of all, I'd like to give you a brief introduction to our city. • Would you like me to offer you some general information about our city? • Do you know how the name of our city came into being?
Providing General Information 介绍城镇的宏观信息	• Hangzhou is the capital of Zhejiang Province. • Lhasa is the capital of Tibet Autonomous Region. 拉萨是西藏自治区的首府。 • Hangzhou has been well-known as "the home of silk and tea". 杭州素有"丝茶之乡"的美誉。

Providing General Information 介绍城镇的宏观信息	• The city boasts numerous tourist attractions, such as well-known scenic spots, historic sites, national nature reserve, and national tourist holiday resort. 该城市有很多旅游胜地，比如著名的风景区、历史古迹、国家自然保护区以及国家旅游度假区。 • Beijing/Shanghai is a world famous metropolis (大都市). • Shanghai is one of the largest and most dynamic cities in China. 上海是中国最大且最有活力的城市之一。 • Wuhan is the center of Hubei Province in politics, economy, culture and information. 武汉是湖北省的政治、经济、文化和信息中心。 • Guangzhou is an affluent, bustling city with a handful interesting sights. 广州是一个富裕、繁华的城市，有很多有趣的景点。
Talking about Population and Area 介绍城镇人口及面积	• The city covers an area of 25,000 square kilometers. 这座城市的总面积为 2.5 万平方千米。 • There are over 24 million people in Shanghai. 上海有 2,400 多万人口。 • The city proper of Hangzhou had a population of over 8 million in 2019. 2019 年，杭州城区的人口超 800 万。 • It's a small town with a population of 12,000. 这是一个有着 1.2 万人口的小镇。 • Beijing, the capital of China, has over 21 million people. 中国首都北京的人口超 2,100 万。 • Beijing's total population topped 21.7 million in 2017. 2017 年，北京总人口达到 2,170 万。
Talking about the Location 介绍城镇的地理位置	• Hangzhou is located in the lower reaches of the Qiantang River approximately 180 kilometers southwest of Shanghai — an easy train ride away. 杭州位于钱塘江下游区域，在上海西南方向约 180 千米处，坐火车很方便到达。 • Beijing is situated at the northern tip of the North China Plain. 北京位于华北平原的北端。 • Lying in the Yangtze River Delta in eastern China, Shanghai sits at the mouth of the Yangtze River in the central coast. 上海位于中国东部长江三角洲中部沿海的长江入海口处。 • Zhejiang borders Anhui to the northwest, Jiangxi to the west. 浙江省西北接安徽省，西接江西省。 • Zhejiang borders Jiangsu and the metropolis Shanghai to the north. 浙江与江苏接壤，北接上海。 • Shanghai is bordered by Jiangsu to the northwest and Zhejiang to the southwest. • Xi'an lies on the Guanzhong Plain in central China. 西安位于中国中部的关中平原。
Talking About Historic Sites 介绍历史古迹	• Beijing has a history of 3,000 years. 北京有着 3,000 年的历史。 • Hangzhou's history spans over 2,200 years. 杭州有 2,200 多年的历史。 • This town is as old as over 1,500 years. 该小镇有 1,500 多年的历史。 • The small town is more than 1,500 years old. 这个小镇有 1,500 多年的历史。 • Its recorded history can be traced back to the Qin Dynasty (221–206 BC). 其有记载的历史可以追溯到秦朝（公元前 221 年–公元前 206 年）。 • Its history dates back 500 years. 其历史可追溯到 500 年前。 • There are many places of historic interest here. 这里有很多历史古迹。 • Rich in relics and natural resources, the city has a long history. 这座城市历史悠久，自然资源丰富，文物古迹众多。

On-the-way Introduction 介绍沿途景观	<ul><li>Please look to the front/right/left.</li><li>We are coming to the largest river in the province.</li><li>The river is best known for its spectacular tidal bore.</li><li>Now we have entered the downtown area.</li><li>It's home to the imperial palace of the Southern Song Dynasty. 这里曾是南宋皇城所在地。</li></ul>
Travel Arrangement （到达酒店前的）旅游安排事宜	<ul><li>Since we'll have a boat tour of West Lake at 9:30 tomorrow morning, is it possible for us to meet together in the hotel lobby at 9:00 tomorrow?</li><li>Shall we set the morning-call at 7:30 am tomorrow?</li></ul>

Part E　English in Use

I. Reading Comprehension

Task 1: Choose the best answer to complete each sentence below.

1. Excuse me, are you the _____ leader of the group from Canada?
   A. traveled　　　　B. main　　　　　C. tour　　　　　D. major

2. _____ behalf of Zhejiang Strait International Travel Service, I'd like to extend a warm welcome to you all.
   A. In　　　　　　B. On　　　　　　C. For　　　　　D. To

3. Suzhou _____ in a sub-tropical zone with four seasons.
   A. situates　　　　B. locates　　　　C. be situated　　D. lies

4. May I _____ myself?
   A. name　　　　　B. tell　　　　　C. introduce　　　D. say

5. It's 9:30 am Beijing standard time. Please _____ the time.
   A. adjusted　　　　B. readjusts　　　C. resets　　　　D. reset

6. I'd like to give you a _____ introduction to our city.
   A. shorter　　　　B. brief　　　　　C. good　　　　　D. great

7. Do you know how the name of our city _____ into being?
   A. came　　　　　B. come　　　　　C. enter　　　　　D. is coming

8. The history of Christmas _____ back over 4,000 years.
   A. was dated　　　B. traced back　　C. dating　　　　D. dates

9. If you have any problems, please _____ to let us know.
   A. feel free　　　　B. do　　　　　　C. remembered　　D. not forget

10. Longjing Green Tea was not only chosen as a _____ to the imperial rulers but also exported overseas.
    A. gift　　　　　B. good　　　　　C. treasure　　　D. tribute

Task 2: Answer the questions concerning the welcome talk given by Chen Yan in Part B.

1. How large is the city of Hangzhou and the Hangzhou metropolitan area? What's the population in 2019?

2. What's Hangzhou's original name? How did it come into being?

3. Who was Marco Polo? When did he first visit Hangzhou? What did he think of Hangzhou then?

4. When was Liangzhu culture prosperous?

5. What's the Qiantang River famous for? When would thousands of people far and near come to watch the natural phenomenon?

Task 3: Decide whether each of the following statements is True or False according to the passage about a good welcome talk in Part C.

1. A welcome talk should be warm, considerate and exciting. (　　)

2. A tour guide should first welcome the tourists who have arrived but greet them later. (　　)

3. After making a self-introduction, the tour guide should assure the tourists that their team will make every effort to make their stay pleasant. (　　)

4. The tour guide should tell the tourists some general information about the city as well as the location and the facilities of the hotel. (　　)

5. The tour guide should remind the tourists to reset their watches now. (　　)

II. Translation

Task 4: Translate the following sentences into English.

1. 很高兴认识你，约翰逊先生，我是你们的地陪，方冰。

2. 请问，您是来自纽约环球旅行社（New York Global Travel Agency）的史密斯先生吗？

3. 我们城市的总面积约为 1.6 万平方公里。

4. 2019 年，杭州城区的人口有 800 多万。

5. 正如孔子所说："有朋自远方来，不亦乐乎？"我们将竭诚使你们在这里的旅行愉快且难以忘怀。

6. 杭州是著名的丝绸之府、茶叶之乡。

7. 这座小镇有 1,200 多年的历史。

8. 上海西北接壤江苏省，西南和浙江省毗邻。

9. 我代表浙江中国旅行社向你们表示热烈的欢迎。

10. 这条江以壮观的潮水著称。

Task 5: Translate the following sentences into Chinese.

1. Xi'an is the center of Shaanxi Province in politics, economy, culture and information.

2. Rich in relics and natural resources, the city has a long history.

3. Its recorded history can be traced back to the Qin Dynasty (221 – 206 BC).

4. Although China spans five zones, the whole country follows Beijing standard time. It's 14:20 Beijing standard time. Please reset your watch.

5. The northern latitude at about 30° runs through some world wonders such as the Great Pyramid in Egypt, ancient Maya, Himalaya Mountains, and some great rivers like the Nile, the Mississippi River, the Changjiang River or Yangtze River in China, etc.

6. Hangzhou is located in the lower reaches of the Qiantang River approximately 180 kilometers southwest of Shanghai — an easy train ride away.

7. Hangzhou is the southern terminus of the 1,794 km-long Beijing-Hangzhou Grand Canal, one of the two greatest man-made projects in ancient China.

8. The Grand Canal, which eventually linked Hangzhou to Beijing, was noted as one of the world's longest artificial waterways, forming one of the country's most important economic arteries.

9. Hangzhou did not take its present name, which means a land accessible only by boat, until 589 in the Sui Dynasty.

10. Hangzhou has been regarded as one of China's six ancient capitals, for it served as the capital of both the Wuyue Kingdom in the 10th century and the Southern Song Dynasty in the 12th and 13th centuries.

III. Role Play

Task 6: Play a role in any of the following situations with your partner(s).

Situation 1: You're a tour guide from Hangzhou Overseas Travel Co., Ltd. (HZOTC). Now you're going to meet a tour group from Australia at the airport in your city. The group tour leader is Jane Thatcher. Make a dialogue with the tour leader, and then give a welcome talk to the tourists on the coach.

Situation 2: You work as a tour guide at a local travel agency. Now you're meeting an American couple Mr and Mrs Donaldson at the railway station in your home town. Make a dialogue with the couple and then give a welcome talk to them in the car.

IV. Problem-solving

Task 7: Analyze the following cases, then answer the questions as required.

Case 1

Situation: You're a local guide from Kanghui International Travel Agency. Now you're to meet a small group of six people from Germany at around 7:00 pm at the railway station. The tour leader is Lucas Schwartz. But only when the group starts to get on the coach do you find that you have picked up the wrong group of Swiss tourists, whose tour leader is named Leo Schwartz.

Question: What would you do if you picked up a wrong group?

Case 2

Situation: Xiao Yang, a local guide from Hongtai International Travel Agency, is to meet a small group of 10 people from Canada at around 13:00 at the airport. The tour leader is Jane Watson. But by mistake, she has picked up a group of Australian tourists, whose tour leader is Lily Watson. It is not until the group gets on the coach that she realizes her big mistake. Fortunately, the wrong group also belongs to the same agency, and their local guide also picks up Xiao Yang's group by mistake and has already left the airport.

Question: Suppose you were Xiao Yang, what would you do then?

Unit 2　Seeing off the Guests

$$\boxed{\textbf{Warm-up}}$$

1. What should a tour guide remind the tourists to remember when checking out at a hotel?
2. As a tour guide, what will you say to the tourists when giving a farewell talk?
3. What emergencies might happen during the tour or the check-out time? How will you handle such emergencies as a tour guide?

Part A　Handling Emergencies During Checkout

Dialogue 1

Situation: *Chen Yan is greeting the tour leader Joe Simpson at the lobby of Deefly Lakeview Hotel before the group checks out.*

Questions for comprehension and discussion:
★ What are Chen Yan and Joe Simpson talking about?
★ Why didn't Joe Simpson sleep well last night?

Chen Yan: Good morning, Joe. How did you sleep?
　　　Joe: Well, actually, I didn't sleep well.
Chen Yan: Sorry to hear that. What's wrong? You look a bit pale.

Joe: Last night when I was in bed, suddenly I was woken up by a call from Jack, a man in our group. He said he had been **vomiting** (呕吐) and had **diarrhea** (腹泻) since a couple of hours after dinner.

Chen Yan: Wow, that's really bad news. Anything wrong with the food?

Joe: I'm not sure. We had some fish yesterday, you know.

Chen Yan: What did you do then? You must have been busy the whole night.

Joe: Yes. It was about 11:00 pm then. I took him to the nearest hospital. The doctor said that he had **bacteria-related** (与细菌有关的) food **poisoning** (中毒) and gave him an **IV drip** (an intravenous drip, 静脉点滴). We came back to the hotel at about 2:00 am early this morning.

Chen Yan: I do feel sorry for him, and you must be very tired since you only had a few hours of sleep.

Joe: That's OK. It's my job.

Chen Yan: How is Jack now? I hope he's fine.

Joe: Yes, he's feeling much better. Thanks.

Chen Yan: Good. How about the others? Is everyone here in the lobby?

Joe: Yes, except Jack, you know the reason. But he told me he'll be here in a few minutes. It's only 8:20 now, and we're leaving for the airport at 8:30, aren't we?

Chen Yan: Right. How about the key cards? Have you got all of them?

Joe: Yes, except Jack's. Aha, there he is.

Chen Yan: Morning, Jack. Joe has just told me about your illness last night. I'm terribly sorry for that.

Jack: Hi, morning. That's OK. It was really horrible last night. But luckily enough, thanks to the great help of Joe and the doctors, I'm recovering now. I should be very careful with the food in China next time.

Chen Yan: Yeah. I'm afraid we all have to. I'm sorry, that's really a shame. But I'll tell the head chef in the restaurant about it and ask them to be more careful about food **hygiene** (卫生). Well, may I have your key card?

Jack: Oh, yes, here it is. Thank you.

Chen Yan: You're welcome. By the way, did you take any drinks or snacks from the **minibar** (小冰箱), with the exception of the **complimentary** (赠送的) mineral water in your room, or the non-food items offered in the bathroom?

Jack: Aha, yes, I've taken one pair of shorts because of the diarrhea.

Chen Yan: Then, I'm afraid you have to pay the extra fee.

Jack: Sure. No problem. Shall I go with you to the receptionist now?

Chen Yan: Yes, please.

Dialogue 2

Situation: *When Chen Yan is helping the group check out at Deefly Lakeview Hotel, Laura, one of the group members, rushes up to her.*

Questions for comprehension and discussion:

★ What's wrong with Laura?

★ Does she have to stay to report the case to the local police?

Laura: Hi, Chen Yan!

Chen Yan: Yes? What's up?

Laura: I'm afraid I've lost my passport. I can't find it now.

Chen Yan: Don't worry, Laura. Can you recall what happened? When and where did you last see it?

Laura: I remember putting it in the safe. I took it out of the safe early this morning and put it into my handbag before heading to the dining hall for breakfast. But now, I can't find it any more.

Chen Yan: Did you check the dining hall then?

Laura: Yes, I was there twice and couldn't find it anywhere.

Chen Yan: How about the safe?

Laura: I've also double checked it. But it's just not there.

Chen Yan: That's strange. Anyway, since you saw it only two hours ago, it must be somewhere else. Don't worry, it will **pop up** (突然出现) somewhere.

Laura: I hope so. But we don't have much time, do we?

Chen Yan: No, I'm afraid we don't. It's almost 8:30. I'm sorry, we have to leave soon, otherwise we'll miss the flight.

Laura: Yes, I see, that's the problem. But what shall I do then?

Chen Yan: If we can't find it in time, then you'll have to stay here and report the loss to the local police before applying for a new passport. Of course, in that case I'll go with you. But anyway, we still have five minutes more. Let's first ask the security guards for help immediately and ask them to help check the places you were to.

(*Turning to Joe*) Joe, will you please take the other guests to the coach? Our coach is just outside the lobby.

Joe: Sure.

(*Just then, a bellboy (侍者) walks towards them.*)

Bellboy: Is this your passport, madam? Someone found it in the lift this morning and turned it in.

Laura: Oh, yes! Thank you very much!

Bellboy: You're welcome.

Chen Yan: Well, do you have all your belongings here? Let's get on the coach right now.

Part B A Farewell Talk

Dialogue

Situation: *Chen Yan is giving a farewell talk to the American group on the way to Hangzhou Xiaoshan Airport.*

Questions for comprehension and discussion:

★ What does Chen Yan say to her American guests?

★ What does the group leader say to the guests?

★ If you were Chen Yan, what would you say to the guests?

Chen Yan: Well, time flies when we're having fun. Your three-day tour of Hangzhou, like all other good things, is coming to an end now, just as a Chinese saying goes: "No feast lasts forever." I would also quote a poem[1] written by an Irish poet: "I love the  simple word hello. It always rings a joyful bell. But one of the saddest words I know, is the oft times tearful word farewell." So it's time to say goodbye to you all though I hate to. But every time we say goodbye, I find it difficult to express myself. It's really my pleasure to have been with you all in the past three days.

---

[1] "The Word Farewell" is written by Francis Duggan, retrieved on Oct. 20th, 2013.(http://www.poemhunter.com/poem/the-word-farewell/)

First of all, thank you for your great interest in Chinese culture. We've had a great time together seeing the world heritage site－the West Lake Cultural Landscape including West Lake, the most charming lake in China; Lingyin Temple, a large Zen Buddhist (禅宗) temple; Six Harmonies Pagoda, a masterpiece of ancient brick-and-wood structure in China. And, in addition to all that, we went to Song Town and experienced the real life of an ordinary person a thousand years ago. We watched the "**Romance of the Song Dynasty (宋城千古情)**", the great live show comparable to the "**Moulin Rouge (红磨坊)**" in Paris or the "**O Show (O秀)**" in **Las Vegas** (拉斯维加斯). From the show, you not only learned a bit about the history of Hangzhou, but also got to know the two beautiful love stories. Can you remember what they are?

Tourist A: Yeah, the butterfly lovers, Chinese Romeo and Juliet.

Tourist B: And the snake lady, Lady White.

Chen Yan: Right. Although the stories are so sad and heartbreaking, we see the beauty of love. Hangzhou is thus renowned as the ideal place for many Chinese lovers to spend time together including their honeymoon. So I hope all the couples here in our group have enjoyed your romantic **stroll** (漫步) on both Bai Causeway and Su Causeway. But if you're still single, I hope you'll soon find your Mr Right or Miss Right after this romantic trip to Hangzhou.

Tourists: Thanks.

Chen Yan: What other places did we go to?

Tourist C: The tea village.

Tourist D: The silk museum.

Chen Yan: Exactly. We also went to the tea village and silk museum to find more about the authentic Longjing tea and Hangzhou silk. It was fun, wasn't it? I'm really glad that you enjoyed yourselves. Your happiness really **makes my day** (让我开心一整天). In a word, thank you again for your great interest and cooperation without which our tour here in Hangzhou wouldn't have been so successful. What's more, I should also like to thank you for your patience and understanding during the **traffic jam** (交通堵塞) for which I was terribly sorry. My special thanks also go to Joe. Thank you, Joe! I really appreciate your help and cooperation. We've been a very good team.

Though I work as a tour guide, I like to make friends with you all. So please call me or email me if you need any help. If you come to Hangzhou again someday with your family or friends, I'll be happy to show you more of the beauty of real Hangzhou.

By the way, I'd like to make a sincere apology for any inconvenience if we weren't able to satisfy some of your needs despite all our efforts. Your comments and suggestions are warmly welcome and will **assist** (帮助) us in continuously improving our service. Last but not least, goodbyes are neither forever nor the end, but rather the moment to start to miss each other. I hope you all will have a pleasant journey back home, and look forward to meeting you again.

Joe: Thank you, Chen Yan. On behalf of my group, I'd like to express my thanks to you and Mr Li for your **professionalism** (职业素养) and efficiency as well as your kindness. You helped solve many difficulties that arose unexpectedly during our trip. We are happy to have been with both of you in the past three days. You're one of the best guides we have ever had, Chen Yan. You really know a lot about Hangzhou and its current status from which we've learned a lot. Before our travel to China, most of us knew little about your country, let alone Hangzhou. After this visit, I'm sure we have a better understanding of what the real China is like and why Hangzhou is called paradise on earth. Someone in our group even

wants to buy a house here if possible. So you see, it's surely one of our **rewarding** (值得的) and unforgettable trips in China. We'll certainly recommend you to anyone travelling to Hangzhou. And I would love to work with you again if possible. Thank you again for all that you have done for us, Chen Yan. So, you guys, let's give Chen Yan a big hand!

Chen Yan: Thank you all! Thank you, Joe! That's very kind of you. It's been wonderful having you all as my guests. Now here we are at the airport. Let's get off the coach, and remember to take all your belongings and keep your passports ready.

Part C   Tips on Giving a Farewell Talk and Handling Emergencies

I. Tips on Giving a Farewell Talk

Questions for comprehension and discussion:
★ What points does a farewell talk normally cover?

A farewell talk is as important as a welcome talk for a guide. It **concludes** (结束) the tour and helps the visitors **rekindle** (激起) their beautiful memories of the whole journey. If you work as a guide, the following tips may be helpful for you when delivering an impressive farewell talk.

☆ To start with, express how much you're going to miss the visitors though you are going to say goodbye. Goodbye is not the end but the moment to keep the beautiful memory of the trip and start to miss each other.

☆ Make a summary of the tour, and express your appreciation for the visitors' interest and cooperation. It's always beautiful to mention in brief the good time you had together, give a brief review of the tour or the whole journey, and show your **gratification** (喜悦) for the visitors' great interest in Chinese culture and support in various activities.

☆ Express thanks to the tour leader for the cooperation. It's important to work well with the tour leader or **escort** (陪同) as a team to offer professional service to the group. Without the leader's help and support, the group tour won't be successful.

☆ Sincerely ask for any suggestions and advice so that you can offer better service in your future work. Make a sincere apology to the visitors if some of their needs were not able to be satisfied due to some emergencies or some other reasons.

☆ Extend your good wishes and try to end with a memorable **closing** (结语) to make your farewell talk a special moment for the guests.

II. Tips on Handling Emergencies

Questions for comprehension and discussion:
★ What kind of emergencies may happen during a trip?
★ What measures should be taken to handle the emergencies?

When travelling abroad, emergencies may occur anywhere and anytime. Severe injuries or even death may not only result from the natural disasters such as flood, earthquake, **tsunami** (海啸), **hurricane** (飓风), storm, heavy snow and other horrible weather, but also from the non-natural causes including fire, violence, road traffic accidents, air crashes, etc. In addition to some **infectious diseases** (传染病) such as **influenza** (流感), **bird flu** (禽流感), **malaria** (疟疾) and **tuberculosis** (肺结核), **Ebola** (埃博拉病毒), **SARS** (非典型肺炎) or **COVID-19** (2019 冠状病毒病), the tourists may also risk getting sick from **contaminated food** (污染的食物) or **poisonous** (有毒的) food with **symptoms** (症状) such as upset stomach, fever, **vomiting** (呕吐) or **diarrhea** (腹泻). Moreover, older tourists may also suffer from various kinds of illness like **stroke** (中风), **heart attack** (心脏病), memory loss and so on. Besides, personal belongings such as the passport, luggage/baggage, handbag and purse/wallet may also get lost during the journey.

Any of the emergencies may cause complaints among tourists, which can ruin the **reputation** (名声) of a tourist guide or even the tour operator. Therefore, on behalf of the tour operator, the guide shall give **top priority to** (高度重视) the safety of the tourists and remind them to be aware of their personal safety and belongings. At all times they should be **alert** (留神的) and well prepared for any possible emergencies.

If you work as a guide, your confidence and professional skills in dealing with both minor and major emergencies will be **reassuring** (令人放心的) to the injured or sick or the one who suffers from the loss of personal belongings. Here follow some tips for handling some common emergencies.

1) Illness, Injuries and Death
As a guide, you shall always care about the tourists' health. In case of any illness or injury, you should help make immediate arrangement for the sick or the injured. First, report the case to your **tour operator** (接待社) for possible **assistance** (支持) without delay. Then send the patient

or the injured person to the nearest hospital, or call the **emergency service** (紧急救援服务, 120 in China and 911 in the US) immediately if it's very serious. In the meantime, you should also help contact the tourist's family members and the local agent for the international insurance company if the tourist has bought travel insurance.

If there is an accident involving severe injuries, call both the police and the emergency service at the same time. While the official **rescuers** (救护人员) are on the way, help the most severely injured first. If someone is suddenly **unconscious** (失去知觉) before the **ambulance** (救护车) arrives, you may try to start **CPR** (Cardiopulmonary Resuscitation, 心肺复苏) to help **revive** (复活) the patient by pressing on the chest and breathing into the mouth. Keep giving at least 100 chest **compressions** (挤压) a minute until the professional rescuer arrives or the person is breathing normally. However, if you are not sure what to do, and think the person may have a **spinal injury** (脊椎受伤), don't move him or her until medical help arrives.

If death occurs, report it to the tour operator and travel agent immediately. If the death is totally unexpected, keep everything on the scene **intact** (原封不动的) and report the situation to the police as well. Besides, you should also help contact the victim's family members and his or her **consulate** (领事馆) or **embassy** (大使馆).

It is very likely that the passengers will experience **panic** (恐慌) when something unexpected happens. Therefore, you should try to calm them down as soon as possible and work with the escort or the tour leader as a team. After handling the emergency, you should continue to take the other tourists to do sightseeing while the tour leader takes care of the sick.

Usually the itinerary should not be **altered** (改变) without the **consent** (同意) of the tourists and the tour operator. However, it is necessary to alter the itinerary due to emergencies. So in this case, you should explain the reasons clearly to the tourists and report it to the tour operator after getting the consent of the tourists.

2) Loss of Property

The loss of property such as handbag, wallet, passport or even luggage often happens during the trip. If it occurs, you should first calm down the worried tourist, and ask him or her to recall the details concerning the lost belongings. Such details as time and places are very **crucial** (关键的) in finding out about the lost item. Then help the tourist search any possible places. If it doesn't work, you should report the case to the local police within 24 hours and leave the tourist's name and contact number in case the lost item is found.

If someone loses a passport and all the search effort fails, you should report it to the tour operator and ask for **identity verification** (身份证明) for the tourist. Then help the tourist report the case to the local police with the identifying information, and apply for a new passport from the **consulate** (领事馆) or **embassy** (大使馆) of his or her home country. Finally, accompany the tourist to the immigration department for a new visa.

What a tourist finds most **intolerable** (无法忍受的) is probably luggage loss or damage while traveling. If this happens, **remedial** (补救的) measures should be taken immediately to minimize the inconvenience for the tourist. First, contact the **bellboy** (行李员) or manager at the hotel to check whether the luggage has been delivered to the right room. If this doesn't prove successful, contact the luggage transport department of the tour operator to check whether the luggage has been delivered to the right hotel for the right group.

If loss of luggage happens after arrival, help the owner contact the **Luggage Service Counter** (行李服务部) at the airport for the missing luggage, and leave the contact number and the name of the hotels as well as your group's itinerary. In the meantime, report it to the tour operator. If the luggage cannot eventually be traced back, help the owner claim **compensation** (赔偿) if travel insurance covers the loss or damage. Last but not least, remember to help the tourist purchase some daily **necessities** (必需品) for the sake of convenience. To avoid such problems, it's advisable for the guide to check the luggage when possible.

3) Tourists Getting Lost

Tourists getting lost is sometimes possible in a crowded place and can be frustrating for a guide as the search may be quite **painstaking** (煞费苦心的) and **time consuming** (费时的). What's worse, there might be a safety risk for the missing tourist. Therefore, if someone gets lost in your group, work together well with the tour leader as a team. Make sure the whole group stay where they are with the tour leader before starting the search. If the tourist is still missing after a long search, report it to both the tour operator and the local police. At the same time, remember to contact the hotel receptionist in case the tourist returns to the hotel.

In a word, whatever happens, you should first keep calm, cope with any of the emergencies properly and remember to report the case to the institutions or departments concerned.

Part D   Language Checklist

A. Vocabulary

emergency service 紧急救援服务 Emergency Center 急救中心	handle/deal with emergency 处理紧急事件	consulate 领事馆 embassy 大使馆
earthquake 地震 tsunami 海啸 hurricane 飓风	illness 生病 injuries 受伤 death 死亡	influenza 流感 bird flu 禽流感 malaria 疟疾 tuberculosis 肺结核
food contamination 食品污染 bacterial food poisoning 细菌性食物中毒	symptoms 症状 upset stomach 肚子疼 fever 发烧 vomiting 呕吐 diarrhea 腹泻 stroke 中风 heart attack 心脏病	IV drip (an intravenous drip) 静脉点滴 CPR (Cardiopulmonary Resuscitation) 心肺复苏

give top priority to 高度重视 food safety 食品安全 hygiene 卫生 personal safety 个人安全	take measures 采取措施 rescuer 救护人员	a spinal injury 脊椎受伤 keep it intact 保持原样
Lost-and-Found Office 失物招领处 loss of property 财物遗失 loss of personal belongings 物品遗失	apply for 申请 identity verification 身份证明	claim compensation 要求赔偿

B. Key Patterns

Expressing Appreciation and Pleasure **表示感谢和高兴**	• Thank you for your cooperation and support in various activities. • Thank you for your help/assistance/support. • I really appreciate all the help you gave me. • Thank you for your great interest and cooperation without which our tour here in Hangzhou wouldn't have been so successful. 感谢你们的极大兴趣和合作，否则的话，我们的杭州之旅不会如此成功。 • Thank you for your patience and understanding during the traffic jam for which I was terribly sorry. 很抱歉，虽然之前交通拥堵，但是你们非常有耐心并表示理解，对此我表示感谢。 • My special thanks also go to Mr Simpson. Thank you, Joe! I really appreciate your help and cooperation. • It's really my pleasure to have been with you all in the past two days. 真的很高兴和大家一起度过了两天的时光。 • Your happiness makes my day. 你们的快乐让我开心一天。 • It's my honor to have been with you. 很荣幸和你们在一起。 • It's been nice meeting you. 见到你们很高兴。
Summarizing the Tour **总结旅游**	• We have had a great time together seeing the world heritage site — the West Lake Cultural Landscape including West Lake, the most charming lake in China; Lingyin Temple, a large Zen Buddhist Temple; Six Harmonies Pagoda, a masterpiece of ancient brick-and-wood structure in China. 我们大家一起开心地游览了世界文化遗产地——西湖文化景观，其中包括中国最迷人的湖泊——西湖，规模宏大的禅宗寺庙——灵隐寺，以及中国古代砖木结构的杰作——六和塔。 • We visited Tian'anmen Square, the Forbidden City, the Summer Palace, and the Great Wall to learn the long history of China. 我们参观了天安门广场、紫禁城（故宫）、颐和园和长城，了解了中国悠久的历史。 • Our visit to Qufu, the birthplace of Confucius, may help you better understand this great ancient thinker and educator in China. 我们游览了孔夫子的出生地曲阜，更加了解这位中国古代伟大的思想家和教育家。 • We began our tour with a trip to Xi'an, taking a good view of the impressive Terracotta Army. 我们在旅程一开始游览了西安，欣赏了壮观的兵马俑。
Making Apology and Asking for Comments and Suggestions **道歉和征求意见及建议**	• We are terribly sorry for any inconvenience caused to you during the trip. 对于在旅途中给你们造成的任何不便，我们感到非常抱歉。 • We do apologize for the delay. 我们对延误感到非常抱歉。 • We're terribly sorry for the accident. 我们对此次事故感到非常抱歉。 • I would like to make a sincere apology for any inconvenience if we weren't able to satisfy some of your needs despite all our efforts. 如果我们无论怎样都无法满足你们的一些要求，对此造成的任何不便我们深感抱歉。 • We've made every effort to tailor the tour to meet your needs. However, we appreciate any of your comments and suggestions. 虽然我们已尽力根据大家的需求安排旅程，但还是欢迎大家多提意见和建议。

Making Apology and Asking for Comments and Suggestions 道歉和征求意见及建议	• Though we've tried our best to make your tour in China enjoyable and informative, your suggestions and advice are highly appreciated. 虽然我们已尽力使大家在中国的旅游愉快而充实，我们还是非常感谢各位的建议和意见。 • Your comments and suggestions are warmly welcome and will assist us in continuously improving our service. 非常欢迎你们提出宝贵意见和建议，并帮助我们继续改善服务。
Saying Goodbye and Giving Wishes 再见和祝愿	• It's time to say goodbye to you all though I hate to. • Your two-day tour of Hangzhou is coming to an end, just as a Chinese saying goes: "No feast lasts forever (天下没有不散的筵席)." • All good things come to an end. 所有好事都会有尽头/天下没有不散的筵席。 • Goodbyes are neither forever nor the end, but the moment to start to miss each other. • "I love the simple word hello. It always rings a joyful bell. But one of the saddest words I know, is the oft times tearful word farewell." "我喜欢简单的问候声，听起来像快乐的银铃。让我最伤感的一个词，就是催人泪下的送行。" • I hope you all will have a pleasant journey back home, and look forward to meeting you again. 希望你们大家都能顺利返程回家，期待下次再见。 • Parting is such sweet sorrow. 离别是甜蜜的愁绪。 • Have a pleasant trip. 一路顺风。 • Goodbye then, and all the very best. 再见了，万事如意。 • Goodbye and thanks again for all you have done. 再见，再次感谢你们所做的一切。 • Hope we'll keep in touch. 保持联系。 • Hope to meet you again. 希望再见到你们。 • I'm looking forward to seeing you again. 很期待再见到你们。
Tour Leader's Comment on the Local Guide 领队对地陪的评价	• Thank you for your courtesy (礼貌) and promptness (机敏). You are one of the best guides we've ever had. 你很懂礼貌，处事机敏，谢谢你。你是我们遇到过最好的导游之一。 • We're very grateful for your professionalism (专业素质) and efficiency. It's one of the best trips we have ever taken. • We're extremely satisfied with your professionalism and excellent service. 我们对你的职业素养和优质服务感到相当满意。 • We really appreciate your competence and efficiency. 我们真的很欣赏你的工作能力和办事效率。 • Thank you for your outstanding service. We've had a wonderful time and seen so much in a short period. • Thank you again for all that you have done for us. • It's a pleasure to have been with you. You're very knowledgeable and have a great history background. 很高兴和你相处。你的知识面很广，也非常熟悉历史。 • You were incredibly organized and left nothing to chance. 你的安排井井有条，服务非常周到。 • You looked after every detail, and made sure we saw everything we had requested. 你的服务细致周到，还带我们游遍所有的景点。 • You've provided us a really enjoyable, informative tour of the main attractions in China. 你安排我们愉快地游览了中国的各大景点，使我们获益匪浅。 • We've learned more from you about Chinese history than we did from the guidebook. • You're very knowledgeable. We've learned a lot of things we didn't know before. • We'll highly recommend you to anyone travelling to China. 我们会把你强烈推荐给任何一位到中国的游客。 • If we travel again with China Travel Service Zhejiang, we would like to have you as our guide again. • We'll surely ask you to be our guide again if we come next time.

Dealing with Illness, Injuries and Death 游客生病/伤亡的 处理	• The tour guide should always care about the tourists' health. • In case of illness or injuries, report it to the tour operator (接待社) for possible assistance (支持) without delay. • Send the patient or the injured person to the nearest hospital, or call the emergency service immediately if it's very serious. • Help contact the tourist's family members and the local agent for the international insurance company if the tourist has bought travel insurance. • If death occurs, the guide should help contact the victim's consulate (领事馆) or embassy (大使馆) in China. 如果发生死亡情况，导游应协助联系受害者所属国的中国领事馆。
Dealing with the Loss of Property 财物丢失的处理	• The guide should give top priority to (高度重视) the safety of the tourists and remind them to be aware of their personal safety and belongings. • If someone loses a passport, report it to the tour operator and ask for identity verification (身份证明) for the tourist. • Help the owner report the case to the local police with the identifying information, and apply for a new passport from the consulate or embassy of their home country. 帮助失主向地方警局报案，出示身份证明，同时向本国领事/使馆申请新护照。 • Accompany the owner to the immigration department for a new visa. 陪同失主到移民部门办理新签证。 • If one's checked luggage is lost, help the owner claim compensation from the airline concerned. 如果有游客的行李丢失，帮助失主向有关航空公司索赔。
Dealing with a Missing Tourist 游客走失的处理	• Ask the whole group to stay where they are with the tour leader before starting the search. 寻找走失游客前，让所有团队成员和领队待在一起。 • Try every effort to search the missing one. 尽力寻找失踪游客。 • If the tourist is still missing after a long search, report it to both the tour operator and the local police. • Contact the hotel receptionist in case the tourist returns to the hotel.

Part E　English in Use

I. Reading Comprehension

Task 1: Choose the best answer to complete each sentence below.

1. The tour leader told the group to hand in their _____ before checking out.
   A. luggage　　　B. passport　　　C. key cards　　　D. money
2. When giving a farewell talk, the guide should also thank _____ for the cooperation.
   A. the driver　　B. the group　　C. the tour operator　D. the tour leader
3. It's necessary for a guide to give a brief _____ of the tour when saying goodbye to the tourists.
   A. opinion　　　B. introduction　　C. speech　　　D. review
4. If some tourists get injured in an accident, the tour guide should first call _____.
   A. embassy　　　　　　　　　B. emergency services
   C. the family members　　　　D. the tour operator
5. If one of the tourists gets sick, the guide should help contact the local agent for the international insurance company if the tourist has bought _____.

A. round tickets   B. luggage   C. healthcare   D. travel insurance

6. If one of the tourists cannot find his/her luggage after arrival, the guide should help the owner contact the Luggage Service Counter at the airport, and leave his contact number and _____.

    A. money

    B. family members' name

    C. the name of the luggage

    D. the name of the hotel

7. If death occurs, the guide should also help contact the _____ of the victim's country in time.

    A. tour operator

    B. police

    C. tour agent

    D. consulate/embassy

8. If someone loses a passport, the guide should report it to the tour operator and local police for identity verification before applying for a new _____ from the consulate of the tourist's country.

    A. visa   B. passport   C. ID card   D. insurance

9. _____ the whole group, the tour leader has to thank the tour guide for his or her service before departing.

    A. On behalf of   B. In behalf of   C. Because of   D. In case of

10. If a tourist gets lost, the guide should ask _____ to stay with the whole group before starting the search.

    A. the tour leader

    B. the driver

    C. the tour agent

    D. the family member

Task 2: Answer the following questions concerning emergencies before checking out in Part A.

1. Why didn't Joe sleep well last night?
2. When did Joe and Jack come back from the hospital?
3. What did Jack take from the non-food items offered in the bathroom?
4. Where was Laura's passport found?
5. What should a tour guide do before seeing the tourists off at the airport or the railway station?

Task 3: Decide whether each of the following statements is True or False concerning tips on handling emergency and delivering a farewell talk in Part C.

1. In case of emergency, the itinerary can be changed without the consent of the tourists. (   )
2. The tour guide should leave the emergencies to be handled by the police. (   )
3. For minor medical emergencies, the guide should take the patient to the nearest hospital. (   )
4. The tour operator should be responsible for identity verification for the tourist losing his or her passport. (   )
5. After dealing with the emergency, the local guide should stay to take care of the sick, and the tour leader would continue to take the other tourists to do sightseeing. (   )

II. Translation

Task 4: Translate the following sentences into English.

1. 您能回忆一下您的手提包是怎么丢的吗？最后见到它是什么时候？在什么地方？
2. 别担心，我们马上去告诉保安，请他们帮忙核查你去过的所有地方。
3. 如果您找不到自己的护照，就得先向当地警方报案，然后才能申领新的护照。
4. 夫人，这是您的手提包吗？有人在商务中心发现后交到了失物招领处。
5. 除了房间里赠送的矿泉水，您还拿过小冰箱里的一些饮料或者点心吗？
6. 先生，对不起，您得另外付费，因为您享受了送餐服务。
7. 我会把这件事告诉餐厅里的厨师长，让他们更加注意食品安全和卫生。
8. 现在到了该说再见的时候，尽管我很不想说。
9. 我真的很高兴这几天大家一直玩得很愉快。
10. 再次感谢你们的大力合作，要不然我们的杭州之行就不会如此成功。

Task 5: Translate the following sentences into Chinese.

1. The doctor said that he had bacteria-related food poisoning and gave him an IV drip.
2. Your two-day tour of Hangzhou is coming to an end now, just as a Chinese saying goes: "No feast lasts forever."
3. Any of the emergencies may cause complaints among tourists, which will ruin the reputation of a tourist guide or even the tour operator.
4. The guide should always be alert and well prepared for any possible emergencies.
5. Thank you very much for your patience and understanding during the traffic jam for which I was terribly sorry during the trip.
6. Your comments and suggestions are warmly welcome and will assist us in continuously improving our service.
7. My special thanks also go to Ms White. I really appreciate your help and cooperation. We were a very good team.
8. I hope you all will have a pleasant journey back home, and look forward to meeting you again.
9. I would like to make a sincere apology for any inconvenience if we weren't able to satisfy some of your needs despite all our efforts.
10. The guide should give top priority to the safety of the tourists and always remind them to be aware of their personal safety and belongings.

III. Role Play

Task 6: Play a role in any of the following situations with your partner(s).

Situation 1: You're a tour guide from Hangzhou China Overseas Travel Service. You're going to see off a tour group from the US on the way to Hangzhou Xiaoshan Airport. The tour leader is Joe Simpson. Now, first make a dialogue with the tour leader, then give a farewell talk to all the tourists on the coach.

Situation 2: Your coach goes out of control and crashes into the back of a lorry. The coach is seriously damaged. The accident leaves three tourists injured and causes panic among others.

Show how you, as a guide, will deal with it.

IV. Problem-solving

Task 7: Make an analysis of the following cases, and answer the questions as required.

Case 1

Situation: An elderly lady happens to have a heart attack when your group is sightseeing. She isn't able to speak and move, indicating something serious and urgent.

Question: If you were the guide, how would you handle the emergency?

Case 2

Situation: When a group is touring around West Lake in Hangzhou, the local guide, Xiao Zhan, finds out that an aged tourist is missing.

Question: Suppose you were Xiao Zhan, what would you do then?

Answers for Reference

Module II
Hotel and Restaurant Services

Unit 3 Hotel Services

Warm-up

1. As a tour guide, what kinds of help can you offer to your tour group checking in at a hotel?
2. What problems might the guests have when staying at a hotel?
3. As a staff member, how will you handle the guests' complaints?

Part A Check-in Service

Dialogue 1

Situation: *Chen Yan helps Joe Simpson, the tour leader of the American tour group, check in at Deefly Lakeview Hotel.*

Questions for comprehension and discussion:
★ What does Chen Yan do first?
★ What's the group's problem?
★ How does Chen Yan help solve the problem?
★ What does Chen Yan tell Joe before leaving the hotel?
★ If you were Chen Yan, what would you do then?

Chen Yan: We made a reservation through our travel agency. I'm going to help you check into the hotel, Joe.

Joe Simpson: OK, thank you.

Chen Yan: Would you please get your group's passports ready?

Joe Simpson: OK, here you are.

Chen Yan: Good. Would you please help fill out the form and sign here?

Joe Simpson: No problem.

Chen Yan: Well, Joe, altogether there are 15 people in your group, aren't there? So I'm afraid one single person in your group will have to pay the price difference for the twin room according to the contract.

Joe Simpson: Yes, I know. That's Sam. But is it possible for him to have a single room instead of the twin room? He'll pay the price difference.

Chen Yan: OK, let me check with the receptionist.

(After some negotiation)

Chen Yan: Well, fortunately there's one single room left for Sam. So everything is done. Here are the 16 passports including yours and the key cards to your rooms, and room 501 is the single room on the fifth floor.

Joe Simpson: Thank you very much. You've been so helpful. Sam is very satisfied as well.

Chen Yan: It's a pleasure. Now the elevator is on the right. Your baggage will be delivered to your rooms soon. Breakfast buffet is served from 7:00 am to 9:30 am on the second floor. And the morning call is set for 7:30 am. Do you need any other help?

Joe Simpson: No, thank you. Everything is perfect.

Chen Yan: And your room number is 312, is that right?

Joe Simpson: Yes, it is, room 312.

Chen Yan: So, see you at 9:00 am tomorrow down in the lobby. Good night.

Joe Simpson: See you. Good night.

Dialogue 2

Situation: *Jim Ralf is checking in at Deefly Lakeview Hotel.*

Questions for comprehension and discussion:

★ What kind of room has Jim Ralf reserved?

★ What time is it then? Can he check in at once? Why or why not?

★ What does the receptionist tell him when giving him the key card?

★ If you were the receptionist, what would you do then?

Receptionist: Good morning, sir. Welcome to Deefly Lakeview Hotel. What can I do for you?

Jim Ralf: Good morning. I'm Jim Ralf from Germany. May I check in now?

Receptionist: Do you have a booking number?

Jim Ralf: Yes, of course. Here's my online reservation.

Receptionist: Thank you. Could you please wait for a moment?

Jim Ralf: OK.

Receptionist: Yes, we have your reservation. So you're from **Allianz** (德国安联保险公司), the global financial services company?

Jim Ralf: Yes.

Receptionist: I see. You've booked one superior room with a lake view for two nights and will check out this Saturday, April 23, is that right?

Jim Ralf: Yes, that's right. Then I can have a good view of West Lake directly from my room, can't I?

Receptionist: Sure. You can see the pagoda on the hill. That's one of the best rooms in our hotel.

Jim Ralf: That's cool! So I can check in now?

Receptionist: Yes, you can, but I'm afraid you have to wait in the lounge for a while, because your room isn't ready yet. The maid is cleaning it now. Our normal check-in time is 2:00 pm, and it's only 11:30 am now.

Jim Ralf: Yes, I see. Then how long exactly am I supposed to wait?

Receptionist: Maybe half an hour, if you don't mind.

Jim Ralf: No problem.

Receptionist: So may I have your passport first?

Jim Ralf: OK. Here you are.

Receptionist: Thank you. Could you please fill out the form and sign it?

Jim Ralf: Fine.

Receptionist: Are you going to pay in cash or by credit card?

Jim Ralf: Credit card, please. Do you take **Euro Mastercard** (欧洲万事达信用卡)?

Receptionist: Yes, of course.

Jim Ralf: Here you are.

Receptionist: Thank you. Now, here's your passport back and your key card. Your room is on the 12th floor. Breakfast service is from 6:30 am to 9:30 am on the second floor. And please remember to tell the breakfast staff your room number when entering the cafeteria.

Jim Ralf: OK.

Receptionist: By the way, we offer room service.

Jim Ralf: Great. Thank you.

Receptionist: We also offer luxurious Western meals and lots of traditional Chinese food.

Jim Ralf: Thanks, I think I'll try the Chinese food, especially the local one.

| Receptionist: | Then you should not miss our Chinese restaurant on the 8th floor. It also faces the lake. You can enjoy the wonderful view of West Lake while having some specialties in Hangzhou. |

Receptionist: Then you should not miss our Chinese restaurant on the 8th floor. It also faces the lake. You can enjoy the wonderful view of West Lake while having some specialties in Hangzhou.

Jim Ralf: Perfect, I'll try the food there. By the way, do I have Internet access in the room?

Receptionist: Yes. The wireless is free. The password is your room number.

Jim Ralf: Good.

Receptionist: Do you have any other questions, Mr Ralf?

Jim Ralf: No, thank you.

Receptionist: Good. The lift is on your left. Enjoy your stay here.

Jim Ralf: Thank you very much.

Dialogue 3

Situation: *Mr Moore and his family are checking in at a hotel.*

Questions for comprehension and discussion:

★ What kind of room has Mr Moore booked?

★ Why should the Moores have to pay for the extra bed?

★ Can they have Internet access in their own room?

★ What does the receptionist tell them when giving them the key card?

★ If you were the receptionist, what would you do then?

Receptionist: Good afternoon, sir. May I help you?

Mr Moore: Yes. We've booked a twin room.

Receptionist: May I have your booking number?

Mr Moore: Here it is.

Receptionist: Thank you. Are you Mr Sam Moore?

Mr Moore: Yes, I am.

Receptionist: Right. You've booked a twin room for three nights. And you're going to check out on May 15?

Mr Moore: Yes, we'll check out this Friday. By the way, can we have a room with a nice view?

Receptionist: It does have a very good view, Mr Moore. It faces the garden with a swimming pool.

Mr Moore: Perfect.

Receptionist: Do you have a child, Mr Moore? How old then?

Mr Moore: Yes, that's my daughter. She's 12 years old.

Receptionist: Well, only a child under 10 is free. I'm sorry, Mr Moore, you have to pay 100 RMB for the extra bed.

Mr Moore: No problem. By the way, can I have access to the Internet in my room?

Receptionist: Yes, you can. Wireless Internet is available in all the hotel rooms, and it's free.

Mr Moore: Great. I love that.

Receptionist: OK, could you please show me your passports?

Mr Moore: All right. Here you are.

Receptionist: Thank you. And here's the form for you to fill out and sign.

Mr Moore: OK. Now, it's done. Here you are.

Receptionist: Thank you. How are you going to pay, cash or credit card, Mr Moore?

Mr Moore: Credit card, please.

Receptionist: Thank you. Now your room is on the sixth floor, and here's your key card. The lift is just over there next to the Business Center. You can have breakfast down in the lobby on the right. Here are your **breakfast coupons** (早餐券) but only for two, I'm afraid. Other person has to pay for the breakfast, 50 Chinese yuan per person.

Mr Moore: I see. Thank you.

Receptionist: It's a pleasure. Have a nice stay here.

Mr Moore: Thank you.

Part B   Housekeeping and Room Service

Dialogue 1: Housekeeping Service

Situation: *Mr and Mrs Moore are having some problems with their room.*

Questions for comprehension and discussion:

★ How many problems does Mrs Moore have?

★ What does the housekeeper say when hearing the complaints?

★ How does she deal with all these problems?

★ If you were the housekeeper, what would you do then?

Housekeeper: Good afternoon, housekeeping service. May I help you?

Mrs Moore: Yes. This is room 602. We have just checked in. But I'm afraid we don't know how to open the safe. Even though we followed the instructions, it still doesn't work.

Housekeeper: Don't worry, madam. I'll send someone up to help you immediately.

Mrs Moore: Thank you very much. By the way, there's a stain on the pillow, and the toilet doesn't flush properly. What's worse, the room has some sort of cigarette smell which we really don't like.

Housekeeper: We're terribly sorry for that. We do apologize for the inconvenience, madam. We'll take care of these problems as soon as possible.

Mrs Moore: Okay, thank you. Actually, we would prefer to have another room.

Housekeeper: Well, our maid will go up to your room right now. She'll be at your service. And the repairman will arrive soon to take care of the toilet. If the **odor** (气味) can't be removed, you can surely have another room after we check with the receptionist, madam.

Mrs Moore: Thank you. That's very kind of you.

Housekeeper: You're welcome. What else can we do for you, madam?

Mrs Moore: Oh, yes. Could we have another pair of **slippers** (拖鞋) for our daughter?

Housekeeper: Of course you can. I'll have them sent to your room in a minute.

Mrs Moore: Thank you very much. By the way, do you have a laundry service?

Housekeeper: Yes, we do. You can put the things in the laundry bag in your room, madam. Our maid will take care of the laundry and will send it back to your room after it's ready. Well, is there anything else we can do for you, madam?

Mrs Moore: Nothing more, thank you very much. You've been very helpful.

Housekeeper: My pleasure. Goodbye.

Mrs Moore: Bye.

Dialogue 2: Room Service

Situation: *Jim Ralf is asking for a room service at Deepfly Lakeview Hotel.*

Questions for comprehension and discussion:
★ What does Jim Ralf want for breakfast?
★ What is the final order?
★ If you worked for the room service, what would you do then?

Room service: Good morning, room service. May I help you?

Jim Ralf: Good morning. This is room 1205. I'd like some breakfast, please.

Room service: Ok. Excuse me for a moment, then is that Mr Ralf speaking?

Jim Ralf: That's right.

Room service: What would you like for breakfast?

Jim Ralf: I'd like **guava juice** (番石榴汁), one **omelette** (煎蛋饼), two pieces of toast and **marmalade** (果酱), one bowl of **muesli** (牛奶什锦干果燕麦片) and a cup of coffee, please.

Room service: Oh, I'm sorry, Mr Ralf, we don't have guava juice, but we have orange juice, apple juice, pineapple juice, and **papaya juice** (木瓜汁). Would you like one of these instead?

Jim Ralf: Some orange juice, please.

Room service: OK, a glass of orange juice. By the way, what kind of milk would you like to go with the muesli, hot or cold?

Jim Ralf: Cold, please.

Room service: And how about the coffee? Black or white?

Jim Ralf: Black, please.

Room service: Okay. Now, may I repeat it? You'd like to have a glass of orange juice, two pieces of toast and marmalade, one omelette, one bowl of muesli with cold milk, and a cup of black coffee. Is that right?

Jim Ralf: Exactly. How long will it take?

Room service: Just a couple of minutes, Mr Ralf.

Jim Ralf: Great, thank you.

Room service: It's a pleasure.

Part C Tips on Handling Complaints

*The following is an excerpt from Doug Kennedy[①]'s article "**Train Your Hospitality Team to Say 'YES!' to Guest Complaints**" written on Thursday, June 3, 2010, retrieved on May 15, 2020 (from https://www.hospitalitynet.org/opinion/4046848.html).*

Questions for comprehension and discussion:
★ How will you deal with a guest's complaints if you serve in a hotel?

---

① 道格·肯尼迪（Doug Kennedy）是美国多家酒店著名刊物的资深撰稿人，经常举办各类酒店培训讲座。2006 年，他创立了肯尼迪培训网络公司并任总裁。该公司专为各类酒店在客房的预订销售、酒店服务礼仪、宾客服务以及优化客房收益的前台工作等方面提供培训。此外，该公司还为各类管理公司、知名酒店和社团定制相关的会议主题和专题讨论培训会。相关介绍及其著作，请详见其主页 https://kennedytrainingnetwork.com。

★ What may be a typical empathy statement when dealing with complaints?

In addition to **tracking** (追踪) complaints, it is of course also important to train your staff on the tools they need to handle complaints properly. Here are some tips on handling complaints for your next meeting:

☆ Listen without interrupting. When guests are first voicing their complaint, it is important to listen interactively without interrupting. Most guests first need to **vent** (发泄) some frustration by telling their "story" completely with some dramatic details.

☆ When in person, demonstrate your attentiveness by maintaining eye contact and having neutral facial expressions. Over the phone, be sure to add some "verbal nods" such as "I see," "okay," and "alright."

☆ Once the guest starts to slow down after **venting** (发泄) their story in full detail, it's time for a statement of **empathy** (同感) followed by an apology. Empathy statements show "I can understand how you must feel; I can imagine I might feel the same way given the circumstance."

☆ To show empathy, **paraphrase** (解释) and re-state their complaint. This not only shows that we understand the details, but also provides **validation** (确认) for the speaker. "Ms Young, I can understand that this must have been frustrating for you. With such a big event planned for this evening I'm sure the last thing you needed was a hotel room without hot water."

☆ Apologize. As simple as it is to apologize, **far too often** (太多时候) guest services **associates** (同事) offer no apology at all, or what's worse, offer a **trite** (老生常谈的), **insincere** (不诚恳的) comment such as "I'm sorry" without meaning it. When you read **negative** (负面的) guest reviews or negative comment card **postings** (评价帖子), a common issue is that "No one seemed to care; no one even apologized." An apology is not an admission of fault; it simply says that the **intentions** (意图) were good.

☆ Restate **option**s (选择). Guests who complain want results. Ideally we can just give them what they want or need. Yet in the real world of hotels, sometimes it isn't that easy. For example, if a guest wants a particular room type when absolutely none is available, try to offer at least two **alternative** (可选择的) choices to pick from. Here is an example: "Unfortunately, Mr Perez, all of our pool view double rooms are occupied this evening. What I can do for you is to put you in a poolside king room and send in a **rollaway** (滚动式折叠) bed, or I can offer you a garden view double room for this evening."

By training your staff to be on the lookout for unvoiced guest complaints, and helping them understand how to draw-out the details and properly resolve the issues, we can reduce the **odds** (可能性) that the incident **surfaces** (出现) in an online posting.

Instead of having a **disgruntled** (不高兴的) guest becoming the hotel's worst **nightmare** (噩梦), we can possibly turn that same guest into an **apostle** (宣传者) to help spread the good news about the great service they received to turn things around.

Part D Language Checklist

A. Vocabulary

online reservation 网上预订 booking number 预订号 online reservation form 在线预订单	check in 入住登记 check out 办理退房手续 fill in/out the form 填表格/填单子 sign the form 在单子/表格上签字 key card 房卡	standard 标准的 superior 高级的 deluxe 豪华的
single room 单人间 twin room 双床房 double room 双人房 queen room 大床房 king room 特大床房 triple room 三人间 suite 套房 family suite 家庭套房 business room 商务房	porter 行李员 bellboy/bellman/bell hop 大堂服务员 maid 客房女服务员 waiter 男服务员 waitress 女服务员 wait staff 餐厅服务员 breakfast staff 早餐厅服务员 server 服务员	morning call 叫醒服务 room service 送餐服务 housekeeping service 客房服务 laundry service 洗衣服务 laundry 洗衣房/洗好/待洗的衣服 pillowcase 枕套 sheet 床单
have access to the Internet 可以上网 wireless Internet 无线上网	Visa 维萨卡 Euro Mastercard 欧洲万事达信用卡 American Express 美国运通卡	safe/safety deposit box 保险箱 price difference 客房差价

B. Key Patterns

Check-in Help 导游协助登记入住	Guide: 协助领队 ● We made a reservation through our travel agency. ● I'm going to help you check into the hotel. ● Will you please get your group's passports ready? ● Would you please help fill out the form and sign here? 协调安排房间 ● I'm afraid a single person in your group has to pay the price difference for the twin room according to the contract. 归还护照，分发房卡 ● Here are the 15 passports including yours and the key cards to your rooms. 介绍酒店设施，告知早餐时间和地点以及行李的去向，确认第二天的叫醒时间 ● Now the lift/elevator is on the right. Your baggage/luggage will be delivered to your rooms soon. Breakfast buffet is served from 7:00 am to 9:30 am on the second floor. And the morning call is set for 7:30 am. Do you need any other help? 确认下一次的见面时间和地点 ● See you at 9:00 am tomorrow down in the lobby.

Check-in 客人自行登记入住	Guest: 告知预订信息 • Good morning. I'm… from… May I check in now? • Good morning, I have a reservation under the name of Jim Ralf. • I made an online reservation. • We booked a twin room in your hotel. • Here's my online reservation. 询问酒店网络设施 • By the way, can I have access to the Internet in my room? • By the way, can I have Internet access in the room? Receptionist: 询问订单号码 • May I have your booking number? • Do you have a booking number? • Could you please wait a moment, sir? 确认预订房间的具体信息（包括确切的离店时间） • Yes, we have your reservation. • You booked one superior room with a lake view for two nights and will check out this Saturday, is that right? • You booked a twin room for three nights. And you're going to check out on May 15, aren't you? 要求填表格和核对护照 • Here's the form for you to fill out and sign. • Could you please fill out the form and sign it? • May I have your passport first? 询问支付方式 • How are you going to pay, cash or credit card, Mr Moore? • Are you going to pay in cash or by credit card?
	介绍酒店设施及相关服务（互联网的使用、房间的景观、早餐时间和地点等） • Wireless Internet is available in all the hotel rooms, and it's free. • The room has a very good view, Mr Moore. It faces the garden with a swimming pool. • The room has a good view of the lake/city/street. • You can enjoy the wonderful view of West Lake while having some specialties in Hangzhou. • It's a large room with a bird's view over the city. • We offer room service. • We also offer luxurious Western meals in Philip Steakhouse and some traditional Cantonese and Sichuan food in Dahua Chinese restaurant. • Now your room is on the sixth floor, and here's your key card. The elevator/lift is just over there beside the business center. You can have breakfast down in the lobby on the right.
Expressing Thanks and Reply 表示感谢和答复	• Thank you very much. • I'm very grateful for your help. • I really appreciate your help. • Thanks./Many thanks./Thanks a lot./Thanks a million. — You're welcome. — It's a pleasure./My pleasure. — Don't mention it. — It was nothing at all.

Expressing Sorry and Reply 表示抱歉和答复	• Sorry, sir. • I'm very sorry, sir/madam. • I'm terribly sorry for it, sir. • Excuse me. • Pardon? • We do apologize for the inconvenience. — It's OK. — Not at all. — Never mind. — No problem. — Forget it. — Don't worry.
Room Service 送餐服务	• Good morning, room service. May I help you? • What would you like for breakfast? • I'm sorry, Mr Ralf, we don't have guava juice, but we have orange juice, apple juice, pineapple juice, and papaya juice. Would you like one of these instead? • Which kind of breakfast do you prefer, continental or American style? • Now, may I repeat it?
Housekeeping Service 客房服务	及时处理客户抱怨和投诉 • We'll take care of/handle/deal with these problems as soon as possible. • Well, our maid will go up to your room right now. She'll be at your service. And the repairman will arrive soon to take care of the toilet. If the odor (气味) can't be removed, you can surely have another room after we check with the receptionist, madam. • We'll send someone up in a minute.

Part E　English in Use

I. Reading Comprehension

Task 1：Choose the best answer to complete each sentence below.

1. — Do you have a _____?
   — Yes, the name is Bill Stephen.
   A. order 　　　　B. reservation 　　　C. check 　　　　D. bookings

2. Excuse me, can I _____ the Internet in my room?
   A. take 　　　　B. used 　　　　C. have access to 　　D. enter

3. — How long will you be staying?
   — I'll be _____ on Saturday.
   A. checking out 　B. checking in 　　C. leave 　　　　D. out

4. — May I have your _____ number?
   — Here it is. We have booked a double room with pool view.
   A. information 　　B. booking 　　　C. room 　　　　D. phone

5. — I really appreciate your help.
   — _____.
   A. It's my duty 　　B. I should help 　　C. Don't mention it 　D. I'd love to

6. — May I have a _____ call for 6:30 am tomorrow?
   — Certainly, sir. What's your room number?
   A. waking   B. alarm   C. wake up   D. morning
7. — Room service, may I help you?
   — Yes, this is Sam Mathew in Room 1221. May I have a tuna sandwich _____ up to my room?
   A. sent   B. send   C. sending   D. being sent
8. Wireless Internet is _____ in all the hotel rooms, and it's free.
   A. used   B. free   C. useful   D. available
9. Your luggage will be _____ to your rooms soon.
   A. take   B. delivered   C. deliver   D. delivering
10. — Thank you. That's very kind of you.
    — _____. What else can we do for you, madam?
    A. Never   B. OK   C. It's all right   D. You're welcome

Task 2: Answer the following questions according to the article on handling complaints in Part C in this unit.

1. When a guest has a complaint, as a staff member, how should you try to listen to it?
2. According to the author, how will you show your attentiveness when listening to the guest's complaint?
3. When answering the phone, what "verbal nods" signal interest and concern?
4. What will you say to show your empathy to the guest's complaint?
5. What kind of problem did the guest have judging from the statement "Ms Young, I can understand that this must have been frustrating for you. With such a big event planned for this evening, I'm sure the last thing you needed was a hotel room without hot water."?

Task 3: Decide whether each of the following statements is true or false according to the article in Part C in this unit.

1. When hearing a complaint, it's important to keep silent and listen carefully. (   )
2. If a guest cannot get the room type as required, it's a good idea to offer alternative choices. (   )
3. Guests always expect your solutions to deal with their problems. (   )
4. We should be more careful about the voiced guest complaints instead of the unvoiced ones. (   )
5. According to the author, the guest might post their complaints online if their problems are not solved. (   )

II. Translation

Task 4: Translate the following sentences into English.

1. 请您填一下表格并签字，好吗？
2. 酒店所有房间都可以无线上网，并且免费。
3. 您的房间在 10 楼，这是您的房卡。电梯就在左边。

4. 自助早餐时间是从上午 7:00 到 9:30，餐厅在三楼。

5. 史密斯先生，您想用现金还是信用卡支付？

6. 您有预订号吗？

7. 您在品尝一些杭州特色菜时可以享受西湖美景。

8. 这里有 10 张护照，包括您的，还有你们房间的房卡。

9. 这个房间的景色不错，面对着一个带泳池的花园。

10. 这间房很大，可以俯瞰整个城市。

Task 5: Translate the following sentences into Chinese.

1. You've booked one superior double room with pool view and one standard twin room for two nights and will check out this Thursday, May 23, is that right?

2. I'd like a glass of orange juice, one omelette and one bowl of muesli, please.

3. I'm afraid one single person in your group has to pay the price difference for the twin room according to the contract.

4. We also offer luxurious Western meals and lots of traditional Chinese food.

5. Our maid will go up to your room right now. She'll be at your service. And our repairman will arrive soon to take care of the toilet. If the odor can't be removed, you can surely have another room after we check with the receptionist, madam.

6. We'll take care of these problems as soon as possible.

7. You can leave your things in the laundry bag in your room, madam. Our maid will take care of the laundry and will send it back to your room after it's ready, madam.

8. You've booked a double room for two nights. And you're going to check out on Sunday, April 10, aren't you?

9. We'll send someone up in a minute.

10. Only a child under 10 is free. I'm sorry, Mrs Simpson, you have to pay 80 RMB for the extra bed.

III. Role Play

Task 6: Play a role in any of the following situations with your partner(s).

Situation 1: You're a tour guide for a British tour group. You're helping the tour leader and his group check into the hotel. Make a dialogue with the tour leader.

Situation 2: You're a receptionist at the front desk of a four-star hotel. A British/French/German guest is checking in at the hotel with a booking number. But unfortunately, all the standard single rooms are occupied until the following day. Make a dialogue with the guest and try to handle the problem.

Situation 3: Mr and Mrs White have just checked in at a hotel. After entering the room, Mrs White finds that there's a stain on the sheet, the bathtub looks dirty, what's worse, there isn't much hot water. So she calls the housekeeper and complains about it. In addition, she asks for room service. Suppose you're the housekeeper, make a dialogue with Mrs White and try to solve the problems.

Situation 4: After checking in at a hotel, Mrs Lincoln doesn't like the room for it smells of cigarette, and the toilet doesn't flush well. Then she calls the housekeeper and complains about it.

Now you're the housekeeper, make a dialogue with Mrs Lincoln and try to deal with the problem.

IV. Problem-solving

Task 7: Make an analysis of the following cases, and answer the questions as required.

Case 1

Situation: An American tourist group has just arrived at a hotel. After entering the room, Mr and Mrs Simpson find that the toilet doesn't flush well in the bathroom and the ceiling is leaking as well. They go downstairs immediately to speak to the tour guide about getting a better room. The guide is still speaking with guests checking in at the reception.

Question: What should a guide do if tourists request better rooms due to inadequate facilities?

Case 2

Situation: A tourist group from Britain has just arrived at a hotel. The guide helps the tour leader hand over the key cards to the tourists. Sue suddenly wants to have a single room because she feels like she needs to have a good sleep and doesn't want to be disturbed by another person. Now she asks the guide for help.

Question: What should a guide do if a tourist asks for a single room instead of the standard room as specified in the contract?

Answers for Reference

Unit 4　Service in a Restaurant

> **Warm-up**
>
> 1. As a server in a restaurant, what are your main duties for customer services?
> 2. How will you handle customer complaints?

Part A　Seating the Guests and Taking Orders

Dialogue 1

Situation: *Richard, a backpacker, comes into a Café.*

Questions for comprehension and discussion:
★ Where does the waiter suggest Richard should sit?
★ Where does Richard prefer to sit?
★ What does Richard finally order?
★ If you were the waiter or waitress, how would you seat the customers and take their orders?

　Waiter:　Good afternoon, sir.

Richard:　Good afternoon. Is it possible to have a meal here?

　Waiter:　Sure. How many in the group?

Richard:　Just me.

　Waiter:　OK, this way please. How about this table in the corner? It's very quiet here.

Richard:　Can I have the table by the window?

　Waiter:　I'm sorry, sir. The one by the window has already been reserved.

Richard: Never mind. Then I'll take this one.

Waiter: May I take your order now?

Richard: Just a moment, please. I'd rather take a look at the menu first.

Waiter: OK, here is the menu.

(A moment later)

Waiter: Are you ready to order now, sir?

Richard: Yes, please. I'd like a Mexican steak and a vegetable salad.

Waiter: How would you like your steak cooked, rare, medium or well done?

Richard: Medium rare, please.

Waiter: And what kind of dressing would you like on the salad?

Richard: What dressings do you have?

Waiter: We have French, Italian, and Thousand Island.

Richard: Then French please.

Waiter: OK. Anything to drink, sir?

Richard: A bottle of Budweiser, please. Oh, by the way, do you have a local beer?

Waiter: Yes, of course. We have Xihu (West Lake) Beer.

Richard: Well, then I'd rather have Xihu Beer.

Waiter: That's all right, sir. A bottle of Xihu Beer, is that all right?

Richard: Exactly.

Waiter: Cold or not cold?

Richard: Cold, please.

Waiter: Anything else?

Richard: No, thank you. That's all.

Dialogue 2

Situation: *Werner and Christel, a German couple, enter a Chinese restaurant. A waitress sees them and goes up to greet them.*

Questions for comprehension and discussion:

★ Where did the couple ask to sit?

★ What kind of view will they have there?

★ Which type of meal do they choose, a la carte or a set meal?

★ How does the waitress recommend Shaoxing Yellow Wine to the couple?

★ How does the waitress recommend the main course to the couple?

★ If you were the waiter or waitress, what would you do then?

Waitress: Good evening, sir. Do you have a reservation?

Werner: Yes. I've made a reservation. I'm Werner Hutterer.

Waitress: OK, just a minute, please. Ah, yes, here it is, Mr Hutterer. A table for two?

Werner: Right, just two of us. We asked for a table by the window.

Waitress: Yes, We reserved one for you, Mr Hutterer. This way, please. Here is your table by the window, is it all right? You have a very good view of the street.

Werner: Oh, perfect! I love it. Thank you.

Waitress: With pleasure. Now here is your menu. Would you like to have a look before you order?

Werner: Yes, please.

(After a while)

Waitress: Are you ready to order now, sir?

Werner: Oh, yes, please.

Waitress: OK, what would you like to drink? Have you ever tried Shaoxing rice wine?

Werner: No, we haven't heard about it. We are new here in China.

Waitress: It's not only our local specialty but also well-known throughout the country. It's different from white wine or red wine. It's made from **sticky rice** (糯米). So it's also called Yellow Wine in China. It tastes quite mellow, sweet and unique. In a word, once you taste it, you will never forget it. It's always a favorite with our regular customers including many foreign guests like you. But one can easily get drunk on it only because of its **tempting** (诱人的) aroma and taste.

Werner: Really? It sounds amazing. I'd love to try some.

Waitress: Good. Then how much would you like, a glass or a bottle?

Werner: A bottle? Oh, no, just a glass, please. I don't want to get drunk, do I?

Waitress: No, you won't. What age wine would you prefer? Three, five, or maybe even ten years old?

Werner: Sorry, I have no idea. What's your suggestion?

Waitress: Well, normally the older the better. But since it's the first time for you to take, you may try the five-year-old one. It tastes perfect.

Werner: OK, I'll take it. What about you, Christel? Would you also like some?

Christel: Sorry, no, not for me. I'd rather have a soft drink, please.

Waitress: We have orange juice, apple juice and corn juice, which one do you prefer, madam?

Christel: Oh, corn juice sounds interesting to me. I've eaten lots of corn at home, but I've never tried the juice.

Waitress: Well, it tastes quite good and is very popular nowadays in China. Would you like some?

Christel: OK, a glass please.

Waitress: Well, would you care for a starter? We have many cold dishes as starters.

Werner: Just a la carte, please.

Christel: What's special for tonight?

Waitress: Today's special is fried crab. It's our chef's personal favorite. Would you try it?

Christel: Fried crab? It sounds unusual to me. I don't know how to eat the crab.

Waitress: Here is the picture of the dish.

Christel: It's **tantalizing** (诱人的), but it might be a bit messy to eat. I'd prefer something else.

Werner: What else can you recommend?

Waitress: Perhaps you might like shrimp meat with crispy fried rice crust. It's called **Xiaren Guoba** (虾仁锅巴) in Chinese.

Werner: It sounds quite special. Let's have a try.

Christel: What vegetable do you have?

Waitress: We've got a variety of fresh vegetables, such as **asparagus** (芦笋) with minced garlic, green peas with ham, **braised bamboo shoots** (油焖笋), etc.

Christel: I love Chinese bamboos, but have never tried bamboo shoots.

Waitress: So would you like to have a try? It's a typical Chinese dish.

Christel: OK, we'll have the bamboo shoots.

Waitress: And if you like hot food, you might also try **Mapo Tofu** (麻婆豆腐), the Chinese **beancurd** (豆腐) in **chili sauce** (辣酱).

Werner: Good. It's always my favorite.

Waitress: Anything else?

Werner: No, thank you. It's enough.

Waitress: OK, let me repeat your order. You'll have a glass of Shaoxing Yellow Wine, a glass of corn juice, the shrimp meat with crispy fried rice crust, braised bamboo shoots and Mapo Tofu, is that all right?

Werner: Yes, that's correct. Thank you.

Waitress: You're welcome.

Part B   Handling Complaints and Settling the Bill

Dialogue 1

Situation: *Judy and her two friends are having some problems while trying to eat at a busy restaurant in China.*

Questions for comprehension and discussion:

★　What problems do Judy and her friends have?

★　What does the waitress give as an excuse?

★　How does the waitress try to solve the problems?

★　If you were the waiter or waitress, how would you solve the problems then?

Judy: Excuse me, how much longer are we going to have to wait for our dinner? I've been trying to catch your attention for almost 15 minutes.

Waitress: I'm terribly sorry, madam. We do apologize for the **inconvenience** (不便). We're quite busy today. What's worse, We're very short of help. By the way, I'm afraid the stewed chicken with mushroom you have ordered really needs quite a while to prepare. Here's our **complimentary** (赠送的) tea.

Judy: That's all right. Thank you, anyway.

(A moment later, the stewed chicken is served. The waitress starts to leave.)

Judy: Just a minute, please. There's too much salt in the soup and the meat is still a bit tough.

Waitress: Oh, I'm quite sorry, madam. Would you like it cooked a little more? I'll speak to the chef right away and see what he can do for you.

Judy: OK. Thank you.

Waitress: It's a pleasure.

Waitress: Here are some Chinese **dates** (枣子), **compliments** (敬意) of the chef.

Judy: Oh, great. Thanks.

Waitress: You're welcome. Enjoy!

(After the meal)

Judy: Oh, may I have the bill, please?

Waitress: Certainly. Would you like one bill or separate bills?

Judy: Please put them together. It's **on me** (我请客) this time. Do you take credit cards?

Waitress: Of course. What kind of credit card do you have?

Judy: American Visa.

Waitress: No problem. By the way, we also take Alipay (支付宝) and Wechat Pay (微信支付).

Judy: Sorry, I don't have them now. But I think I might try to have one of them if I decide to extend my stay.

(After a while)

Waitress: Here is the bill. Just sign here, please.

Judy: OK.

Waitress: Thank you very much. Good night. Hope to see you again.

Dialogue 2

Situation: *A waitress offers a wrong dish to Mr and Mrs Smith, a British couple.*

Questions for comprehension and discussion:

★ What did Mr Smith order?

★ What does the waitress bring to them?

★ Does Mr Smith refuse to take it?

★ What compensation does the waitress offer for her mistake?

★ If you were the waiter or waitress, what would you do then?

Waitress: Here you are, sir, **the stir-fried shrimp, Shanghai style** (上海油爆虾).

Mr Smith: Pardon? The stir–fried shrimp? Sorry, this is not what I ordered.

Waitress: Oh, I'm terribly sorry. I must have made a mistake. What did you order?

Mr Smith: I asked for **salty boiled shrimp** (盐水虾).

Waitress: I'm really sorry. I misunderstood you. I'll change it right now.

Mr Smith: That's all right. Well, it doesn't look bad; I think I'll take it anyway.

Waitress: Thank you very much, that's very kind of you. But if it really bothers you, I'll exchange it for you.

Mr Smith: No, thanks. That's fine with me. By the way, the dish here **shredded pork with vegetables, Sichuan style** (川味小炒) is too oily for me.

Waitress: Oh, I'm sorry. May I take it back and ask the chef to make a lighter one?

Mr Smith: That would be lovely. Thank you.

Waitress: You're welcome.

(After the meal)

Mr Smith: Could you please bring the bill?

Waitress: How are you going to pay, in cash or by credit card?

Mr Smith: In cash, please.

Waitress: Altogether, it's 95 Chinese yuan. We do apologize for the inconvenience and would like to offer you a 10% discount for the food.

Mr Smith: Thanks, that's very nice of you.

Waitress: Thank you too. Hope to see you again. Goodbye!

Part C   Tips on Restaurant Service Etiquette

*The following article on "**Top 10 Unspoken Rules of Restaurant Service Etiquette**" was written by Erika Strum on Feb 20, 2010, retrieved on May 10, 2020 (from http://www.winemag.com/ 2010/02/20/opinion-top-10-unspoken-rules-of-restaurant-service-etiquette).*

Questions for comprehension and discussion:

★ What do you think are some rules of restaurant service etiquette?

★ What do you think of the 10 unspoken rules mentioned in the text?

If you dine out with any **regularity** (规律), it's likely you have an opinion on how restaurant service should be. Whether you feel service is of prime importance or not, we all have our **gripes** (牢骚). Recently, I had a particularly poor experience at a **2-Michelin-Star** (米其林二星) restaurant in NY. Since posting my **recap** (简要概述) this morning, I've been amazed at the number of people **corralling** (集中) to support me. And it makes sense! When you pay top dollars for a meal, people should treat you nicely. Oddly enough, I think too many people take service **etiquette** (礼节) for granted. Not wanting to be **curmudgeonly** (坏脾气的) they keep opinions to themselves, making these rules unspoken.

Anyone who has dined with me knows I'm not shy about discussing these **sticking points** (困惑的问题). So why not share them with all of you? These are my top ten rules for providing great service, in no particular order. What are yours?

☆ If a reserved table is not ready when the customers arrive and they have to wait longer than 15 minutes, apologize and offer a **complimentary** (免费赠送的) **cocktail** (鸡尾酒) or glass of wine.

☆ When asking about water **preferences** (爱好), be as clear as possible. No one will be happy when they order a $20 bottle of **Perrier** (法国产的毕雷矿泉水) by accident. Also, don't make the customer feel bad if they want **tap water** (自来水). Asking "Bottled water or just tap?" creates this feeling.

☆ Never make **assumptions** (猜测) about someone's wine knowledge. Ask a few questions to **gauge** (判断) their experience. (Just because I'm young and female, doesn't mean I'm a novice!)

☆ There is a certain **rhythm** (间隔) to water and wine refills. Both need to be handled with enough frequency that the customers never pour for themselves but rarely enough, that they won't feel **rushed** (匆忙的) or **intruded** (侵入) upon.

☆ Good wait staff are always available for **patrons** (老主顾) who might be seeking attention. Even when focused on something else, they should **have their eyes peeled** (警觉). Customers should not have to **flail** (挥动) their arms to get somebody's attention.

☆ Do not ask if someone is finished when others are still eating that course. It makes those eating feel guilty and rushed.

☆ Please do not clear plates until everyone is finished.

☆ If I clean my plate, don't make a comment about it. Yes, this girl likes to eat!

☆ Please do not bring the bill until someone requests it.

☆ Wait until the customer leaves to take the signed bill. It makes them feel rushed and it's awkward to say goodbye after the tip is signed, even if the service was perfect.

In the end, your waiter/waitress is a person too and nobody is perfect. These are **mere** (仅仅) guidelines. But no matter what your profession is, we should all aim to do a good job of it!

Part D   Language Checklist

A. Vocabulary

		speciality/specialty 招牌菜/特色菜 Chef's Special 主厨特色菜 Chef's Soup 主厨特色汤	fry 油煎 sauté 嫩煎 stew 炖 braise 炖/焖 simmer 炖/慢煮 boil 煮/steam 蒸
rare 二至三分熟 medium rare 三至四分熟 medium 五分熟 well done 全熟	a la carte 照菜单点菜 table d'hote 套餐 set meal 套餐		
bake 烘焙/roast 烘烤 broil 烤炙（高温） grill （烤架）烧烤 barbecue 烧烤野餐	tasty/delicious 美味的 yummy 好吃的 palatable 可口的 appetizing 开胃的	bland/tasteless/flavorless/ unsavory 无味的 oily/greasy 油腻的	awful/terrible/disgusting/ distasteful/ yucky 难吃的

B. Key Patterns

Seating the Diners/Guests 安排座位	• Could you follow me, please?/Could you please follow me? • This way, please. • Would you like to come with me, sir? • Here's your table, sir. It's by the window. • Yes, we have a window table reserved for you. • Would you like to sit here? It's very quiet. • Would you like to take the one in the corner? • How about this one? You can have a good view of the lake. • What about the one that is further back but still offers a view of the lake? 有靠后一点但是仍能欣赏到湖上景色的桌子，行不行？ • Will this table be all right? • There is a table for six over there. Would you like it? • I'm sorry, there is only one table near the door available now. Would you mind sitting over there? Or you may wait in the lounge if you like and we'll let you know when we have a table available. • I'm sorry, sir, the one by the window has already been reserved. • I'm sorry to say that we haven't got any vacant seat at present/at the moment. • I'm sorry, the house is full now. But if you would like to wait, you are more than welcome to do so. 对不起，餐厅现在客满了。但是如果您愿意在这儿等的话，我们非常欢迎。 • Would you please wait in the lounge for about five minutes? 请您在休息室等 5 分钟左右好吗？ • I'm sorry to have kept you waiting, madam. Your table is ready now.
Asking If the Dinner is Ready to Order 询问是否点菜	• Are you ready to order now, sir? • May I take your order, sir? • Would you like to order now, sir? • Have you decided on something, sir?/Have you decided what you'd like, sir?

Asking What to Have 询问吃什么	• What would you like to have/drink?/Would you like something to drink/eat? • What kind of drink would you like to have? • What would you like to start/begin with? • Would you like a la carte or table d'hote/a set meal? 您想单点还是点套餐？ • Would you care for a drink before you order, sir? • What soup would you like to have/prefer? • How about the drink/soup/dessert/vegetables? • How do you like your steak cooked, rare, medium or well done? • And any vegetables? • And what to follow? 接下来还要什么？
Asking What to Offer 询问菜肴	• What are your specialties? • What's your specialty?/What's today's special?/What's good today? • What's Chef's Special? • What soup would you recommend?/What would you recommend for soup? • Let's look at the menu first. • What else have you got on the menu?/What have you got? • What kind of seafood/soup/dessert do you have/serve?
Recommending the Dishes 介绍菜肴	• Shaoxing Yellow Wine (Shaoxing Rice Wine) tastes quite mellow, sweet and unique. 绍兴黄酒味道香醇甜美，很独特。 • I would recommend Dongpo Cubed Pork. It's our specialty. It tastes very special and you may have a try. 我向您推荐东坡肉这道菜，这是我们的特色菜，味道特别，您可以尝一下。 • Perhaps you might like shrimp meat with crispy fried rice crust. It's called Xiaren Guoba in Chinese. 也许您可能喜欢虾仁和松脆的油煎锅巴，中文叫虾仁锅巴。 • We've got a variety of fresh vegetables, such as asparagus with minced garlic, green peas with ham, braised bamboo shoots, etc. 我们有各种新鲜蔬菜，如蒜泥芦笋、火腿豌豆和油焖笋等。 • Maybe our fish cutlet will be to your taste. 我觉得我们的鱼片可能合您的口味。 • If you like hot food, you may/might try Mapo Tofu, the Chinese beancurd in chili sauce. 如果您喜欢辣的菜，不妨尝试一下麻婆豆腐。 • So why not have a try? It's a typical Chinese dish. • Well, would you care for some starter? We have many cold dishes as the starters.
Handling the Complaints 处理抱怨	• We do apologize for the inconvenience and would like to offer you a 10% discount for the food. 真的很抱歉给您带来不便，现在给您点的食物打九折。 • Oh, I'm quite sorry. May I take it back and ask the chef to make it less greasy? 非常对不起。我能把这道菜拿回去让厨师做得清淡一点吗？ • I'm terribly sorry. I must have made a mistake. What did you order? • I'm really sorry. I misunderstood you. Let me change it for you right away. • Here are some Chinese dates, compliments of the chef. 这些是厨师赠送的红枣。 • Here's our complimentary (赠送的) tea. 这是我们赠送的茶。 • I'm really sorry. I'll be happy to change it for you. 真的抱歉，我会（很愿意）给您换菜。
Settling the Bill 结账	• How are you going to pay, in cash or by credit card? 您想怎么支付，现金还是信用卡？ • Would you like one bill or separate bills? 你们一起付账还是分开付账？ • What kind of credit card do you have? • Here is the bill. Will you please sign it here? • By the way, we also take Alipay and Wechat Pay. 顺便提一下，我们也可以接受支付宝和微信支付方式。

Part E　English in Use

I. Reading Comprehension

Task 1: Choose the best answer to complete each sentence below.

1. — May I take your _____?
   — I'd like the rocky mountain oyster.
   A. menu　　　　　B. order　　　　　C. dish　　　　　D. food

2. — How would you like your steak _____?
   — Well done please.
   A. cooked　　　　B. cooking　　　　C. to cook　　　　D. to be cooking

3. — I'm sorry, sir. Would you like your egg sunny-side up or _____?
   — Sunny-side up please.
   A. scrambling　　B. over easy　　　C. over sided　　D. rare

4. What kind of dressing do you like _____ the salad? We have French, Italian, and Thousand Island.
   A. for　　　　　B. at　　　　　　C. on　　　　　　D. with

5. Would you like one bill or _____ bills?
   A. separate　　　B. differ　　　　C. many　　　　　D. same

6. Would you like to take _____ or a set meal?
   A. individuals　　B. separated meal　C. different　　　D. a la carte

7. We have various _____, such as beans, peas, cabbage, eggplant and cauliflower. Which one do you prefer?
   A. dish　　　　　B. food　　　　　C. vegetables　　D. cuisine

8. What would you like to _____, orange or apple juice?
   A. drink　　　　B. eat　　　　　　C. /　　　　　　D. favor

9. How many people do you have? A table _____ ten?
   A. for　　　　　B. at　　　　　　C. of　　　　　　D. with

10. Here is the _____. Are you ready to order?
    A. a la carte　　B. menu　　　　　C. drink　　　　D. dish

Task 2: Answer the following questions concerning the restaurant service etiquette in Part C.

1. What shall a server do if the reserved table is not ready when the customers arrive and they have to wait for a long time?

2. What is the best time to refill the customer's water or wine?

3. Why shouldn't the server ask if someone is finished while others are still eating?

4. When will the server bring the bill?

5. What might be the other rules you may keep in mind when offering service in a restaurant?

Task 3: Decide whether each of the following statements is True or False according to the article on restaurant service etiquette in Part C.

1. You only say sorry to the customers when they have to wait for a long time to have dinner. (   )
2. It is very important to be as clear as possible when asking about water preferences. (   )
3. A good server will always be at the customer's service. (   )
4. As a server, you can make a comment as "Well, do you like the food?" when the customer is cleaning his or her own plate. (   )
5. When serving in a restaurant, you should always wait until a customer waves wildly to get your attention. (   )

II. Translation

Task 4: Translate the following sentences into English.

1. 您想先来点什么？
2. 对不起，所有靠窗的位子都已经被预订了。
3. 请走这边，好吗？角落这边的桌子怎么样？这儿很安静。
4. 我向您推荐东坡肉，它是我们的特色菜，味道很特别，您可以尝一下。
5. 我重复一下您的订单好吗？您想要鸡肉面条、西兰花和酸辣汤，对吗？
6. 您想单点还是点套餐？
7. 您希望牛排怎么烧？嫩一点，不老不嫩，还是老一点？
8. 对不起，目前没有空位。
9. 请您在休息室等5分钟左右，好吗？
10. 先生、女士，对不起，让你们久等了，现在，你们的桌子已准备好了。

Task 5: Translate the following sentences into Chinese.

1. We have various salad dressings, such as French, Italian, and Thousand Island. Which one do you prefer?
2. You have ordered a tuna, a sandwich, a black coffee, and a glass of orange juice.
3. I'm sorry, since it has been served according to your order, I'm afraid we cannot replace it with Mapo Tofu for you, unless you agree to bear the extra expense.
4. We have very nice assorted vegetables, such as asparagus with minced garlic, green beans with ham, braised bamboo shoots, etc.
5. Shaoxing Yellow Wine (Shaoxing Rice Wine) tastes quite mellow, sweet and unique. It is always a favorite with our regular customers including many foreign guests like you.
6. How are you going to pay, in cash or by credit card?
7. By the way, the dish here shredded pork with vegetables, Sichuan Style is too oily for me.
8. Here are the Chinese dates, compliments of the chef.
9. Would you care for a starter? We have many cold dishes as starters.
10. I'm afraid the stewed chicken you have ordered really needs quite a while to prepare. Here's our complimentary tea.

III. Role Play

Task 6: Play a role in any of the following situations with your partner(s).

Situation 1: You're a receptionist at a hotel restaurant. A guest called Angela Thatcher is calling you to reserve two tables for 16 people for Friday evening at 6:00 pm. She's requesting for both tables by the window. But unfortunately, all the tables except one by the window have been taken by the others. Now you negotiate with the guest and try to meet her needs.

Situation 2: You're working in a nice restaurant in your local area. One day, a group of foreign tourists come in. They haven't made a reservation. Greet and seat them, take their orders, and settle the bill.

Situation 3: A group of American tourists enter a restaurant. All of them make their own choices. But when the food is served on the table, Lily, one of the group members, finds that she gets a wrong dish. What's worse, another member Bob's order seems to be totally forgotten, and he has to wait until almost all the others at the table have finished their own food. Now they complain to the server. You're the server and feel terribly sorry for the mess and try your best to deal with all these problems.

IV. Problem-solving

Task 7: Analyze the following cases, and then answer the questions as required.

Case 1

Situation: Linda has reserved a table for five people at a busy restaurant at 6:00 pm. Now it's 6:15 pm, Linda calls the wait staff that she and her friends would be one hour late due to the traffic jam. However, it's in the peak season, and there is a long waiting list in the restaurant.

Question: Suppose you were the server receiving Linda's call, what would you say to her? If Linda and her friends finally arrived, what would you do then?

Case 2

Situation: Since the restaurant is crowded with diners, Sue has been waiting for a long time for her dish. However, a small group of people next to her table are lucky enough to get their food much quicker than her, though they entered the restaurant much later than her. Now she complains to one of the wait staff.

Question: If you were serving Sue, how would you handle the complaint?

Answers for Reference

Unit 5　Chinese Cuisine

Warm-up

1. People often say "fashion in Europe, living in America, but eating in China." **Now can you think of one or two sayings concerning food in Chinese culture and explain what they mean in English?**

2. Are you a **gourmet** (美食家), a person who knows a lot about food and drink? Do you like cooking? **Now check how much you know about Chinese cuisine. Write the name of the dish you know under each of the pictures.**

1) _____

2) _____

3) _____

4) _____

5) _____

6) _____

7) _____

8) _____

9) _____

Part A　Four Major Cuisines in China

Dialogue

Situation: *Sam, an American university student who is very interested in Chinese cuisine, is with a tour group in Hangzhou. After visiting Lingyin Temple and Feilai Peak, they are now having a short rest. Sam takes the chance to ask their tour guide, Chen Yan, something about Chinese cuisine.*

Questions for comprehension and discussion:

★ Why does Sam love Chinese food?

★ What are the main features of Chinese cuisine?

★ What are the "four or eight major cuisines" commonly known to us?

★ What other cuisine do you know in China which is worth mentioning?

Sam: Excuse me, Chen Yan. Can I ask you some questions about Chinese cuisine? I'm preparing a paper on it.

Chen Yan: Sure. What would you like to know?

Sam: Well, I come from New York. There's a wide choice of Chinese restaurants there. Whenever possible, I go there either by myself or together with my Chinese friends. I love Chinese food very much. Cooked in various ways with diversified colors, these Chinese dishes are full of flavor and taste really good.

Chen Yan: I'm glad you love Chinese food. In fact, you've already mentioned the main features of Chinese cuisine — diversified colors, characteristic flavor, and distinctive taste. However, Chinese cuisine is not only tasty but also a work of art for people to appreciate. That's why Chinese cuisine is ranked among the best of the world's cuisines and Chinese restaurants can be found today in many countries and regions throughout the world.

Sam: So, typical Chinese food should include the features of color, flavor, taste and **food presentation** (食物展示/形) as well?

Chen Yan: Right, we call it "a perfect combination of color, flavor, taste and food presentation".

Sam: Could you please explain them in more details?

Chen Yan: Sure. First, food with lots of colors can usually arouse people's **appetite** (胃口). To have pleasant and harmonious colors is one of the main principles when cooking Chinese food. To achieve this, two or three ingredients with different colors make a wonderful presentation. To put it simply, if the food doesn't look good, few people would like to try it, right?

Sam: That's true. The first impression is very important. Personally, I wouldn't try any ugly foods.

Chen Yan: You've got it. Then the food should smell good. The **aroma** (香味) of the food

can be very **inviting** (诱人的). Various herbs and spices are used to add flavor to the food. Spices such as **aniseed** (茴香), Chinese **prickly ash seeds** (花椒籽) and **cinnamon** (桂皮) are also used to **dispel** (消除) unfavorable **odors** (气味) of some ingredients like **mutton** (羊肉) or fish. Other herbs like **scallions** (细葱), ginger, garlic or **chili** (红辣椒), together with **cooking rice wine** (料酒) and **sesame oil** (芝麻油), are also added to give the food a fragrant flavor.

Sam: I see. It's interesting that the herbs and spices used in your country are quite different from ours at home. For example, we seldom use ginger or scallions, but often use **parsley** (香菜), **rosemary** (迷迭香), **thyme** (百里香), etc.

Chen Yan: Just as what your beautiful song "**Scarborough Fair** (斯卡布罗集市)" tells? That's why Chinese food has its unique flavor. Now let's come to the taste. Distinctive taste is regarded as the soul of Chinese cuisine. Some 3,000 years ago, Chinese people already knew how to "deliciously" blend the **five tastes** (五味) — sweet, sour, bitter, spicy and salty. **Condiments** (调料) such as soy sauce, sugar, vinegar and salt are added in proper **proportion** (比例) at different times to enhance the flavor of the food.

Sam: Got it. Thank you very much. By the way, I once read about eight major Chinese cuisines, but just lately I've heard of four major cuisines in China. Now I'm getting confused about them. Are they **interrelated** (互相关联的)?

Chen Yan: There are thousands of different local cooking styles in China due to the differences in **geography** (地理), climate, resources, **produce** (物产) and eating habits. Chinese cuisine is usually divided into eight regional cuisines[①], among which Sichuan, Guangdong, Shandong, and **Huaiyang** (淮扬) cuisines are the first four original and popular ones. Besides, sometimes Beijing and Shanghai cuisines are also now included. In addition, there are some special cuisines like **imperial cuisine** (御膳), **vegetarian cuisine** (素膳), and **medicinal cuisine** (药膳). Chinese medicinal cuisine is unique and has a long history. It's a combination of **therapeutic** (益于健康的) Chinese herbs and food. In China, it is widely believed that **food tonic** (食补) is much better than medicine in strengthening one's health.

Sam: Oh, really? What are the characteristics of the four major ones then?

Chen Yan: Let's begin with Sichuan Cuisine, which is called **Chuan Cai** (川菜) in Chinese. It's well-known in China and overseas for its **tongue-numbing** (麻) and mixed spicy tastes. For example, **Poached Fish Fillet in Chili Oil** (水煮鱼)**, The Couple's Sliced Beef and Ox Tongues in Chilli Sauce** (夫妻肺片) and Sichuan

---

① 中国由于不同的地理气候、资源物产，以及由此形成的饮食习惯，形成了各具特色的地方菜系，有"四大风味""八大菜系"之说。"四大风味"是指以鲁（山东）、川（四川）、粤（广东）、淮扬（扬州）为代表的地方风味；"八大菜系"是指由上述四种有代表性的风味发展而来的地方菜系，包括鲁菜（山东菜）、川菜（四川菜）、湘菜（湖南菜）、粤菜（广东菜）、闽菜（福建菜）、苏菜（江苏菜）、浙菜（浙江菜）、徽菜（安徽菜）。——北京市人民政府外事办公室和北京市民讲外语活动组委会办公室. 美食译苑——中文菜单英文译法[M]. 北京：世界知识出版社，2011：4。

hotpot (火锅) are very spicy and **appetizing** (开胃的).

Sam: Oh, yeah, I love hotpot. It's very delicious. But by the way, why is there the couple's dish? Maybe I have tried this dish but have never heard the name.

Chen Yan: You mean the sliced beef? Because it was first invented by a couple almost 100 years ago, who happened to put together some of the delicious **innords or offals** (内脏) such as ox tongues, **tripe** (牛肚), hearts, etc. in one dish. The dish has turned out to be very popular throughout the world, even in your country. Actually, the dish made by a Chinese Sichuan restaurant in **Huston** (休斯顿) ranked top in the **list of American Food in 2017** (美国 **2017** 餐饮排行榜) in the magazine "*Go*", and was voted as the **Appetizer of the Year (**年度开胃菜**)**. It got its name, Mr and Mrs Smith, after the well-known movie. Isn't that cool?

Sam: Wow, that's really cool. I can't wait to try it. Besides, I once had a dish called **Mapo Tofu** (麻婆豆腐). Is that a typical Sichuan dish too?

Chen Yan: Exactly. It's tofu **sautéed** (嫩煎) in a hot, spicy sauce. In a word, Sichuan chefs select their ingredients with great care, use a variety of seasonings and cook each dish differently. Thus, Sichuan dishes are known as "a hundred dishes with a hundred tastes", earning the reputation of "**food in China, taste in Sichuan**" or "**Chinese food with Sichuan flavors** (食在中国，味在四川)".

Sam: I see.

Chen Yan: Have you ever tried a Cantonese dish?

Sam: I think so, but I'm not quite clear about its features.

Chen Yan: Cantonese or Guangdong Cuisine, also called **Yue Cai** (粤菜) in Chinese, takes a great variety of ingredients from seafood to **poultry** (家禽). They emphasize freshness and tenderness. One of their most famous dishes is **Crispy Roasted Suckling Pig** (脆皮烤乳猪). Sounds mouth-watering, doesn't it?

Sam: Yeah! I'd try that. How about Shandong Cuisine then?

Chen Yan: Shandong Cuisine, or **Lu Cai** (鲁菜) in Chinese, also uses a wide selection of ingredients. Shandong soups are very famous, and green onions are commonly used to add flavor to the food. They are known for various seafood dishes. For instance, some dishes like **Braised Sea Cucumber with Scallions** (葱烧海参), **Crab Roes with Shark's Fin** (蟹黄鱼翅), **Dezhou Deboned Chicken** (德州扒鸡), and **Creamy Walnut Soup** (核桃奶油汤) are very **delectable** (美味可口的) and nutritious.

Sam: Wow! I wish I had the chance to try all this tasty food.

Chen Yan: Yes, you could if you stayed here for quite a long time.

Sam: Well, there's one more cuisine we haven't talked about, right?

Chen Yan: Yes. That's **Huaiyang Cuisine, or Huaiyang Cai** (淮扬菜) in Chinese.

Sam: Is there a province called Huaiyang in China?

Chen Yan: No. Huaiyang Cai is the famous cuisine of the **middle and lower reaches of the Yangtze River** (长江中下游) including Jiangsu, Zhejiang, Anhui, and parts of Jiangxi and Henan Provinces as well as Shanghai. Today Huaiyang Cuisine centers on **Yangzhou** (扬州), **Zhenjiang** (镇江) and **Huai'an** (淮安). Zhejiang Cuisine and Anhui Cuisine are included in the Eight Cuisines of China.

Huaiyang Cuisine has taken center stage in several international **banquets** (宴会). Huaiyang dishes have light flavors, retaining the original taste of the ingredients, and are very healthy and **organic** (有机的). They tend to be a bit sweet and are scarcely spicy, in contrast to those of Sichuan or Hunan. Most dishes are more **meticulously** (精细的) prepared with beautiful presentation, but their portions are not as generous as those of northern cuisines.

Sam: Any characteristic dishes?

Chen Yan: The most traditional and typical one I know is **Braised Pork Balls in Brown Sauce** (红烧狮子头). In its Chinese name, the meatball is compared to a lion's head, hence the name "Lion's Head-like Meatball Stew". A funny name, isn't it? I'm particularly fond of breakfast items like **Crab Roes Dumplings** (蟹黄汤包), **Thousand-layer Cake** (千层糕), **Steamed Jiaozi** (蒸饺) and **Cai Baozi** (Steamed Buns Stuffed with Vegetable, 菜包子).

Sam: Mm, yummy, my mouth is watering. Thanks for telling me so much about Chinese cuisines.

Chen Yan: My pleasure. This evening, you'll have a chance to taste our local specialties — Zhe Cai, that is Zhejiang Cuisine, specifically Hangzhou regional dishes.

Sam: Really?

Chen Yan: Yes. We're going to have dinner at Louwailou Restaurant, the most famous restaurant in Hangzhou.

Sam: Great!

Part B   Local Specialties

Monologue 1

Situation: *After a boat tour around West Lake, the American tour group are in Louwailou Restaurant (楼外楼餐馆) for dinner. Now everybody is at the dinner table waiting to be served. Chen Yan talks about Louwailou and its specialties.*

Questions for comprehension and discussion:

★ How does Chen Yan begin with her introduction?

★ What does she say about the history of Louwailou?

★ Can you pick out the adjectives used to describe the main features of Zhejiang Cuisine and Hangzhou Cuisine?

★ What are some of the specialties of Louwailou Chen Yan mentions at the end?

Good evening, everyone! We're now at Louwailou, Hangzhou's most famous restaurant, located at the foot of **Solitary Hill** (孤山) facing the beautiful West Lake near **Zhongshan Park** (中山公园), the former **temporary imperial palace** (临时行宫) in the Qing Dynasty. It's noted for its "delicious food and beautiful scenery". People in Hangzhou have a custom: guests are often invited to Louwailou to try **authentic** (正宗的) Hangzhou dishes if money allows. It's believed that one hasn't been to Hangzhou unless they have been to Louwailou.

The name of the restaurant, Louwailou, means "a building outside another building" or "building beyond building", which is said to be inspired by an ancient Chinese poem. Louwailou is a restaurant with a history of more than 160 years. It was founded in 1848 in the 28th year of **Emperor Daoguang** (道光皇帝，在位 1821 – 1850) in the Qing Dynasty. The

owner of this building is **Hong Ruitang** (洪瑞堂), a **man of letters who failed in the imperial examination** (落第文人). He and his wife moved from Shaoxing (绍兴) to Hangzhou after their parent's death, and lived at the bank of **Xiling Bridge** (西泠桥) at the foot of the Solitary Hill, making a living by boating and fishing. Their specialty was cooking fresh fish and shrimp. When they noticed that there was no restaurant in that area, they began to save money and opened a small restaurant. The restaurant was rebuilt on the site we are now in about forty years ago. This is not the original site.

Louwailou has long been a go-to restaurant for tourists at home and abroad. Its previous **patrons** (顾客) were **Sun Yat-sen** (孙中山), **Lu Xun** (鲁迅), etc. As far as I know, the former

Premier Zhou Enlai (周恩来总理) was here nine times, which has become a favorite tale for local people. Many foreign VIPs also dined here during their visit. Now for most people, a visit to Louwailou is a must during their tour in Hangzhou. With a wonderful view of West Lake outside, one can surely delight in dining here at the restaurant.

The restaurant features **authentic** (真正的) Hangzhou cuisine. As I've told you, Zhejiang Cuisine is one of the eight major cuisines in China. With exquisite preparation and various ways of cooking, Hangzhou food is quite light and fresh, and thus has become the most important part of Zhejiang Cuisine.

The most famous traditional specialties served here are **West Lake Vinegar Fish** (西湖醋鱼), **Fried Shelled Shrimps with Longjing Tea Leaves** (龙井虾仁), **Beggar's Chicken** (叫花鸡), **Sister Song's Fish Broth** (宋嫂鱼羹), **Dongpo Pork** (东坡肉), **Fried Stuffed Tofu Skin Rolls** (Fried Ring Bell, 干炸响铃) and many other typical dishes. This evening, you'll have all these dishes just mentioned. Now dinner is ready. Please help yourselves.

Monologue 2

Situation: *Chen Yan continues to make a brief introduction to the dishes at the table.*

Questions for comprehension and discussion:
★ How does Chen Yan introduce each dish at the table?
★ What different cooking methods can you find in her introduction?
★ Almost every famous dish has a story behind it. Can you tell some of them?

Here is Sister Song's Fish Broth. It's appetizing because it's **piquant** (辛辣开胃的) and smooth. It's usually served before a meal or as the first course as an appetizer. The dish has a history of more than 800 years. It was originally cooked by a woman called Sister Song whose family made a living on fishing. She made a special fish soup for her sick **brother-in-law** (小叔) to help him recover soon. The soup with fresh tender fish meat without any bones, tastes like crab meat or even better, and is thus considered one of the most delicious fish dishes in Hangzhou.

Now comes Dongpo Pork. This dish is named after Su Dongpo, an **eminent** (杰出的) poet in the Song Dynasty. When working as the governor in Hangzhou, Su Dongpo had the most tender and **premium** (优质的) pork braised with good rice wine, soy sauce and sugar, and then had it **distributed** (分发) in cubes to reward the workers **dredging** (疏浚) West Lake. Now you can see the cubed pork has very thin skin with almost half fat and half lean meat in a **deep**

reddish brown color (色泽鲜亮). Although it looks a little fatty, it tastes extremely delicious and not greasy at all. However, it takes time to cook. At least three hours is needed, for it's **simmered**

(炖) twice, and then **braised** (烧) and **sautéd** (快炒) before it's ready. The meat is so tender that you can easily break it into small pieces with chopsticks.

Next is **West Lake Vinegar Fish**, one of the must-eat dishes here. It's fresh and tender with **sweet** and sour flavor. All the fish is especially **bred** (饲养) in West Lake outside the restaurant. Legend says that the fish was originally created by a man's sister-in-law to inspire him the essence of the true life with the sweet-sour flavor. Since the man's surname is Song, it's also called "**Sister Song's Treasure** (叔嫂传珍)". The same surname as the fish broth, isn't it interesting?

Here is Fried Shelled Shrimps with Longjing Tea Leaves. It's made up of fresh shrimps and cooked with Longjing tea leaves picked around **Qingming Festival** (清明节). The shelled shrimps look white and fresh, and the tea leaves are green with good aroma. It was believed to have been created by chance. In the Qing Dynasty, while cooking shrimp, a chef made the mistake of adding Longjing tea leaves to the dish as a condiment. It happened that the dish was ordered by **Emperor Qianlong** (乾隆皇帝, 1711–1799), one of the longest reigning monarchs in China, who was then in Hangzhou during his visit in the South of

the Yangtze River known as **Jiangnan** (江南). To the chef's surprise, however, the emperor enjoyed it, hence the dish.

Well, Beggar's Chicken is coming. You may be very surprised at its special wrapping. According to legend, once Emperor Qianlong had a tour of the lower reaches of the Yangtze River in plain clothes. Walking alone in the open field one day, the emperor felt quite hungry. Just then, a beggar nearby was wrapping a chicken with mud and

roasted it in the fire. Later when the beggar stripped off the mud, the aroma of the chicken **wafted** (飘荡) towards the emperor. Seeing the stranger's mouth watering, the beggar kindly offered the emperor the chicken. The emperor thanked him and wolfed it down quickly. From then on, the emperor had the chicken cooked in the same way in memory of the beggar's chicken. Look, it's very tender with a special aroma of lotus leaves. Can't wait?

This dish has a special name called **Fried Ring Bell**. It's actually stir-fried Tofu or beancurd skin rolls stuffed with minced pork. When the crispy rolls are **crunched** (嘎巴作响地咀嚼) it sounds like the ringing of a bell, hence the name. Funny name, isn't it? It usually goes with sweet sauce, scallions or ground pepper.

OK, I think I'd better stop talking to let you enjoy the delicious food.

Part C   Major Traditional Chinese Festival Food

Questions for comprehension and discussion:

★ What traditional festivals are mentioned here?

★ What particular food is associated with each festival? Why?

★ What other traditional Chinese festival food do you know?

An important part of Chinese culture, traditional festivals reflect Chinese people's ancient beliefs and customs. Listed below are the four most popular traditional festivals with their **festivities** (节庆活动).

Festival	Date	Festivities
Spring Festival 春节	1st day of the first lunar month to the Lantern Festival 15 days later	• hang up or paste **Spring (Festival) couplets** (春联), the character **Fu** (Happiness, 福) and paper-cuts • set off firecrackers and fireworks • express New Year greetings and make or have visits • eat Jiaozi or **Nian'gao/New Year Cake** (年糕) • a big meal with family members
Lantern Festival 元宵节	15th night of the first lunar month	• eat Tangyuan (汤圆), mainly special sweet dumplings made of glutinous rice • watch colorful lanterns, lantern dragon dance (龙灯舞) • solve riddles on the lanterns (猜灯谜)
Qingming Festival 清明节	around April 5th of the solar calendar	• offer **sacrifice** (祭祀) • tidy up or sweep the tomb • go on outing/**Spring Outing** (踏青) • fly kites • eat **Qingtuan/Qingmingguo** (Herbal Rice Rolls, 青团/清明果)
Duanwu Festival/ Dragon Boat Festival 端午节	5th day of the 5th lunar month	• commemorate ancient poet **Qu Yuan** (屈原) • go in for dragon boat race • eat **Zongzi** (粽子)
Mid-autumn Festival 中秋节	15th day of the 8th lunar month	• legend of **Chang'e** (嫦娥) • worship and enjoy the moon • eat moon cakes

As you can see from the above table, traditional Chinese festivals are always associated with some particular food. In fact, the food plays an important role in celebrating the festival, without which the celebration may not be as perfect as it is.

1. Spring Festival Food

Spring Festival is regarded by the Chinese people as the grandest and most important annual festival, a time for family reunion, similar to Christmas Day for westerners. On New Year's Eve, no matter where they are, family members will try their best to come back to enjoy the family reunion dinner. People from north and south have different habits about the food they eat on this special day.

In northern China, people usually eat Jiaozi, dumplings stuffed with different fillings. As it is shaped like the Chinese **Yuanbao** (元宝), a kind of money used in ancient times, eating Jiaozi means wealth in the coming year. While the northerners eat Jiaozi, southerners like to eat **Nian'gao** (年糕), a kind of sticky rice cake. Nian'gao, is a **homonym** (同形同音异义词) for "growing up each year", symbolizing progress and promotion at work, and improvement in life year by year.

2. Lantern Festival Food

Lantern Festival falls on the night of 15th day of the Chinese New Year when the moon is full. It is celebrated with various fantastic lanterns on display as well as **lantern dragon dance** (龙灯舞) for people to enjoy. There are also lots of **riddles** (字谜) on the lanterns that people can have fun solving. In the meantime, before going out of their home to watch the colorful lanterns, people would have a big dinner with their family members and eat Tangyuan (汤圆), a kind of special dumplings made of glutinous rice mainly with sweet fillings, which symbolizes family reunion, as the moon does.

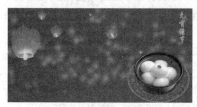

3. Qingming Festival Food

The **Qingming Festival** (清明节), also known as Tomb-sweeping Day or Pure Brightness Festival, is one of the **Chinese 24 Solar Terms** (24 节气) [1], the crucial time for plowing and sowing in the spring. Therefore, it has a close relationship with agriculture. However, it's more than a seasonal symbol; it's a festival with unique characteristics — a combination of sadness and happiness.

On this day, sweeping tomb, also called **Shang Fen** (to visit a grave in memory of the dead, 上坟), is the most important and popular activity for offering sacrifice and showing respect to the ancestors. Besides, it's also the best time for people to enjoy themselves outdoors by appreciating early blossoms before summer and flying kites, which we call it **Taqing** (Spring Outing, 踏青/春游), one of the most popular **festivities** (庆祝活动) in China. The traditional popular food for the occasion is a variety of **Qingtuan/Qingmingguo** (Herbal Rice Rolls, 青团/清明果), a kind of pastry or dumpling made of glutinous rice mixed with some herbs and usually stuffed with savory or sweet filling.

---

① The 24 Solar Terms are determined by changes in the sun's position in the zodiac during the year, showing the changes of climate and natural phenomena. They are closely related to farming and people's daily life. 中国农历 24 节气是根据太阳一年中在黄道（地球绕太阳公转的轨道）上的位置来划分的，反映了气候和自然现象的变化，与农事以及人们的日常生活息息相关。为方便记忆，人们编了 24 节气歌：春雨惊春清谷天，夏满芒夏暑相连，秋处露秋寒霜降，冬雪雪冬小大寒。

4. Duanwu Festival Food

The **Duanwu Festival** (端午节), also called the Dragon Boat Festival, has a history of more than 2,000 years with a number of legends explaining its origin. The most popular and widely accepted version is associated with **Qu Yuan** (屈原), a minister during the **Warring States Period** (475–221 BC, 战国时期).

As a minister in the **State of Chu** (楚国), Qu Yuan supported the decision to fight against the powerful **State of Qin** (秦国). However, he was **exiled** (流放) by the King. In order to show his love and passion for his country, he wrote many **remarkable** (非同凡响的) poems and is therefore regarded as a famous poet in China's history. In 278 BC, he drowned himself in the

river to show his loyalty. People searched for his body by sailing their boats down the river and threw food into the water to attract fish and other animals and keep them from destroying Qu Yuan's body. Thus dragon boat racing and eating **Zongzi** (粽子), which is mode of sticky rice with various fillings wrapped in bamboo or reed leaves have become the major festivities.

5. Mid-Autumn Festival Food

The Mid-Autumn Festival, or Moon Festival, is the second grandest festival next to the Spring Festival. It's a popular harvest festival dating back over 3,000 years. On this day, the moon is supposed to be the biggest, roundest and brightest. As the round moon implies family reunion in Chinese culture, this festival is another time for family members to get together wherever possible.

People will bring their family members back to their parents' home, and have dinner together.

Eating moon cakes is the most popular celebration of the day. Moon cakes are traditional Chinese pastries made with various kinds of sweet fillings. The moon cake is also a symbol of family reunion.

Another festivity is to worship and enjoy the moon. People watch the bright full moon while eating moon cakes with their family, or express homesickness if staying far away from home.

Part D   Language Checklist

A. Vocabulary

sour 酸，sweet 甜，bitter 苦	hot/spicy/piquant/pungent 辛辣的
salty/savory 咸味的	sweet-and-sour 糖醋的
aromatic/fragrant 香的	fresh and tender 鲜嫩的
juicy/succulent 多汁儿的	soft and smooth 柔滑的
plain/light/mild 温和清淡的	appetizing 开胃的
delectable/palatable 美味可口的	delicious/tasty/tasteful/flavorful/yummy 好吃的
appealing/inviting/tempting 诱人的	delightful/pleasing 宜人的
crisp and refreshing 酥脆爽口的	mouthwatering 令人垂涎的

B. Popular Chinese Foods[①]

Types of Cuisine	Names of the Dishes
Guangdong Cuisine/Yue Cai 粤菜	Roasted Suckling Pig 烤乳猪
	Boiled Chicken Slices with Sauce 白切鸡
	Crispy Chicken 脆皮鸡
	Soup with Various Ingredients 老火靓汤
	Chicken-bone Herb and Aged Chicken Soup 鸡骨草煲老鸡
Shandong Cuisine/Lu Cai 鲁菜	Beijing Roast Duck/Peking Duck 北京烤鸭
	Braised Sea Cucumber with Scallions 葱烧海参
	Crab Roes with Shark's Fin 蟹黄鱼翅
	Dezhou Braised Chicken 德州扒鸡
	Creamy Walnuts Soup 核桃奶油汤
Sichuan Cuisine/Chuan Cai 川菜	Mapo Tofu 麻婆豆腐
	Gongbao Diced Chicken 宫保鸡丁
	Poached Fish Fillets in Chili Oil 水煮鱼
	Sautéed Pig's Kidney 火爆腰花
	Sliced Beef and Ox Offal in Chili Sauce 夫妻肺片
	Twice (Double) Cooked Pork Slices 回锅肉
Huaiyang Cuisine/Huaiyang Cai 淮扬菜	Squirrel-shaped Mandarin Fish 松鼠鳜鱼
	Stewed Pork Ball in Brown Sauce 红烧狮子头
	Crab Roe Dumplings 蟹黄汤包
	Thousand-layer Cake 千层糕
	Steamed Jiaozi 蒸饺
	Yangzhou Fried Rice 扬州炒饭
Zhejiang Cuisine/Zhe Cai 浙菜 Hangzhou Dishes 杭帮菜	West Lake Vinegar Fish 西湖醋鱼
	Fried Shelled Shrimps with Longjing Tea Leaves 龙井虾仁
	Beggar's Chicken 叫花鸡
	Sister Song's Fish Broth 宋嫂鱼羹
	Dongpo Pork 东坡肉
	Pian'er Chuan (Noodles with Preserved Vegetables and Sliced Pork and Bamboo Shoots in Soup) 片儿川
	Fried Ring Bell (Fried Stuffed Tofu Skin Rolls) 干炸响铃
	Noodles with Fried Eel Slices and Shrimps 虾爆鳝面

---

① 菜名翻译原则：具有中国特色且被外国人接受的传统食品，本着推广汉语和中国餐饮文化的原则，使用汉语拼音；具有中国特色且被外国人接受的，使用方言拼写或音译的菜名仍保留其拼写方式；无法体现烹饪手法和主配料的菜肴，采用汉语拼音加英文注释的形式。具体请参见由北京市人民政府外事办公室和北京市民讲外语活动组委会办公室编著的《美食译苑——中文菜单英文译法》（2011 年由世界知识出版社出版）。

Types of Cuisine	Names of the Dishes
Fujian Cuisine/Min Cai 闽菜	Fotiaoqiang 佛跳墙-Steamed Abalone (鲍鱼) with Shark's Fin (鱼翅) and Fish Maw (鱼鳔) in Broth (汤)
	Chicken in Rice Wine 醉糟鸡
Snacks 小吃	Jiaozi 饺子，Steamed Jiaozi 蒸饺，Guotie (Pan-Fried Jiaozi) 锅贴
	Mantou (bun) 馒头，Huajuan (twisted buns) 花卷
	Baozi (Steamed Stuffed Bun) 包子
	Wotou (Steamed Corn Bun) 窝头
	Youtiao (Deep-Fried Dough Sticks) 油条
	Chow mein/fried noodles 炒面
	Plain Noodles 阳春面 (清汤面)
	Yuanxiao (sweet dumplings made of glutinous rice for Lantern Festival) 元宵
	Zongzi (glutinous rice wrapped in bamboo leaves) 粽子
	Nian'gao/New Year Cake (Sticky Rice Cake) 年糕

C. Key Patterns

Features 特色	• Sichuan cooks select their ingredients with great care, use a variety of seasonings and cook each dish differently. 川菜选料讲究，调味多变，菜式多样。 • Sichuan Cuisine often reminds people of tongue-numbing and spicy tastes. Seasonings are very important in Sichuan Cuisine with different flavors which mostly include scallion, ginger, garlic, chili, pepper, Chinese prickly ash, vinegar, etc. 一提起川菜，人们常会想到麻、辣两味。川菜特别注重调味品，风味丰富。常见的调味品有葱、姜、蒜、辣椒、胡椒、花椒、醋等。 • Zhejiang Cuisine also uses rice wine's lees (酒糟) as seasoning and stresses the cooking skills of simmering, braising, stewing and so on. 浙菜也用酒糟调味，注重煨、焖、烩、炖等烹调技法。 • Guangdong Cuisine takes a great variety of ingredients from seafood to poultry (家禽). 粤菜取料广博，从各种家禽到海鲜，应有尽有。 • Shandong Cuisine uses a wide and fine selection of ingredients. Shandong soups are most famous, and green onion is commonly used as a seasoning. 鲁菜选料广而精，特别有名的是汤，最常用的调料是大葱。 • Huaiyang Cai tends to be a bit sweet and are scarcely spicy, in contrast to those of Sichuan or Hunan. 淮扬菜偏甜，几乎不辣，与一些其他的中国菜不同，如川菜或湘粤菜。 • Most Huaiyang dishes are light and more meticulously prepared with beautiful presentation but their portions are not as generous as those of northern cuisines. 大多数淮扬菜看和中国北方的菜肴相比要显得更加清淡、精美，但菜量不如北方菜多。
	• Sichuan dishes are known as a hundred dishes with a hundred tastes, earning the reputation of "food in China, taste in Sichuan". 川菜素以"一菜一味，百菜百味"而闻名，享有"食在中国，味在四川"的美誉。 • No wonder it's said that Cantonese eat almost anything that walks, crawls, flies or swims. 难怪说广东人什么都吃，走的、爬的、飞的或游的，一应俱全。 • The fresh, tender, soft, and smooth dishes accompanied by its mellow fragrance have won a widespread reputation in the culinary world. 鲜嫩、柔滑、醇香的各式菜肴早在烹饪界赢得了广泛的声誉。

Reputation 声誉	• One of their most famous dishes is crispy roasted suckling pig. 其中最著名的菜是脆皮乳猪。 • Shandong soups are most famous. 鲁菜中的汤特别有名。 • The spicy cooking has become the region's dominant cuisine. 辛辣的菜肴已经成为这个地区的主要美食了。 • It's best represented by its variety of seafood. 最有代表性的是其各式海鲜菜肴。 • As the symbol of family union, moon cakes are traditional Chinese pastries made with various kinds of sweet and savory fillings. 月饼象征着家庭的团聚，是传统的中国糕点，有各种甜和咸的馅料。

Part E   English in Use

I. Reading Comprehension

Task 1: Choose the best answer to complete each sentence below.

1. _____ is known to all, Chinese cuisine enjoys an international reputation for its appeal to the senses through color, flavor and taste with optimal presentation.
   A. As   B. That   C. Which   D. What

2. So _____ pleasant and harmonious colors is one of the main principles when Chinese food.
   A. have, cook   B. have, cooking   C. to have, to cook   D. to have, cooking

3. Sichuan cuisine is well-known in China and overseas for its _____ taste.
   A. salty   B. tongue-numbing and spicy
   C. bitter and sour   D. sweet and sour

4. The dish is named _____ Su Dongpo, a noted poet, artist and calligrapher in Song Dynasty.
   A. in   B. for   C. after   D. before

5. How I wish I _____ the chance to taste all these delicious dishes.
   A. will have   B. have   C. had   D. shall have

6. For most people, it's _____ to visit Louwailou restaurant while having a tour in Hangzhou.
   A. a necessary   B. always   C. need   D. a must

7. I'd like to _____ you the following restaurants for sampling and enjoying Hangzhou Cuisine at its best.
   A. remind   B. warn   C. help   D. recommend

8. On New Year's Eve after the dinner, the whole family will sit together, _____.
   A. chatting and watching TV   B. chat and watch TV
   C. chatted and watched TV   D. to chat and to watch TV

9. When friends meet, they will _____ each other happiness and prosperity with a big smile.
   A. hope   B. wish   C. tell   D. say

10. Minorities celebrate their Spring Festival almost the same day _____ the Han people, _____ they may have different customs.
    A. that, which   B. on which, although
    C. which, though   D. as, though

Task 2: Answer the following questions concerning Chinese Cuisines and local specialties in Part A and Part B.

1. What are the main features of Chinese Cuisine? And what do five tastes refer to in Chinese Cuisine?
2. What are the eight major Chinese Cuisines and what do four major Chinese Cuisines refer to?
3. What do the special cuisines include in China? What do you think of medicinal cuisine?
4. What's the story about Beggar's Chicken?
5. How did the dish Fried Shrimps with Longjing Tea Leaves come into being?

Task 3: Decide whether each of the following statements is True or False in terms of Chinese Festival Food in Part C.

1. Qingming Festival is a time when people pay respect to their ancestors, and in the meantime, they can enjoy a spring outing. (   )
2. People all over China have the same habits about the food they eat at Spring Festival. (   )
3. Qingming Festival is one of the Chinese 24 Solar Terms, the crucial time for plowing and sowing in the spring. (   )
4. Dragon boat racing and eating Zongzi are two festivities for the Duanwu Festival. (   )
5. The Mid-Autumn Festival is a popular harvest festival celebrated by Chinese people dating back over 5,000 years. (   )

II. Translation

Task 4: Translate the following sentences into English.

1. 众所周知，中国菜因其诱人的色、形、香、味而誉满全球。
2. 难怪有人说，"时尚在欧洲，生活在美国，饮食在中国"。
3. 色泽艳丽的食物通常能使人们的食欲大增。
4. 最后同样重要的是，美味被认为是中国菜的灵魂。
5. 让人惊叹不已的不仅仅是中国菜的口味，还有它的审美价值。
6. 据初步统计，中国有五千多种不同的地方烹饪风格。
7. 楼外楼是一家具有一百六十多年历史的老店，建于 1848 年，即清朝道光二十八年。
8. 人们普遍认为，不到楼外楼就不可能真正品尝到美味可口的杭帮菜。
9. 春节是中国人最盛大和最重要的节日，是家人团聚的日子，类似于西方人的圣诞节。
10. 端午节也可称作龙舟节，有着两千多年的历史，关于它的起源有着许多不同的传说。

Task 5: Translate the following sentences into Chinese.

1. As food occupies a very important part of daily life in China, it's not only considered a source of nutrition and enjoyment, but also has a special meaning to the Chinese people.
2. With diversified colors, aromatic flavor and distinctive taste, Chinese cuisine is not only tasty but also a work of art for people to appreciate.

3. That's why Chinese cuisine is ranked among the best of the world cuisine and Chinese restaurants can be found today in many countries and regions throughout the world.

4. In China, it's widely believed that food tonic (食补) is much better than medical tonic in strengthening one's health.

5. What is worth mentioning here is that Chinese medicinal cuisine is unique in China and has a long history.

6. Sichuan dishes are known as a hundred dishes with a hundred tastes, earning the reputation of "food in China, taste in Sichuan".

7. Huaiyang dishes have light flavors, retaining the original tastes of ingredients, and are very healthy.

8. Fried Ring Bell is actually stir-fried Tofu or beancurd skin rolls stuffed with minced pork. Crunching the crispy rolls sounds like the ringing of a bell, hence the name.

9. Mapo Tofu is a traditional flavorful dish in Sichuan. It is said that towards the end of the reign of **Tongzhi** (同治, 1862–1874) of the Qing Dynasty, a **pockmarked** (有麻点的) woman surnamed Chen was a very good cook in a restaurant.

10. Yunnan's **Crossing the Bridge Noodles** (过桥米线) is said to have been created by the wife of a scholar in the Qing Dynasty to prevent the noodles cooling on the way to her husband studying in an island pavilion. It consists of a chicken broth with a hot, **insulating** (隔绝的) layer of oil on top with noodles, slices of ham, vegetables, and egg to be added to it at the table.

III. Role Play

Task 6: Play a role in any of the following situations with your partner or partners.

Situation 1: You're a local guide for a group of foreign tourists who are very interested in Chinese cuisine. Introduce some of the most popular specialties to them in your area.

Situation 2: You're a local guide. Make a brief introduction to Sam about some of the most popular traditional Chinese festival food.

IV. Problem-solving

Task 7: Analyze the following cases, then answer the questions as required.

Case 1

Situation: You're a local guide. You've arranged a dinner for a tour group from Germany. But just before the dinner starts, one of the tourists wants to change the dishes already served on the table, because the food is not favorable.

Question: What should you do in such a case?

Case 2

Situation: You're Chen Yan. You've just had a nice talk with Sam about Chinese cuisines. Sam is so fascinated by what you've told him, especially after you made an excellent introduction to the local Hangzhou Cuisine, that he wants to explore Hangzhou by himself to experience different kinds of local dishes.

Question: Now that he's unwilling to have meals together with other tourists, what should you do?

Answers for Reference

Unit 6　Banquet Service

$$\boxed{\text{Warm-up}}$$

1. What is a banquet? How many types of banquet service do you know?
2. What is the service process of Western banquet?
3. What is a formal table setting like at a dinner party in the West?
4. Can you name the following glasses?

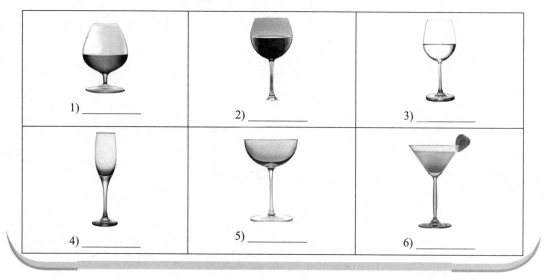

1) _____

2) _____

3) _____

4) _____

5) _____

6) _____

Part A　Western Cuisine and Beverage Service

Monologue: Western Cuisine

Situation: *Robbie Kelder, Director of Food and Beverage, is training the new wait staff in a Crowne Plaza (皇冠假日酒店) in China.*

Questions for comprehension and discussion:
★ What is Spanish cuisine well-known for?
★ What are the features of French cuisine?
★ What typical dishes is Italian cuisine famous for?
★ What is British cuisine renowned for?
★ What are the characteristics of American food?

Hello, ladies and gentlemen, I would like to share with you Western cuisine which is definitely different from Chinese cuisine. Now let's start with Spanish Cuisine. Spanish food is greatly influenced by Roman, Greek, Jewish and **Moorish culinary traditions** (摩尔人的美食传统). It's characterized by a wide selection of meat and seafood. However, the world-famous **Paella** (什锦菜肉/海鲜饭) is always at the top of the list of people's favorite Spanish food. It's a rice dish either with meat, fish or other seafood, together with vegetables, and features the use of **saffron** (番红花) to give it a yellow color and unique flavor. **Tapas** (西班牙餐前小吃) are also outstanding. They are small plates of food served with drinks or before a main meal, and thus serve as appetizers or snacks. There's a breathtaking variety of tapas. One of the typical Spanish tapas is the **tortilla (Spanish omelet,** 西班牙式煎蛋饼). It's an omelet-like potato dish, fried in olive oil. It's a filling and flavorful dish with the addition of chopped onions and can be served in slices, warm or cold. **Fried Calamari** (炸小鱿鱼) is also distinctive and delicious, and various kinds of shrimps are equally memorable. **Jamon**

serrano (a typical ham, 西班牙火腿) and **chorizo** (西班牙香辣肠) are often used in Spanish food. In addition to these, **gazpacho** (西班牙冷汤) is also very popular. It's made of bread, cucumber, tomato, garlic in vinegar and olive oil, and is served cold. **Flan** (西班牙果馅饼), a special pudding, is a wonderful dessert. Moreover, a wide selection of Spanish wine is served with the meal.

Next is French cuisine. No one would deny that French food is distinctive and delicate. It's noted for **exclusive (**独有的) ingredients and cooking techniques, and has contributed significantly to Western cuisines. Its **criteria** (标准) are used widely in Western **culinary** (烹饪的) education, and has been on the list of the UNESCO's world's "**intangible cultural heritage** (非物质文化遗产)".

One typical French dish is **Boeuf Bourguignon** (勃艮第酒炖牛肉). It's beef cooked in red wine from Burgundy, usually with mushrooms and carrots. Another popular dish is **Escargots**, meaning **snails** (蜗牛) in French. They are typically prepared with butter and garlic, which makes them absolutely delicious.

Besides, lobsters, oysters, goose liver and **truffles** (松露块菌菇) are also world-renowned.

When talking about French food, one should also consider the various French breads, especially French **baguette** (法式长棍面包) and **croissant** (羊角面包). Another typical French pastry is **crepe** (法

式薄饼). It's a thin pancake, and can be topped with anything, such as fresh strawberries or ham and cheese. French cheese also enjoys a good reputation for its incredible variety. There are at least 500 different kinds of cheese in France. One of the most famous and oldest cheeses is Roquefort (洛克福羊乳干酪).

Italian cuisine boasts regional diversity and rich tastes, and is the most preferred, and copied cuisine in the world. It's generally characterized by its simplicity, for many dishes have only two

to four main ingredients. Italian cooks put more stress on the quality of the fresh or seasonal ingredients rather than on elaborate preparation. Cheese, olive oil, **balsamic vinegar** (香醋), **prosciutto** (意式五香火腿) and spices are commonly used. In addition to meat, seafood and vegetables, various pastas in different shapes are particularly popular. Pizza is probably the most popular Italian food all over the world. It

has numerous varieties with different ingredients. Each pizza has different topping. **Pizza Margherita** (玛格丽特披萨) was created **resembling** (相似) the colors of the Italian flag, **red** for tomato, **white** for mozzarella and **green** for basil (罗勒), and was named after the queen **Margherita** (玛格丽塔).

In addition, **lasagne** (lasagna, 意式千层面) and **ravioli** (意式馄饨/小方饺) as well as **macaroni** (通心粉) and **spaghetti** (意大利实心面条) are delightful too. **Lasagne** is made of several layers of pasta sheets alternated with cheese, sauce, minced meat or

various ingredients. **Ravioli** looks like Chinese Jiaozi or dumpling but is typically square-shaped with different fillings, though other forms are also used. Most spaghetti is served with cheese, garlic, tomato, meat, and different sauces.

It's a pity that many people assume English cuisine is simple and uninteresting, the quality being far below that of French or Italian food, for they may not know the real delights of English food. Actually, traditional English cuisine is **acclaimed** (受到赞扬的) as fresh and healthy food. It features bread and cheese, roasted and stewed meats,

pies and puddings, boiled vegetables and **broths** (肉汤), as well as seafood. Now it's much influenced by foreign ingredients and cooking styles, especially Indian food, and has become more flavorful with many **herbs** (香草) and spices. Briefly speaking, the most popular English foods are **Fish & Chips** (炸鱼薯条), **Steak & Kidney Pudding** (牛肉腰子布丁), **Shepherd's Pie** (牧羊人羊肉饼), **Cottage Pie** (村舍牛肉饼) and **Yorkshire Pudding** (约克郡布丁), etc.

Fish and Chips (炸鱼和薯条) earns the same reputation in England as Pizza in Italy, and is thus regarded as the English national dish. Pieces of fish, usually **Atlantic cod** (大西洋鳕鱼) or **haddock** (黑线鳕), are dipped in **batter** (面糊) and fried, giving a **crunchy** (脆的) outside coating while the fish remains soft and juicy. Steak & Kidney Pudding is perfect for

English dinner. It's a steamed pudding where diced beef and kidney are enclosed in a crust made of **suet pastry** (牛油糕). Served with mashed potatoes and steamed vegetables, it makes a warming, filling dinner. Onions and button mushrooms can add additional flavor to the wonderful gravy produced inside the pastry crust.

Besides, English food is distinguished by its full breakfast and the traditional, formal afternoon tea. **Tarts** (果馅饼), cakes and other **pastries** (糕点) are also very common.

Finally, let's talk about American food. The United States is called a melting pot of many different cultures, so is its cuisine. It's difficult to define what typical American food is like. Every single dish could be traced back to some group of immigrants or another. For example, like the famous country song "Jambalaya" written in the 1950s, **Jambalaya** (什锦饭) is popular in the southern US. It's a **Louisiana Creole** (路易斯安那克里特人) dish of Spanish and French influence. Similar to Spanish paella, it is traditionally made of three parts: meat (chicken and Andouille sausage) with shrimp, vegetables (a trinity of celery, pepper, and onion), and is completed by adding **stock** (肉汤) and rice.

Anyway, when talking about American food, you might come up with those items in Mac Donald's or KFC, such as hamburger, sandwich, hotdog, popcorn, potato chips, all of which are commonly regarded as unhealthy food. However, there are some other foods which are also really American and you should not miss a chance to try them. One typical food is **Roast Turkey** (烤火鸡) which is perfect for thanksgiving dinner. Another special one is apple pie. It's occasionally served with **whipped cream** (鲜奶油) or ice cream on top, or alongside **cheddar cheese** (切达奶酪). It's also regarded as an **iconic American food.** (标志性的美国食物).

To sum up, the cuisines of Western countries share some common characteristics. For example, they **place importance on** (重视) seasonal produce and fresh ingredients. Many dairy products such as cheese and butter are widely used in cooking, so are various kinds of seasonings, sauces and other **condiments** (调味品). Compared with Asian cuisines, meat is more often used and the servings are larger. In addition, grains such as wheat, flour, oats and others types are the most important ingredients in European cuisine.

Dialogue: Beverage Service

Situation: *Robbie continues to talk about beverage and beverage service.*

Questions for comprehension and discussion:

★ How much do you know about beverage and beverage service?

★ Which wine goes with white meat or fish?

★ What is the main difference between the white and red wine glass?

★ What are the popular cocktails?

Robbie: Hello, ladies and gentlemen, today we're going to learn about beverage and beverage service at a banquet. Let's talk about beverage first. It's very important to have some knowledge about what beverages are like. Beverage is a formal term for a drink of any type. It falls into two groups: alcoholic and nonalcoholic beverage.

Trainee A: Sorry, are soft drinks nonalcoholic, Robbie?

Robbie: Yes. Soft drinks include iced tea, **lemonade** (柠檬水), coke, **soda** (汽水) and other **carbonated drinks** (碳酸饮料). But soft drinks don't usually include water, milk, hot tea, hot chocolate and **milkshake** (奶昔).

Trainee B: Then the hot tea and chocolate are called hot drinks because they are served warm?

Robbie: You got it. Coffee-based beverages are also hot drinks, including **cappuccino** (卡布奇诺), **espresso** (意式浓咖啡), and **latte** (拿铁).

Trainee A: Fruit juices are not hot drinks.

Robbie: Right, but they are also nonalcoholic beverages.

Trainee B: Alcoholic beverages are just wines, is that right?

Robbie: Oh, many other people would think so too. Wines, made from **fermented** (发酵的) grapes or other fruits, are alcoholic drinks, but so are beers, **distilled liquors** (烈性蒸馏酒) and sweet **liqueurs** (烈性甜酒).

Trainee C: I see.

Robbie: Well, at a formal dinner, especially a banquet, alcoholic beverages may vary according to the serving times.

Trainee B: Wow, sounds complex.

Robbie: You bet. Does anyone know about an **aperitif** (开胃酒)?

Trainee D: A pre-dinner drink. It's taken before a meal to **stimulate** (刺激) the appetite.

Robbie: Very good. It's used to **whet** (刺激) the appetite. It's a starter drink that opens a meal, and we often call it a welcoming drink to greet our guests. **Champagne** (香槟酒) or other sparkling wine, cocktail, **vermouth** (苦艾酒), **sherry** (雪利酒) and bitters are good choices. Actually, any alcoholic drink can be the aperitif as long as it's **refreshing** (神清气爽的).

Trainee A: I know cocktail is a mixed drink and quite popular in the West. But I have no idea of what it mainly contains.

Robbie: It usually contains one or more types of alcoholic drinks or spirits such as brandy, **vodka** (伏特加), **rum** (朗姆), **gin** (杜松子), **tequila** (龙舌兰) or whisky together with other ingredients like fruit juice, **bitter** (苦啤酒), honey/sugar, milk, soda, or other flavorings. It's served with ice cubes or crushed ice.

Trainee C: Sounds amazing. What are the famous cocktails?

Robbie: The list of cocktails is extremely long. Some notable cocktails include **Bloody Mary** (血腥玛丽), **Martini** (马提尼) and **Margarita** (玛格丽特), just to name a few. However, cocktails vary in their ingredients from **bartender** (酒吧侍者) to bartender. Even though two cocktails have the same name, they could taste fairly different. OK, so much for the cocktail. Let's move on to **digestifs** (餐后酒). What's that then?

Trainee A: Well, I know. It's an alcoholic drink served after a meal in contrast to the aperitif.

Trainee C: That's the after-dinner drink. Brandy can be one, is that right?

Robbie: Exactly. It's a French word literally meaning "digestive" (有助消化的), so it helps warm the belly and ease the mind after the dinner. It's used to end the meal or dinner. The most popular digestifs may include various sweet liqueurs and liquors like brandy, **scotch** (苏格兰威士忌), **bourbon** (美国波本威士忌) and other whiskeys.

Trainee B: What about the drinks with the food during the dinner then?

Robbie: Usually wine or beer. Now, let's turn to wine made from grapes. Wine has a long history of over 8,000 years. It consists of red and white wine. Wines tend to be named and classified by **place of origin** (原产地) such as **Bordeaux** (波尔多), **Bourgogne** (勃艮第), while many non-European wines tend (倾向于) to be classified by grape such as **Cabernet**

Merlot (解百纳洛红葡萄酒) and **Pinot Noir** (黑皮诺葡萄酒).

Trainee A: There's a certain rule concerning food and wine, is that right?

Robbie: Yes. Generally speaking, white wine goes well with seafood and white meat, while red wine is good with red meat.

Trainee A: I see. If our customer orders some chicken or fish, we could recommend some white wine, otherwise, red wine is suitable.

Robbie: Right. In a word, good wine, white or red, can **complement** (补充) and balance the flavors of a meal. But remember to serve different wines in different glasses.

Trainee A: Does it mean the shape of the glass has an effect on the taste of drink?

Robbie: Good question! It's believed that the shape of the glass is essential to **concentrate** (聚集) and keep the wine's **aroma** or **bouquet** (酒香). People would use the glass to appreciate and taste the wine, so it must be plainly clear with a **stem** (酒杯脚) and of a suitable size.

Trainee B: Why is a stem so important?

Robbie: It's used for people to hold so that no fingerprints will be left on the bowl. Besides, it ensures that the wine is not warmed by the hands cupped around the bowl.

Trainee B: I see. If we serve the wine next time, we should remember to pick up the glass by the stem instead of the bowl.

Robbie: Exactly. A good wine glass **tapers** (逐渐变细) slightly at the top with the bowl at the bottom "fatter" than the top, so that the aroma of the wine **wafts** (飘进) to the nose after being **swirled** (轻晃).

Trainee C: Excuse me, Robbie. Just now you mentioned the temperature of the wine. Why should the wine be kept cool? Do we have to serve the wine at certain temperature?

Robbie: Ah, yes. The temperature for wine is very important. Usually, white wine should be served chilled around 7-10° Celsius or around 45° Fahrenheit, while red wine should be kept around 15-18° Celsius or around 60° Fahrenheit or at room temperature. Otherwise, the colder or higher temperature would **overwhelm** (淹没) the taste.

Trainee C: Now I understand the reason why the wine is always kept in the cellar, refrigerator or an ice bucket.

Robbie: You got it.

Trainee A: What kind of glass is perfect for wine then?

Robbie: There are mainly three types of wine glasses for white wine, red wine and champagne. The round-bowled, **stemmed glasses** (高脚杯) are right for red wine and the smaller **tulip-shaped** (郁金香型的), stemmed glasses are for white wine. The **flute** (细长香槟杯) and the **coupe-shaped** or **saucer-shaped** (浅腹大口杯/浅碟型大口杯) wine glasses are two shapes of glasses for the **sparkling wine** (气泡的) champagne. The slim flute tends to prolong the bubbles of the wine, while the round, shallow coupe helps people drink it quickly especially for celebration. By the way, when opening the bottle of champagne, be sure to wrap the bottle in a towel or napkin in case the champagne **spills** (溢出) over if the **cork** (塞子) **pops** (喷弹出) too fast.

Trainee A: Okay, thank you. How about cocktail glasses?

Robbie: A cocktail glass is also called a **martini glass** (马提尼酒杯). It's a stemmed glass with a **cone-shaped** (锥形的) bowl. It's important to note that not all cocktails are served in a martini glass. Each type of cocktail can have its own type of glassware.

Trainee C: Brandy is generally served in a **snifter** (小口矮脚杯) which is a short stemmed glass with a wide bottom and a narrow top. Am I right?

Robbie: You got it！ The narrow top **retains** (保留) the aroma inside the glass, while the bowl-shaped bottom makes the glass accessible to be cupped in the hand. Any other question?

Trainee A: No more questions, thank you, Robbie. We've learned a lot.

Robbie: Great! See you tomorrow then.

Trainees: Thank you again, Robbie. See you!

Part B　Table-setting for a Western and Chinese Banquet

Dialogue 1: Western Table Setting

Situation: *Xia Li is a new waitress in the Western restaurant in* **Crowne Plaza**. *She's consulting with Robbie Kelder, director of food and beverage, about how to set a banquet table.*

Questions for comprehension and discussion:

★　In which order are the **cutlery, glasses and dishes** placed?

★　How are the wine glasses positioned?

Xia Li: Hi, Robbie, are you free?

Robbie: Yes, sure. What can I help you with?

Xia Li: If you are free, can I ask you some questions about table setting? I am still confused about it.

Robbie: I am free now. What are your questions?

Xia Li: Thank you! When serving a formal banquet in the West, I should put forks, butter plate and napkin to the left of the dinner plate, then the knives including butter knife, spoon, wine glasses and coffee cup to the right. Is that right?

Robbie: Not exactly. The butter knife should be placed **diagonally** (斜地) on the butter plate to the upper left of the dinner plate. You can put the coffee cup to the right of the plate, but it's usually brought in after the meal. Anyway, it depends on the host's intention and preference.

Xia Li: I see. Thank you. It's really complex.

Robbie: Yes, it is. By the way, the ways of table-setting vary even in Europe.

Xia Li: That's interesting. Well, would you please tell me what a formal table setting is really like?

Robbie: OK. As far as the place setting is concerned, keep one rule in mind: "everything should be geometrically spaced: the **centerpiece (**餐桌中央摆设**)** in the actual center, the place settings at equal distances, and cutlery balanced. "[1] Now let's start with the tablecloth. It should be clean and **well-pressed** (熨烫平整). If necessary, decorate the table with a vase of fresh flowers to make a good impression on the guests. Then place the **service plate** (大托盘) in the center of the place setting.

Xia Li: Is the service plate a dinner plate?

Robbie: No, it's a large decorative plate used to dress up the dinner table for the dinner plate. The **tableware** (餐具) is usually arranged in a particular order so that the **flatware** (扁平的餐具，指刀叉等) is used first farthest from the plate. The first course flatware is placed most furthest out and then work your way inwards. Remember to place knives with **blades** or **cutting edges** (刀刃) facing the plate.

Xia Li: What about the soup spoon?

Robbie: Set the soup spoon farthest to the right side of the plate outside the knives, so is the fruit spoon if there is some fruit.

Xia Li: I always see a fork on the right of the plate outside the spoon. What is it used for?

Robbie: It's called **oyster fork** (生蚝叉) for some **shellfish** (贝类). It's the only fork set on the right. Besides, the dessert spoon and fork are usually brought in on the dessert plate just before dessert is served at a formal banquet. If the banquet is less formal, then place them above the service plate, with the handle of fork facing left and the handle of spoon facing right.

Xia Li: Now I get it. Thank you very much. What about the glassware then?

Robbie: At a formal banquet, always set the glasses according to size, with the largest one on the left, starting with the water goblet. For example, place the **water goblet** (水杯) one inch above the tip of the dinner knife. The other glasses are arranged right next to the water glass in the order of use: a champagne

---

① PEGGY POST. *Emily Post's Entertaining*[M]. New York: HarperResource, 1998: 22.

flute or coupe is set to the right at a slight distance. The red wine or white wine glass is positioned between the water goblet and flute or coupe. The sherry glass is placed either to the right or in front of the wineglass. The glass for dessert wine like brandy glass is usually brought in when dessert is served.

Xia Li: I see. How about the napkin?

Robbie: A cloth napkin should be placed on the center of the dinner plate, or to the left of the forks. The napkin can be folded artfully. By the way, make sure that the lower edges of the cutlery and the bottom rim of the plate should be **in alignment** (成一条直线) one inch up from the edge of the table. Besides, flatware shouldn't be hidden under the rim of **hollowware** (浅口的盘、碟), and it should be put one inch away from the side of the plate.

Xia Li: OK. Thank you very much, Robbie. Now, I'm quite clear about the table-setting. You've been very helpful. Thank you again for your help.

Robbie: You're welcome.

Dialogue 2: Chinese Table Setting

Situation: *Li Qi is a manager in a Chinese restaurant. He is telling Gloria, a newly-recruited American waitress about Chinese table setting. Gloria is an international student in a university in China and works at the restaurant part-time so that she could have a better understanding of Chinese catering (饮食服务).*

Questions for comprehension and discussion:

★ What is the function of a Lazy Susan?

★ What is a Chinese table setting like?

Gloria: Hi, Mr Li, are you free now?

Li Qi: Yes, is there anything I can do for you?

Gloria: I'm wondering if you could spare a few minutes to tell me something about Chinese table setting for a banquet? I'm quite interested in it. It's totally different from ours, you know.

Li Qi: Oh, yes. That's my job. I should have told you about it earlier. I'm sorry, Gloria.

Gloria: It's alright. That's very kind of you to say so. Thank you indeed.

Li Qi: Well, let's begin with the table. Since Chinese people like to share the meal with each other, a round table with a **Lazy Susan** (圆转盘) set in the middle is a must,

so that everyone at the table has the chance to get the food and enjoy the conversation. At a banquet, each round table is ready for ten people and is covered with a clean pressed table cloth.

Gloria: I like the Lazy Susan. It's so **nifty** (灵便). I'd love to have one like that at home.

Li Qi: Now the dishes. The rice bowl is usually set on a service plate or to the upper left of the plate at a fancy banquet. The service plate is used to discard bones or put food until it is eaten. The wine glass or beer glass is placed to the top right of the service plate.

Gloria: Do you have pre-dinner drinks or after-dinner drinks?

Li Qi: No, we don't, except for various teas. People like to have a cup of tea before the meal or after the meal. People in the north usually like to have distilled liquors, while those in the south prefer rice wine or wine. With strong alcohol, liquor is served in a small cup or glass, and wine or rice wine is in a wineglass.

Gloria: Are there any other specific glasses for different liquors or wines?

Li Qi: No, there aren't. We do have various kinds of alcoholic, nonalcoholic drinks and fruit juices, but all these drinks may be served in any kinds of glasses. Usually, a small cup or glass for the liquor is placed to the left of the wine glass or beer glass, while the glass for any fruit juice or nonalcoholic drinks is to the right of the wine glass or beer glass. It's much simpler than your Western style.

Gloria: Yes, definitely. And you only have a pair of chopsticks instead of knives and forks. Chopsticks are amazing! But it takes time to learn how to handle them.

Li Qi: Right. All we have for utensils are the chopsticks and spoons. The chopsticks are placed on the right of the service plate with the tips on a **chopstick rest** (筷子架), while the spoon is in the bowl. The folded napkin is set to the left of the service plate or directly on it if the bowl is placed outside the plate.

Gloria: I see. How about the tea cup?

Li Qi: It's placed to the top left of the service plate. By the way, if you serve the main dishes, put them on the edge of the Lazy Susan for easy reach by guests, but place the soup in the middle with a ladle. However, it varies slightly in different restaurants. Well, that's all for the table setting. Isn't it easy for you to learn?

Gloria: I think so. Thank you very much.

Li Qi: It's a pleasure.

Part C　Tips on Banquet Service

Questions for comprehension and discussion:

★ In which order should the wait staff serve their guests?

★ How should the wait staff serve the food and beverage properly?

Serving a banquet means to provide food and beverage to a group of people in a timely, courteous and professional way. If you work as a server, you should observe some important rules of etiquette. These rules include setting the table correctly, greeting the guests politely, serving food and beverages properly, and clearing the table skillfully. Here are some useful tips concerning banquet service.

☆ Make suitable preparation for the table setting. Make sure each plate, fork, knife, spoon or glass is clean and placed properly.

☆ Get to know about each course to be served in advance.

☆ Greet the guests politely with a friendly smile. Pronounce and describe the dish when serving it to the guest.

☆ Remember to begin the service always by starting with the **female guest of honor** (女主宾), the woman on the host's right, or the **guest of honor** (男主宾), the man on the hostess's right, and move around **counterclockwise** (逆时针).

☆ Pass the first course to the female guest of honor or the guest of honor, and then pass it counterclockwise. Remember to always serve from the left side of the guest with your left hand.

☆ Serve the wine at a cool room temperature. And chill the white wine in the refrigerator at least two hours before the meal, or chill the white wine in a **wine cooler** (冷酒器) for twenty-five minutes in a bath of ice cubes and ice water.

☆ Serve the wine from the right side of the guest, where the wine glasses are in place. Pour wine first into the glass of the female guest of honor, unless she doesn't want any. Then fill the others' glasses by moving around the table counterclockwise. If only the guest of honor is present, then serve him first instead.

☆ Fill the red wine glass no more than 1/3, and the white wine glass 2/3 or less full.

☆ If there are more than eight or ten guests, two servers are needed. One begins serving the female guest of honor; the other begins serving the guest of honor at the other end of the table. Each server ends up serving the host or hostess last.

☆ If a serving dish is hot, place a folded napkin under it to protect your hand.

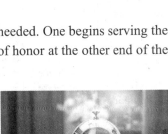

☆ Once a course is finished, remove each used plate from the right side of the guest with your right hand. If there's a fork and knife or spoon on each plate, **clamp down** (压住) on them with your right thumb to keep them from falling off the plate.

☆ Bring in the clean plates for the next course, and put down each in front of the guest from the left side.

☆ Make sure you lift the heavy tray with grace and serve food steadily and quickly.

☆ When it's time for dessert, clear the table by removing the entrée or salad course plates as well as the knives and forks.

☆ Bring in the dessert plates. Then ask each guest if they would care for coffee or tea. If yes, put down a three-quarter-filled coffee cup and saucer with the coffee spoon on the right side of the saucer from the right side of each guest. Then pass to each guest the tray containing the cream, sugar, and artificial sweetener.

☆ During the after-dinner coffee hour, when everyone has been sipping their coffee, offer a tray bearing a bottle of **cognac** (白兰地) and one or two sweet liqueurs, plus several snifters and small liqueur glasses.

☆ After a while, carry a tray of tall glasses of ice water first to the host so that he knows what is going on. Then pass the glasses around the entire group in case some guest prefers a **highball** (掺有冰水的威士忌饮料), a mixed drink made of Scotch and ice water or soda served in a tall glass.

Part D   Language Checklist

A. Vocabulary

strong 烈性的 stout 浓烈的 tart 酸涩的 vinegary 酸的 bitter 苦的 pale 味淡的	high/low in alcoholic strength 酒劲高/低 heady 易使人醉的 powerful 酒劲足的 have a high/low alcoholic content 酒精含量高/低	sparkling 起泡的 foamy 泡沫的 fizzy 冒泡的 bubbling 冒气泡的	thick 醇厚的 full-bodied 浓郁的 mellow 甘美的 refreshing 神清气爽的

B. Cultural Notes

Popular Western Foods 受欢迎的西方美食	French Food 法式食物	baguette 法式长棍面包，croissant 羊角面包，crêpe 法式薄饼，truffles 松露块菌菇，oysters 牡蛎，snails 蜗牛，scallops 扇贝，Fried Fresh Scallop with Goose Liver Jam 鹅肝酱煎鲜贝，Quiche Lorraine 洛林乳蛋饼，French Onion Soup 法式洋葱汤 • Quiche Lorraine refers to a type of savory pie served with a filling of savory custard, cheese, meat, and/or vegetables. • Crêpe is a thin pancake made of either wheat flour, or buckwheat flour. 法式薄饼是由小麦粉或荞麦粉做的。 • Originated in Brittany, crêpes are filled with different fillings, which can be sweet, or savory, and are served with cider (苹果酒).
	Italian Food 意大利食物	pizza, macaroni 通心粉，spaghetti 实心面条，lasagne/lasagna 意式千层面，ravioli 意式馄饨/小方饺，pasta 意大利面食，cappuccino 卡布奇诺，espresso 意式浓咖啡，prosciutto 意式五香火腿 • Lasagne is a food dish that consists of layers of pasta, sauce, and a filling such as meat or cheese, baked in an oven. 千层面是一种多层面条，里面含酱汁和肉或乳酪做的馅，在烤炉里烤制而成。

Popular Western Foods 受欢迎的西方美食	Spanish Food 西班牙食物	Tapas 餐前小吃，Paella 肉菜饭，Spanish omelette 西班牙式煎蛋饼，Chorizo 西班牙辣香肠，Calamares fritos 炸小鱿鱼，spider crab 蜘蛛蟹，Gazpacho 西班牙冷菜汤 • Tapas are small plates of food that are served with drinks before a main meal. 在西班牙，餐前小吃指的是上主菜前就提供的小盘食物，一般配酒水饮料吃。 • Paella is a dish cooked especially in Spain, which consists of rice mixed with small pieces of vegetables, fish, and chicken. • Gazpacho is a soup made with chopped tomatoes and onions and cucumbers and peppers and herbs and is served cold. 西班牙冷汤主要由切碎的西红柿、洋葱、黄瓜、香草和辣椒制成，应冷吃。
	English Food 英国食物	breakfast cereal 早餐牛奶麦片，muesli 牛奶什锦果仁麦片，poached 煮的，fried or scrambled eggs, toast, bacon 培根，fried or grilled tomatoes, fried mushrooms, fried bread or toast with butter, sausages and black pudding, tarts 果馅饼，Bubble and Squeak 卷心菜煎土豆，Steak Kidney Pudding 牛肉腰子布丁，Fish & Chips 炸鱼排薯条，Shepherd's Pie 牧羊人羊肉饼，Cottage Pie 村舍牛肉饼，Yorkshire Pudding 约克郡布丁，Creamy Mushroom Soup 奶油蘑菇汤 • A Cottage Pie is made with ground beef or minced beef with mashed potato on top, and if using ground lamb, then it would be called a Shepherd's Pie. • Yorkshire Pudding is made by baking a thick liquid mixture of flour, milk, and eggs and is often eaten with roast beef. 约克郡布丁由面粉、牛奶和鸡蛋烘烤而成，常与烤牛肉同食。
	American Food 美国食物	hamburger, cheeseburger, hotdog, Big Mac 巨无霸，roast turkey 火鸡，apple pie, New York-style pizza, barbecue, fried chicken, Reuben sandwich 鲁本三明治 • Reuben sandwich is made of corned beef, Swiss cheese, Thousand Island dressing and sauerkraut (德式泡菜).
Beverages 饮料	**Non-alcoholic Beverages 不含酒精的饮料**	
	Soft Drinks 软饮	soda 苏打水，lemonade 柠檬水，coke, Sprite and other carbonated drinks 碳酸饮料 • A nonalcoholic drink contains very little alcohol content, usually less than 0.5% of the total, or none. 非酒精饮料不含酒精或酒精浓度少于 0.5%。
	Hot Drinks 热饮	hot tea and chocolate，cappuccino 卡布奇诺，espresso 意式浓咖啡，mocha 摩卡，latte 拿铁
	Other Drinks 其他饮料	fruit juices, tap water, mineral water, milkshake 奶昔
	Alcoholic beverages 含酒精的饮料	
	Aperitifs 餐前酒	cocktail, vermouth 苦艾酒，Champagne 香槟酒，sherry 雪利酒 and any dry light white wine or liqueur • Other sparkling wines (气泡酒/汽酒) include Prosecco (普西哥，又名普洛赛克汽酒, Italy), Cava (卡瓦汽酒, Spain), and Sekt (赛克特汽酒, Germany and Austria). • Most sparkling wines pair beautifully with a range of foods, so they can also accompany appetizers. 大部分汽酒能很好地搭配多种食物，所以也能搭配各种开胃菜。 • Champagne is classically associated with parties, celebrations and New Year's festivities. 香槟酒往往是社交聚会、各种庆祝和新年节庆活动中的喜庆酒。
	Digestifs 餐后酒	sweet liqueurs and liquors like brandy, scotch 苏格兰威士忌，bourbon (美国波本威士忌) and other whiskeys: Cognac 科尼亚克白兰地，Jim Beam 占边美式玉米威士忌，Johnnie Walker 尊尼获加威士忌

Beverages 饮料	Drinks with the Meal 餐中酒	wine, beer and ale 麦芽啤酒 • Generally speaking, white wine goes well with seafood and white meat, while red wine is good with red meat and game (野味). • Red meat is meat such as beef or lamb, which is dark brown in color after it has been cooked. • White meat is meat such as chicken, usually carved from the breast of a fowl, which is pale in color or light-colored after it has been cooked. 白肉指烹饪后颜色显淡色的鸡肉等，通常指鸡脯肉。 • Usually, white wine should be served chilled around 7-10° Celsius or around 45° Fahrenheit, while red wine should be kept around 15-18° Celsius or around 60° Fahrenheit or at room temperature. 白葡萄酒通常要在温度 7-10℃ 或 45°F 左右的时候端上，红葡萄酒则要在 15-18℃ 或 60°F 或在室温下保存。
	White Wines 白葡萄酒	French Bordeaux Blanc 波尔多干白，Chablis 夏布利干白，Muscadet 麝香干白，sweet Sauternes 苏特恩/苏玳白葡萄酒，Liebfraumilch 莱茵干白 • **Bordeaux Blanc**①(波尔多干白) from south-west France, **Chablis** (夏布利干白) and **Muscadet**②(麝香干白) from central France are quite popular dry wines. • German **Liebfraumilch**③(莱茵干白) is also perfect with the seafood. But the sweet **Sauternes**④ (苏特恩/苏玳白葡萄酒) is suitable with desserts.
	Red Wines 红葡萄酒	Burgundy 勃艮第红葡萄酒，Cabernet Merlot 解百纳洛红葡萄酒，Pinot Noir 黑皮诺葡萄酒，Italian Chianti 基安蒂红葡萄酒，Lambrusco 兰布鲁斯科红葡萄酒 • French **Burgundy** (勃艮第红葡萄酒) is a **full-bodied** (醇厚的) red wine and pairs with red meat and game. • Italian **Chianti**⑤ (基安蒂红葡萄酒) is strong and good with pasta and red meats. • Another Italian red wine is **Lambrusco**⑥ (兰布鲁斯科红葡萄酒). It's very light and can go well with almost any food.
	Cocktails 鸡尾酒	• Popular cocktails are Bloody Mary (血腥玛丽), Martini (马提尼) and Margarita (玛格丽特). • It contains one or more types of alcoholic drinks or spirits such as brandy, vodka (伏特加), rum (朗姆), gin (杜松子), tequila (龙舌兰) or whisky together with other ingredients like fruit juice, bitter (苦啤酒), honey/sugar, milk, soda, or other flavorings.
Table Setting 餐具摆台	Western Table Setting 西餐餐具摆台	• The tableware is usually arranged in a particular order so that the flatware is used first farthest from the plate. • Set the glasses according to size, with the largest one on the left, starting with the water goblet, then the red wine and white wine glass, and last followed by Champagne glass. • Put the forks on the left side of the service plate in the order that they will be used, and the knives on the right side of the plate as well.

① 产自法国西南部波尔多地区的白葡萄酒。

② 产自法国中部卢瓦尔河河谷（Loire Valley）的白葡萄酒。

③ 产自德国境内莱茵河地区的白葡萄酒，名为"圣母之乳"。

④ 产自法国波尔多南部地区的白葡萄酒，一般配甜点。

⑤ 产自意大利托斯卡纳地区的红葡萄酒。

⑥ 产自意大利中部的红葡萄酒。

Table Setting 餐具摆台	Western Table Setting 西餐餐具摆台	• The service plate is positioned in the center with the forks to its left and the knives to its right. The fish fork, meat fork and salad fork are placed from farthest to nearest, so are the fish knife, meat knife and salad knife. The soup spoon is put outside the knives. • The butter plate is set above the forks at the left of the place setting with the butter knife diagonally (斜地) placed at its top. • The oyster fork is the only fork set on the right beyond the spoon. • Place a small dessert fork above the service plate with its tines (叉齿) pointing to the right, and set a dessert spoon horizontally with its head facing left. • Put cloth napkins on the dinner plate, and fold them in a simple triangle or square shape to enforce the impression that they have not been handled. 把餐巾放在餐盘上，将其简单折成三角形或正方形，以示没有用过。
	Chinese Table Setting 中餐餐具摆台	• Since Chinese people like to share the meal with each other, a round table with a Lazy Susan (圆转盘) set in the middle is a must, so that everyone at the table can reach the food and enjoy the conversation. • Usually, a small cup for the liquor is placed to the left of the wine glass or beer glass, while the glass for any fruit juice or nonalcoholic drink is to the right of the wine glass or beer glass. • Chopsticks and spoons are the main utensils. • The chopsticks are placed on the right of the service plate with the tips on a chopstick rest (筷子架), while the spoon is in the bowl. The folded napkin is set to the left of the service plate.

Part E　English in Use

I. Reading Comprehension

Task 1: Choose the best answer to complete each sentence below.

1. Snails and truffles are the typical _____ food.
   A. French　　　　　B. Italian　　　　　C. British　　　　　D. Spanish

2. English food is distinguished by its full _____ and the traditional, formal afternoon tea.
   A. lunch　　　　　B. breakfast　　　　　C. supper　　　　　D. buffet

3. In general, _____ is perfect for drinking with red meat dishes.
   A. white wine　　　B. champagne　　　　C. beer　　　　　D. red wine

4. The soup spoon and knives should be placed to the _____ of the service plate.
   A. left side　　　　B. upper left　　　　C. right side　　　　D. upper right

5. Which of the following dishes is typical Spanish food? _____
   A. Lasagna　　　　B. Paella　　　　C. Fish & Chips　　　　D. Turducken

6. Which of the following dishes is typical English food? _____
   A. Macaroni　　　　B. Quiche Lorraine　　C. Fish & Chips　　　D. Chorizo

7. One of the famous Italian pasta is _____.
   A. bacon　　　　　B. tarts　　　　　C. ravioli　　　　　D. muesli

8. What glass is usually brought in when dessert is served? _____

    A. Flute   B. Coupe   C. Snifter   D. Stemmed glass

9. European wines tend to be classified by _____, while non-European wines are classified by grape.

    A. grape   B. country   C. region   D. brand

10. The only fork set on the right outside the knives is _____.

    A. oyster fork   B. butter fork   C. fish fork   D. dinner fork

Task 2: Answer the following questions concerning the beverage service in Part A and the table-setting in Part B.

1. Why is a stem of a wine glass so important?

2. What is the proper temperature served for white wine and red wine? How is wine kept?

3. How should the wineglasses be placed at a formal banquet?

4. What is a table setting like at a Western banquet?

5. What's the major difference between the Western and Chinese table setting?

Task 3: Decide whether each of the following statements is True or False according to the passage on banquet service tips in Part C.

1. Begin serving the woman on the host's right or the man on the hostess's right, and move around clockwise. (　　)

2. Pour wine into each glass, moving around the table counter clockwise after first filling the female guest of honor's glass. (　　)

3. Serve the coffee cup and saucer from the left side of the guest. (　　)

4. Serve the food and wine from the left side of the guest, and remove the used plate from the right side. (　　)

5. Fill the red wine glass less than one-third, and the white wine glass two-thirds full. (　　)

II. Translation

Task 4: Translate the following sentences into English.

1. 餐前酒是一种刺激食欲的饭前开胃酒。

2. 香槟酒是餐前开胃酒，我们经常称之为欢迎客人的迎宾酒。

3. 一般来说，白葡萄酒配海鲜和白肉，红葡萄酒配红肉。

4. 波尔多干白（Bordeaux Blanc）产自法国西南部，是吃白肉或鱼时最理想的搭配了。

5. 葡萄酒杯高脚的一个原因是供人们用手握住杯子，以免在酒杯身上留有指印。

6. 记住，要用不同的酒杯装不同的葡萄酒。

7. 无论是白葡萄酒还是红葡萄酒，只要是好酒，都能搭配并调和食物的风味。

8. 把水杯放到最靠近盘子餐刀的上方，接下来放红葡萄酒杯和白葡萄酒杯，最后是香槟酒杯。

9. 按使用的顺序把叉放在餐盘的左边，刀放在盘子的右边。

10. 生蚝叉用来吃贝壳类食物，这是唯一放右边的叉。

Task 5: Translate the following sentences into Chinese.

1. Paella is a dish cooked especially in Spain, which consists of rice mixed with small pieces of vegetables, fish, and chicken.

2. Quiche Lorraine refers to a type of savory pie served with a filling of savory custard, cheese, meat, and vegetables.

3. Traditionally a Cottage Pie is made of ground beef or minced beef with mashed potato on top, and if using ground lamb, then it would be called a Shepherd's Pie.

4. White meat or light meat refers to some poultry meat such as chicken which is pale in color before cooking. Red meat is meat such as beef or lamb that is dark in color before cooking.

5. White wines are usually served with white meats such as seafood, chicken, etc.

6. French Burgundy (勃艮第红葡萄酒) is a full-bodied (醇厚的) red wine and pairs with red meat and game.

7. It is believed that the shape of the glass is essential to concentrate and keep the wine's aroma or bouquet (酒香).

8. Popping the cork and toasting with sparkling, fizzy champagne as the clock strikes midnight on New Year's Eve is a tradition in many households around the world.

9. The stem allows you to hold your wine glass without heating your wine by cupping your hands around the bowl, and without leaving fingerprints on the bowl which will distract from the visual enjoyment of your wine.

10. Place a small dessert fork above the service plate with its tines (叉齿) facing right, and set a dessert spoon horizontally with its head facing left.

III. Role Play

Task 6: Play a role in any of the following situations with your partner(s).

Situation 1: Sam Martin, a French **maitre d'hotel** (领班), is training the new wait staff of a **Radisson Hotel** (雷迪森酒店) in China about beverage service.

Situation 2: Chen Ling is a new waitress in the Western restaurant in a five-star hotel. She's consulting with Richard Cooper, the maitre d'hotel, about how to set a banquet table.

Situation 3: Xu Qing is a manager in a Chinese restaurant. She's telling Susan, a newly-recruited American waitress about Chinese table setting.

IV. Problem-solving

Task 7: Make an analysis of the following cases, and answer the questions as required.

Case 1

Situation: You work as a waitress/waiter at a restaurant. You're busy serving a sit-down banquet for a group of people from a big company. They are having an annual celebration for their company and enjoying themselves. Just then, one of the guests accidentally breaks a plate or a glass, you happen to be near.

Question: What would you do then?

Case 2

Situation: A group of people are having a birthday party at a restaurant. The dinner party begins at 6:30 pm, and now it's already past 10:00 pm. These people are having a good time by talking and drinking, and the party doesn't seem to end yet. Your restaurant is supposed to close soon.

Question: If you were the waiter or waitress, how would you deal with the problem?

Case 3

Situation: You're busy serving a wonderful meal to more than 30 people at a dinner party. While offering the soup, you happen to spill it over a guest.

Question: What should you do then?

Answers for Reference

Module III
Introduction to Cultural Sites

Unit 7　Lake, Garden and Grottoes

1. Can you name the following scenic spots or historic sites in both Chinese and English and tell where they are in China?

1) _____
2) _____
3) _____
4) _____
5) _____
6) _____
7) _____
8) _____
9) _____

2. What are the four major gardens in China? How about the four in Suzhou?
3. What are the three major sites for Buddhist grotto art in China?
4. Can you make a nine-day tour plan in China? Now read the following itinerary and translate it into Chinese.

Tour the Highlights in China

Day 01 Arrival in Beijing
Arrive at 4:00 pm in Beijing. Free time.

Day 02 Beijing
Visit Tian'anmen Square, the Forbidden City in the morning, and the Summer Palace in the afternoon. Free evening.

Day 03 Beijing
Climb Juyongguan Pass of the Great Wall in the morning, and take a tour of the "Bird's Nest" and "Water Cube" in the afternoon.

Day 04 Beijing to Xi'an
Fly to Xi'an after a visit to the Temple of Heaven where Ming and Qing emperors worshiped the God of Heaven and prayed for good harvests.

Day 05 Xi'an
Visit the Terracotta Warriors & Horses in the morning, and the Huaqing Pool Hot Spring in the afternoon. Free evening.

Day 06 Xi'an
Visit the Great Wild Goose Pagoda, the Forest of Stelae in the day time, then the 600-year-old ancient city wall in the evening.

Day 07 Hangzhou
Fly to Hangzhou, the paradise city in China in the morning. Take a boat tour of West Lake and visit the Huagang (Red Carp Pond) Park in the afternoon. Watch the evening show — "Most Memorable is Hangzhou (最忆是杭州)".

Day 08 Hangzhou
Visit Lingyin Temple and Feilai Peak (Peak Flown from Afar) in the morning, Tiger Spring and Tea Village in the afternoon. Take the express train to Shanghai in the evening.

Day 09 Shanghai
Visit the classical Ming Dynasty Yu Garden, and **Pudong** (浦东), the new economic district across from the Bund. Take a cruise on the Huangpu River and then a stroll along the Bund in the afternoon. Free evening.

Day 10 Shanghai Departure
Fly back home in the morning.

Part A   Discussing the Itinerary

Dialogue 1

Situation: *On the coach from the airport to the hotel, the national tour guide Su Ling is discussing the itinerary with the tour leader Mark from the US.*

Questions for comprehension and discussion:
★ What time is the group supposed to have supper?
★ What are many of the group members interested in seeing in Beijing?
★ What's Su Ling's suggestion since the group has plenty of time before supper?
★ What's Su Ling's requirement after the suggestion?
★ If you were Su Ling, what suggestions would you make?

Su Ling: Hi, Mark, what do you think of the tour plan in Beijing?

Mark: It's great on the whole. By the way, we'll have free evening today, won't we?

Su Ling: Yes, of course.

Mark: What time will we arrive at our hotel?

Su Ling: Probably 4:00 pm if the traffic is smooth.

Mark: Right, it's still early for supper, isn't it?

Su Ling: Yes, it is. We're supposed to have supper at around 6:30 pm, is that all right?

Mark: Good. So we have plenty of time before supper. Many people in our group would be quite interested in seeing the local people's life here. By the way, we can have supper a little bit later, say 7:00 pm. That's our usual supper time back home.

Su Ling: OK, then a visit to **Hutong** (胡同), the alleys in **Houhai** (后海). It's not far away from the hotel, only a 10-minute walk.

Mark: Perfect.

Su Ling: Houhai Hutong area is the best protected district, for there are many traditional Beijing-style courtyard dwellings such as **Siheyuan** (四合院). I'm sure your group will enjoy the experience.

Mark: Definitely.

Su Ling: In that case, rather than taking a rest after we check in at the hotel, we ought to go directly to the Hutong area to save the time. Is that OK?

Mark: That's great.

Su Ling: Since this is the additional tour, I'm afraid you have to bear the extra expense. But first let me check with our travel service.

Mark: Fine.

Dialogue 2

Situation: *The tour guide Chen Yan is explaining the next day's itinerary and discussing it with the tourists on the coach.*

Questions for comprehension and discussion:

★ According to the tour guide Chen Yan, what's the schedule for the tour group the next day?

★ Does the tour group agree to the plan?

★ What are some of the tourists interested in?

★ How does Chen Yan solve the problem? What's her final suggestion?

★ If the plan is not totally agreed on by the group, how would a guide solve the problem?

Chen Yan: Hi, everyone, after a whole day's sightseeing, you might need time to have a rest. Before you go back to your hotel, I'd like to say a few words about our schedule for tomorrow. We'll visit **Lingyin Temple** (灵隐寺) and **Feilai Peak** (飞来峰) in the morning, and have lunch at **Huazhong Cheng Restaurant** (花中城餐馆) near **Leifeng Pagoda** (雷锋塔). After lunch at about 1:00 pm, we'll visit Leifeng Pagoda, and then at about 3:00 pm, we'll head for the **Six Harmonies Pagoda** (六和塔). It's not far away from Leifeng Pagoda, and it's towering over the Qiantang River.

Tourist A: Sorry to bother you, but do we have to visit both pagodas the whole day? Can we just choose one so that we have more time to visit the Tea Village? I have been looking forward to seeing how the green tea grows here.

Tourist B: Yeah, I quite agree. I'm not so interested in the tea myself, but one of my friends is crazy about it. Personally, I would love to see the Silk Museum.

Tour Leader: Well, Chen Yan, could you please give us a better suggestion? Or please just make a choice for us.

Chen Yan: Well, each of the pagodas has its own special features, if we have enough time, it's better to see both of them. Now since most of you want to visit one pagoda, I would recommend the Six Harmonies Pagoda, as it's a perfect symbol of brick-and-wood structure built in the ancient China, while Leifeng Pagoda was  reconstructed after the old original one collapsed in 1924. In that case, we'll have to change our schedule so that we may have a better itinerary. That is, we'll first visit Six Harmonies Pagoda in the morning, then have a cup of green tea at the Longjing Tea Village. After that, we'll have lunch at **Tianwaitian restaurant** (Heaven Beyond Heaven, 天外天餐馆) near Lingyin Temple. After lunch, we'll go directly to visit the temple. Is that all right?

Tourist A: Great.

Tourist B: Fine. But is there any chance for us to visit the Silk Museum? I'd love to see those little tiny silk worms.

Tourist C: So would I. Those worms must be cute.

Chen Yan: Don't worry, you won't miss it. The day after tomorrow we can visit it in the morning.

Tourist B: Thank you very much. That's so nice of you.

Part B   West Lake, Summer Palace and Mogao Grottoes

Dialogue 1: West Lake

Situation: *The tour guide Chen Yan is introducing West Lake to the American group on the coach on the way to the lake.*

Questions for comprehension and discussion:

★ How much do you know about West Lake?

★ Do you know the folktale in which West Lake is compared to a pearl?

★ Can you recite the poem in which West Lake is compared to an ancient beauty Xizi?

Chen Yan: Hi, good morning, everyone! We'll take a 50-minute lake **cruise** (坐船游览), probably the highlight of your tour in Hangzhou. As the saying goes, "Above is paradise, and below are Suzhou and Hangzhou." Hangzhou has long been praised as paradise on the earth mostly because of West Lake. But do you know how many West Lakes there are in China?

Tourist A: Two or three?

Tourist B: Ten?

Tourist C: Sorry, no idea.

Chen Yan: Well, there are actually thirty-six West Lakes in the whole country. All of them are beautiful and special. **Kunming Lake** (昆明湖) in the Summer Palace is also called West Lake, as it's an imitation of the lake in Hangzhou.

Tourist A: Really?

Chen Yan: Yes. The largest of these thirty-six is in **Guilin** (桂林) noted for its unique landscape. However, there's a popular saying: "Of the thirty-six West Lakes east or west, the West lake in Hangzhou is the best. "

Tourist B: Amazing!

Chen Yan: Almost 1,200 years ago, when serving as the local governor, **Bai Juyi** (白居易, 772–846), the famous Tang Dynasty poet governor once said in one of his numerous poems: "I cannot bear to depart from Hangzhou, half of the reason is the lake." The West Lake Cultural Landscape of Hangzhou has been included on the list of UNESCO's World Heritage Sites since 2011.

The lake lies to the west of the city, hence the name. It used to be a **lagoon** (潟湖) about 12,000 years ago. It was not until the **Sui Dynasty** (隋朝, 581–618) about 1,400 years ago that a fresh-water lake came into being. Since then, it has become famous because of its natural beauty. What's more, it has been **likened**

(比作) to a dazzling pearl accidentally falling from the heaven once upon a time, according to folklore. Its owners were **Jade Dragon** (玉龙) and **Golden Phoenix** (金凤) living on the bank of galaxy or **the Milky Way** (银河) as you call it. They had spent thousands of years carving a shining **pebble** (卵石) found on a fairy island into a magic pearl. Fascinated by the bright pearl, the **Queen Mother of the West** (西天王母娘娘) obtained the pearl by sending her guards to steal it from the couple while they were sleeping. Shocked that the pearl was missing, the couple searched for it everywhere in sorrow. Finally, they happened to find it at the birthday party held for the Queen Mother who was showing off the pearl to all the guests. Out of anger, the couple hurried to snatch it. The three **grappled** (扭打) with each other, but all of a sudden, the pearl fell off to the earth and changed into a lake. To protect the pearl, the couple flew and danced down to the earth and changed themselves into two hills — presently known as the **Jade Emperor Hill** (玉皇山) and the **Phoenix Hill** (凤凰山) by the lake. So there's a popular folk saying: "The West Lake, a dazzling pearl, falling from the sky; the Flying Dragon and Dancing Phoenix forever standing by." A beautiful story, isn't it?

Tourist A: Yes, it sure is. I love this story.

Chen Yan: As far as the beauty of the lake is concerned, the Northern Song Dynasty poet Su Dongpo compared the lake itself to a legendary ancient beauty, **Xizi** (西子/西施), kind of Chinese **Helen of Troy** (特洛伊的海伦) ①, in a poem of praise for the lake.

"The shimmering ripples delight the eye on sunny days,
The dim hills present a rare view in misty rain.
West Lake may be compared to Beauty Xizi at her best,
She is gorgeous, richly clothed or plainly dressed."

Tourist B: I see. In terms of scenic splendor or natural beauty, many lakes around the world may rival the West Lake here. I've learned that the essence of the lake lies not on the surface, but in the rippled reflections of legend and myth that have **enthralled** (吸引) Chinese visitors for **millennia** (千年).

Chen Yan: You're right. Many of us here in Hangzhou grew up with legends and classic poems about the lake, for the lake together with the hills surrounding its three sides, has inspired numerous poets, scholars and artists since the 9th century.

Tourist B: No wonder **the West Lake Cultural Landscape of Hangzhou** (杭州西湖文化

---

① Helen of Troy：特洛伊的海伦，源自荷马史诗《伊里亚特》（*Iliad*）中的希腊神话故事。希腊南部邦城斯巴达国王墨涅拉奥斯（Menelaus）的王后海伦美艳无比，是希腊的绝代佳人。后来，她被特洛伊王子帕里斯诱拐去特洛伊。墨涅拉奥斯发誓报仇雪恨。此事也激起了希腊各部族的公愤，从而引发著名的特洛伊战争。

景观) is on the list of UNESCO World Heritage Sites.

Chen Yan:　Exactly. The West Lake Cultural Landscape now covers 33 square kilometers. The lake is divided into five sections with the Outer Lake being the largest by two **crisscrossing** (交叉的) causeways — **Bai Di** (Bai Causeway, 白堤) and **Su Di** (Su Causeway, 苏堤), together with three artificial islets, which are compared to the fairy islands in the eyes of our local people. It originally covered

5.6 square kilometers. Since 2008, the lake has been expanded to the west to restore its original size, as it was 300 years ago. Now the new large lake covers a total area of 6.5 square kilometers with a **circumference** (周长) of 15 kilometers. The third causeway, called **Yanggong Di** (Yanggong Causeway, 杨公堤), is included. It's named after the former governor **Yang Mengying** (杨孟瑛) in the 16th century. You'll get to know most of the "Top Ten Views" during the cruise.

Now we're passing by the **Broken Bridge** (断桥)**,** the most popular bridge on the lake, linking the downtown area to Bai Causeway. You may wonder why it's called broken as it's definitely not. It's actually a heart breaking bridge where one of the most romantic folklores happened in China, a love story of Xu Xian (许仙), a secular scholar, and the **White Snake Lady** (白蛇娘子). Another reason is related to the snow. It's widely believed that West Lake looks more beautiful in the snowy time than in the sunny or rainy time. The bridge is the best place to have a unique view of the lake in the snow. Moreover, when the sun comes out after the snow, the snow melts first on the sunny side of the bridge, while on its shady side, the snow still **lingers**（未消散）. Viewed from a distance, the bridge appears to be broken. Hence the name "**Lingering Snow on the Broken Bridge** (断桥残雪)" for the unique view in the snow.

Well, to your left, at the other end of Bai Causeway is Gushan, the **Solitary Hill** (孤山), the largest island in the lake. It's home to over 30 scenic spots and historic sites such as **Zhejiang Provincial Museum** (浙江博物馆), **Xiling Seal Engravers' Society** (西泠印社), **Zhongshan Park** (中山公园), the

former imperial vacation palace in the Qing Dynasty and the century-old **Louwailou** (楼外楼) restaurant, etc. By the way, can you see the pavilion over there? It's dedicated to Lin Hejing (林和靖, 967–1028), a **hermit poet** (隐逸诗人) who lived about 1,000 years ago. He loved plum trees and cranes so much that both of them were compared to be his wife and sons.

Well, we'll soon arrive at the **wharf** (码头). Our boat cruise will start from Gushan for you to have a view of the hill as well as the two beautiful causeways, and then go round the three islets, finally stop at the southern end of Su Causeway so that you can visit the **Red Carp Pond** (红鱼池) in Huagang Park (花港公园) after landing.

OK, here we are. Please don't forget your belongings and follow me. We'll get on the boat.

Dialogue 2: Summer Palace

Situation: *The tour guide Han Bin is showing a couple Sue and Jim around the Summer Palace.*

Questions for comprehension and discussion:

★ What was the Summer Palace originally named? Why was it built?

★ Where did the Empress Dowager Cixi get the money from to have the destroyed garden rebuilt?

★ What's the highlight of the Summer Palace?

★ What is the long corridor mainly famous for?

★ If you were Han Bin, what would you briefly tell the couple about the Summer Palace?

Han Bin: Now, we're in the Summer Palace.

Sue: Is it also called Yi… Yuan?

Han Bin: Yes, it's **Yihe Yuan** (颐和园), meaning "the Garden of Health and Harmony".

Jim: Is it called the Summer Palace because of the empress?

Han Bin: Yeah, you're right. It was supposed to serve as a summer resort for the **Empress Dowager Cixi** (慈禧太后, 1835–1908) in the Qing Dynasty, who had **misappropriated** (挪用) some funds from the Imperial Navy and other sources to rebuild it.

Sue: Excuse me, how much of the funds was used?

Han Bin: Well, there are many different calculations. Some experts estimate over five million **taels of silver** (银两), while others believe three million.

Sue: I see.

Han Bin:

The domain had long been a royal garden before the 18th century. It was then named "**Garden of Clear Ripples**" (清漪园) and was **embellished** (修缮) by Emperor Qianlong to celebrate his mother's birthday in 1750. Unfortunately, it was **vandalized** (肆意破坏) by the **Anglo-French Allied Force** (英法联军) in 1860 at the end of the Second Opium War (1856–1860). Then it was rebuilt in 1888 in favor of Cixi. And it was a shame that it was again **plundered** (洗劫), this time by the **Eight-Power Allied Forces** (八国联军) in 1900.

Now, it covers an area of 2.9 square kilometers, two thirds of it is water. It mainly consists of Kunming Lake and **Wanshou Hill** (Longevity Hill, 万寿山), including **Hall of Benevolence and Longevity** (仁寿殿), **the Tower of the Fragrance of the Buddha** (佛

香阁), **Marble Boat** (石舫) and **the Long Corridor, 17-arch Bridge** (十七孔桥) as the highlight. It's the largest and the best preserved of the imperial gardens still existing in China. In other words, it's the masterpiece of Chinese gardens, and is well-known around the world.

Jim: Wow, we're so glad to be in the largest imperial garden now in China.

Sue: No wonder it's gorgeous here! I like the lake, it's so peaceful!

Han Bin: Let me show you one of the highlights first. This way, please.

Sue: I know. It's the Long Corridor, isn't it?

Han Bin: Yes, it is. You seem quite familiar with this place.

Sue: Not really, but we have a travel **brochure** (小册子).

Han Bin: I see. It was first built in the middle of the 18th century. It's the longest corridor in the gardens in China and was regarded as the longest painted corridor in the world in 1990. Do you know how long it is?

Jim: Not quite sure.

Han Bin: It's 728 meters long and is divided into 273 sections. It's famous for its rich painted decoration. All these paintings are quite vivid.

Jim: There are numerous paintings here, aren't there?

Han Bin: Yes, there are over 14,000 paintings in all.

Sue: Incredible! I love these paintings, though I don't know much about the stories.

Han Bin: Many of them are landscapes with flowers and birds, and others are figure paintings, which illustrate some famous classical works of literature and folk tales.

Monologue: Dunhuang Mogao Grottoes

Situation: *A tour guide is introducing the Mogao Grottoes in Dunhuang to the tourists. Dunhuang is one of the three major sites for grotto art in ancient China.*

Questions for comprehension and discussion:

★ Where are Dunhuang Mogao Grottoes?

★ What are the caves noted for?

★ Why are they also called "Caves of a Thousand Buddhas"?

★ If you were the guide, how would you introduce Mogao Grottoes to the tourists?

Hi, everyone, we're now on the way to Dunhuang Mogao Grottoes which are famous for numerous delicate **sculptures** (雕/塑像) and colorful **murals** (壁画). These caves, covering an area of 1,600 meters from the north to the south, are located within the cliffs of the **Mingsha Hill** (meaning Singing Sand Hill, 鸣沙山) 25 kilometers southeast of **Dunhuang** (敦煌) city, Gansu Province. Being an **oasis** (绿洲) at a religious and cultural crossroads on the Silk Road, Dunhuang serves as a strategic point along the road, an important gateway to the West, as well as a **refuge** (避难所) or a **staging post** (补给站) for **weary** (疲倦的) Silk Road travelers.

As a **dazzling** (耀眼的) pearl along the Silk Road, the cave complex in Mogao is the largest, most fascinating **repository** (储藏库) of Buddhist grotto art in the world. It was listed as a UNESCO World Heritage Site in 1987, followed by **Longmen Grottoes** (龙门石窟) in Henan in 2000 and **Yungang Grottoes** (云岗石窟) in Shanxi in 2001.

According to historical records, a monk named Lezun or **Yuezun** (乐尊) had a vision of thousands of Buddhas bathed in golden rays at the site in 366 AD. Inspired, he began to build the first cave in this area. From then on, numerous caves were constructed over one thousand years spanning ten dynasties until the 14th century. Thus, Mogao Grottoes are also commonly known as "**the Caves of a Thousand Buddhas** (千佛洞)". The caves **initially** (起初) served only as a place of **meditation** (坐禅，静思) for hermit monks, but later became a place of **worship** (崇拜，尊崇) and **pilgrimage** (朝圣) for the public.

There are 492 caves or grottoes in existence with some 45,000 square meters of murals, and over 2,400 painted clay figures. In addition, up to 50,000 **manuscripts** (手稿) in the **Library Cave** (藏经洞) known as Cave 17, discovered recently in 1900, are part of the greatest treasure trove of ancient documents found. Although some of them have been **dispersed** (散落) and now many of them are on display in **British Museum** (大英博物馆), the remaining **fabulous** (难以置信的) collection is one of the essential sources of Asian history. The **astounding** (令人震惊的) discovery, which has been acclaimed as the world's greatest discovery of ancient Oriental culture, inspired hundreds of scholars to study the Buddhist art displayed in these grottoes in Dunhuang area.

The caves in Mogao vary in size, with Cave 37 being the smallest with an area of less than one square meter, and Cave 16 the largest covering an area of 268 square meters. Cave 96 presently is as high as 40 meters with nine-tiered **wooden fore** (木制遮檐) housing the largest sitting **Maitreya Buddha** (弥勒佛) at 35.5 meters high. In the Tang Dynasty, the art of the Mogao Grottoes were at its **heyday** (全盛时期). Despite the **erosion** (侵蚀) caused by wind and **drifting sand** (流沙) for over a thousand years, many of the painted clay figures are still in good condition, and the murals are in bright colors.

All the painted clay figures in various poses, showing a variety of gestures, range in size from 0.1 meter to 35.5 meters. The Buddha is generally shown in the middle, often **flanked** (两侧) by **bodhisattvas** (菩萨), **heavenly kings** (天王), **devas** (提婆，天神), along with **yaksas** (夜叉) and other mythical creatures. Cave 158, also called **Nirvana Cave** (涅槃洞), features a large **reclining Buddha** (卧佛) covering the entire hall with a total length of 15.6 meters.

Some **venerable images** (尊像), **donors** (供养人) can also be found.

Make sure you diret your attention to the fantastic murals on the walls in the caves, as well. They span a long period of history, from the 5th to the 14th century, and are valued for the scale and richness of content as well as their artistry. They mainly depict **Buddhist**

themes (佛教主题), such as the illustrations of **Buddhist sutras** (佛经), **Jataka**① (《本生经》), etc. While earlier works were influenced by Indian Buddhist art, more recent works depict all walks of life and activities in a local setting. However, the most remarkable images are **Flying Apsaras** (飞天), or the **celestial beings** (仙人，天神), the symbol of Dunhuang art. They fly with the support of floating cloth and colored ribbons in the ceiling or above the Buddhas. They are an **embodiment** (化身) of **Gandharva**② (乾闼婆), the singer in the court of gods, and **Kinnara**③ (紧那罗), the celestial musician, in **Indian mythology** (印度神话). Flying Apsaras have thousands of forms and postures but change over time. However, They are the mixture of Chinese and foreign characteristics.

In a word, it's believed that Mogao Grottoes constitute an **anthology** (集萃) of Buddhist art with paintings and sculptures spanning a period of a thousand years, which is of unmatched historical value.

Now we've arrived at our destination. The grottoes here can be divided into two sections, the northern and southern ones. The southern section contains the highlight of the grottoes, but there are only five existing caves containing the murals or statues in the northern one. So, first, I'll show you around the southern section, and then you'll have free time for about 40 minutes. And after that, we'll meet at the exit. Now, this way, please.

Part C   Tips on Oral Presentation

Questions for comprehension and discussion:
★ Who may the tourists be?
★ What do you think is the most important point to include when making an oral presentation?
★ How will you make an effective oral presentation?

It's very important to have good guiding skills to be an excellent tour guide. The guide may use different methods of oral presentation with regard to the characteristics of tourist attractions. A good presentation should always try to **cater to** (满足) the various requirements of the tourists with different nationalities, ages, genders, occupations, educational backgrounds, interests, especially purposes of travel. In other words, as people may travel for adventure, recreation, education, pilgrimage or other purposes, various requirements for the guide's presentation are expected. For example, those intellectual people would expect professional service, experienced guiding skills and good presentation with specific information, while those people mostly seeking pleasure and fun favor a simple, interesting or even humorous introduction.

---

① Jataka：《本生经》，是印度佛教文学中最重要的经文，讲述佛陀释迦牟尼在成佛之前的故事。成佛之前，释迦牟尼经过了无数次轮回转生，如做过国王、王子、婆罗门、商人、妇人、大象、猴子、鹿等。他每一次转生，便有一个行善立德的故事，这些故事被称为"本生故事"。
② Gandharva：乾闼婆，印度教中半人半马或鸟，会歌舞的天神。
③ Kinnara：紧那罗，印度教中半人半马持乐器并崇尚爱情的音乐天神。

Therefore, it's necessary for a guide to bear the following points in mind when showing the tourists around the tourist attractions.

☆ Always keep active, energetic and lively.

☆ Choose a good or appropriate place or site for the introduction.

☆ Face the tourists, use the microphone correctly, and make yourself clearly understood.

☆ Offer both general and specific information of the tourist attractions correctly.

☆ Show the tourists the highlight of the visiting place.

☆ Try best to arouse the interests of the tourists by keeping your talk short and to the point.

☆ Use a method of question-and-answer properly to avoid a long boring talk.

☆ Tell properly some legends, fairy tales, folklores, stories, well-known sayings, quotes of literature and remarks of some celebrities, etc.

☆ Tell possibly some humorous but not dirty stories to cheer up the tourists who seem to feel a bit bored, tired or dismayed for various reasons.

☆ Advise the tourists of the best time and best place to enjoy the views of the scenery.

☆ Always confirm the time and meeting place when allowing free activities in the visiting place.

☆ Always remember to remind the tourists to keep safe when touring a place.

Part D   Language Checklist

A. Tourist Attractions

Tourist Attractions	中 文 名	城　　市
Forbidden City	紫禁城	北京
Summer Palace	颐和园	北京
Mountain Resort in Chengde	承德避暑山庄	承德
Badaling/Juyong Pass of the Great Wall	八达岭/居庸关长城	北京
Birds' Nest and Water Cube	鸟巢和水立方	北京
Heaven Temple	天坛	北京
Terracotta Army	兵马俑	西安
Huaqing Hot Spring	华清池	西安
Great Goose Pagoda, the Forest of Steles	大雁塔，碑林	西安
West Lake	西湖	杭州
Lingyin Temple	灵隐寺	杭州
Six Harmonies Pagoda	六和塔	杭州
Leifeng Pagoda	雷峰塔	杭州
The Bund	外滩	上海
Yu Garden	豫园	上海
Canglang Pavilion	沧浪亭	苏州

Tourist Attractions	中 文 名	城 市
Shizi Lin (Lion Grove Garden)	狮子林	苏州
Zhuozheng Garden (Humble Administrator's Garden)	拙政园	苏州
Liu Yuan (Lingering Garden)	留园	苏州
Mountain Villa with Embracing Beauty	环秀山庄	苏州
Wangshi Garden (Net Master's Garden, Hermit's Garden)	网师园	苏州
Mogao Grottoes	莫高石窟/莫高窟	敦煌
Longmen Grottoes	龙门石窟	洛阳
Yungang Grottoes	云冈石窟	大同
Maiji Grottoes	麦积山石窟	天水

B. Vocabulary

Xizi/Xishi 西子/西施 Chinese Helen of Tory 中国的特洛伊海伦	lagoon 潟湖 a dazzling pearl 一颗璀璨的明珠 the Milky Way 银河 grapple 扭打	Jade Dragon 玉龙 Golden Phoenix 金凤 Jade Emperor Hill 玉皇山 Phoenix Hill 凤凰山
Bai Causeway 白堤 Su Causeway 苏堤 Yanggong Causeway 杨公堤	Summer Palace 颐和园 Kunming Lake 昆明湖 Longevity Hill 万寿山	Queen Mother of the West 西天王母娘娘 Empress Dowager Cixi 慈禧太后
Mogao Grottoes 莫高窟 Caves of a Thousand Buddhas 千佛洞 nine-tiered wooden fore 九层木制遮檐	Buddhist themes 佛教主题 sutras 佛经 scriptures 经文 Jataka 本生经	Flying Apsaras 飞天 celestial beings 仙人，天神 Gandharva 乾闼婆 Kinnara 紧那罗 Indian mythology 印度神话
meditation 坐禅/静思 embodiment 化身	mural 壁画 statues 雕/塑像 illustration 插图	venerable image 尊像 donor 供养人
pilgrimage 朝圣 worship 崇拜	heyday 全盛时期	manuscript 原稿
fabulous 难以置信的	anthology 集萃	alley 胡同，小巷 courtyard dwellings 四合院

C. Key Patterns

Introducing a Lake 介绍湖泊	• Above is paradise, and below are Suzhou and Hangzhou. 上有天堂，下有苏杭。 • Of the thirty-six West Lakes east or west, the West lake in Hangzhou is the best. 天下西湖三十六，此中最美是杭州。 • I cannot bear to depart from Hangzhou, half of the reason is the lake. 未能抛得杭州去，一半勾留是此湖。 • The West Lake, a dazzling pearl falling from the sky; the Flying Dragon and Dancing Phoenix, forever standing by. 西湖明珠从天降，龙飞凤舞到钱塘。

Introducing a Lake 介绍湖泊	• The shimmering ripples delight the eye on sunny days, The dim hills present a rare view in rainy haze. West Lake may be compared to Beauty Xizi at her best. She is gorgeous richly clothed or plainly dressed. 水光潋滟晴方好，山色空蒙雨亦奇。欲把西湖比西子，淡妆浓抹总相宜。
Introducing a Garden 介绍园林	• The World Heritage Committee has inscribed the West Lake Cultural Landscape of Hangzhou, comprising West Lake and the hills surrounding its three sides, on the UNESCO's *World Heritage List*. 世界遗产委员会已把包括西湖及其周边山峰的杭州西湖文化景观列入联合国教科文组织的《世界遗产名录》。 • West Lake is surrounded on three sides by "cloud-capped hills" and on the fourth by the city of Hangzhou. Its beauty has been celebrated by writers and artists since the Tang Dynasty (618–907). (West Lake Cultural Landscape of Hangzhou, UNESCO World Heritage Site description). 西湖三面云山一面城。自唐朝以来，西湖之美一直被文人墨客称颂。（杭州西湖文化景观，联合国教科文组织世界遗产地说明） • The key components of West Lake still allow it to inspire people to "project feelings onto the landscape". 西湖的核心要素依然能够激发人们"寄情山水"的情怀。 • West Lake is an outstanding example of a cultural landscape that displays with great clarity the ideals of Chinese landscape aesthetics, as expounded by writers and scholars in the Tang and the Song dynasties. The landscape of West Lake had a profound impact on the design of gardens not only in China but further afield, where lakes and causeways imitated the harmony and beauty of West Lake. 西湖是文化景观的一个杰出典范，正如唐宋文人墨客所描述的那样，它极为清晰地展现了中国景观的美学思想，其创设的一种与自然和谐的美被很多湖泊和湖堤所模仿，对中国乃至世界的园林设计影响深远。 • The Summer Palace is the largest and the best preserved of the imperial gardens still existing in China today. 颐和园是中国当今现存最大且保护得最好的皇家园林。 • Classical Chinese garden design, which seeks to recreate natural landscapes in miniature, is nowhere better illustrated than in the nine gardens in the historic city of Suzhou. They are generally acknowledged to be masterpieces of the genre. Dating from the 11th-19th century, the gardens reflect the profound metaphysical importance of natural beauty in Chinese culture in their meticulous design. (Classical Gardens of Suzhou, UNESCO World Heritage Site description) 历史名城苏州的九座园林绝美地体现了中国古典园林设计思想，采用微缩景观，以小见大，苏州园林被公认为实现这一设计理念的典范。这些建造于11—19世纪的园林，以其精雕细琢的设计，折射出中国文化中取法自然而又超越自然的深邃意境。（苏州古典园林，联合国教科文组织世界遗产地说明） • The four classical gardens of Suzhou are masterpieces of Chinese landscape garden design in which art, nature, and ideas are integrated perfectly to create ensembles of great beauty and peaceful harmony, and four gardens are integral to the entire historic urban plan. 这四座苏州古典园林的设计完美地融合了艺术、自然和人文思想，使其达到自然和谐美的高度统一，系统而全面地展示了苏州古典园林城市建筑的整体布局，是中国园林设计的典范。 • The Humble Administrator's Garden, Lingering Garden, Net Master's Garden (Hermit's Garden) and the Mountain Villa with Embracing Beauty were on the list of UNESCO's World Heritage Sites in 1997. 苏州园林中的拙政园、留园、网师园和环秀山庄于1997年被联合国教科文组织列入世界遗产地名录。 • The Humble Administrator's Garden is the largest garden of the city and the masterpiece of Chinese landscape garden design in Suzhou. 拙政园是苏州最大的一处园林，也是苏州园林的代表作。

Introducing Grottoes 介绍石窟

- The Mogao Grottoes, covering an area of 1,600 meters from the north to the south, are located within the eastern cliffs of the Mingsha Hill (Singing Sand Mountain, 鸣沙山), 25 kilometers southeast of Dunhuang city, Gansu Province. 莫高窟位于甘肃省敦煌市东南 25 千米的鸣沙山东麓崖壁上，南北长 1,600 米。

- There are 492 grottoes in existence with some 45,000 square meters of murals, and over 2,400 painted clay figures. It's worthy of the name of treasure house for Chinese art. 现存有 492 个石窟，壁画总面积为 45,000 平方米，彩塑达 2,400 多尊，堪称中华艺术宝库。

- A monk named Lezun or Yuezun (乐尊) happened to vision thousands of Buddhas bathed in golden rays at the site in 366 AD. Then inspired, he began to build the first cave in this area. 公元 366 年，僧人乐尊路经此山，忽见金光闪耀，如现万佛，于是便在岩壁上开凿了第一个洞窟。

- The art of Dunhuang covers more than ten major genres, such as architecture, stucco sculpture, wall paintings, silk paintings, calligraphy, woodblock printing, embroidery, literature, music and dance, and popular entertainment. 敦煌艺术涉及的类型有十几种，如建筑、泥塑、壁画、丝绸画、书法、木刻印刷、刺绣、文学、音乐和舞蹈，以及流行的娱乐活动。

- Situated at a strategic point along the Silk Route, at the crossroads of trade as well as religious, cultural and intellectual influences, the 492 cells and cave sanctuaries in Mogao are famous for their statues and wall paintings, spanning 1,000 years of Buddhist art. 莫高窟地处丝绸之路的一个战略要塞。它不仅是东西方贸易的中转站，同时也是宗教、文化和知识的交汇处。莫高窟的 492 个小石窟和洞穴庙宇，以其雕像和壁画闻名于世，展示了延续千年的佛教艺术。

- The cave complex in Mogao is the largest, most fascinating repository (储藏库) of Buddhist grotto art in the world. 莫高窟是世界上最大的、最令人惊叹的佛教洞窟艺术宝库。

- The Mogao Grottoes are the best and largest of the Buddhist caves in China and the world. 莫高窟是中国也是世界上保存得最好、规模最大的佛教洞窟。

- Along with Longmen Grottoes and Yungang Grottoes, the cave complex in Mogao is one of the three famous sites for Buddhist grotto art in China. 莫高窟、龙门石窟和云冈石窟并称为中国三大著名的古代佛教石窟群。

- In a word, the Mogao Grottoes constitute an anthology (集萃) of Buddhist art with paintings and sculptures spanning a period of a thousand years.

- The caves contain some of the finest examples of Buddhist art spanning a period of 1,000 years. 这些洞窟拥有一些体现跨越千年的佛教艺术的精美杰作。

- The Mogao Grottoes vary in sizes, with Cave 37 being the smallest with an area of less than one square meter, and Cave 16 the largest covering an area of 268 square meters. Cave 96 presently is as high as 40 meters with a nine-tiered wooden fore. 莫高窟内的洞窟大小不一，最小的 37 号洞窟，面积不到 1 平方米，最大的 16 号洞窟的面积却有 268 平方米。96 号洞窟目前高达 40 米，有 9 层高的木制遮檐。

- The Yungang Grottoes, in Datong city, Shanxi Province, with their 252 caves and 51,000 statues, represent the outstanding achievement of Buddhist cave art in China in the 5th and 6th centuries. 山西省大同市的云冈石窟共有大小窟龛 252 个，造像 51,000 余尊，代表了公元 5~6 世纪时中国杰出的佛教石窟艺术。

- The Five Caves created by Tan Yao (昙曜), with their strict unity (严谨统一) of layout and design, constitute a classical masterpiece (经典杰作) of the first peak of Chinese Buddhist art.

- The grottoes and niches of Longmen contain the largest and most impressive collection of Chinese art of the late Northern Wei and Tang Dynasties. These works, entirely devoted to the Buddhist religion, represent the high point of Chinese stone carving. 龙门地区的石窟和佛龛展现了中国北魏晚期至唐代最具规模和最为优秀的造型艺术。这些翔实描述佛教中宗教题材的艺术作品代表了中国石刻艺术的最高峰。

Introducing Grottoes 介绍石窟	• The Grand Vairocana Buddha (卢舍那大佛) sits in the middle of the niche, 17.14 meters tall. Her head is 4 meters long and her ear 1.9 meters wide. Her lips are slightly upturned, and a slight smile makes her look like a graceful lady. 壁龛正中的卢舍那大佛通高17.14 米，头部高 4 米，耳宽 1.9 米。她嘴唇微翘，面露微笑，像一位优雅的贵妇。 • Altogether there are more than 2,100 grottoes at Longmen with more than 100,000 statues.

Part E   English in Use

I. Reading Comprehension

Task 1: Choose the best answer to complete each sentence below.

1. In addition to Dunhuang Mogao Grottoes, what are the other two major grottoes in China? _____

   A. Longmen Grottoes in Gansu, Yungang Grottoes in Shanxi.

   B. Longmen Grottoes and Yungang Grottoes in Shanxi.

   C. Longmen Grottoes in Hebei, Yungang Grottoes in Datong city.

   D. Longmen Grottoes in Henan, Yungang Grottoes in Shanxi.

2. The Summer Palace was supposed to serve as a _____ for the Empress Dowager Cixi in the Qing Dynasty.

   A. summer resort   B. winter resort   C. royal house   D. palace

3. The Summer Palace in Beijing, the Mountain Resort of Chengde in Hebei Province, the Lingering Garden in Suzhou, _____ are considered as China's four major gardens.

   A. West Lake in Hangzhou

   B. Ge Yuan in Suzhou

   C. Zhuozheng (the Humble Administrator's) Garden in Suzhou

   D. Canglang Pavilion in Suzhou

4. Many of them are the landscapes with flowers and birds, and others are _____ the paintings.

   A. person   B. figure   C. people   D. human

5. The largest of these thirty-six West Lakes is in Guilin _____ for its unique landscape.

   A. well know   B. well-known   C. noting for   D. fameful

6. We are _____ to have supper at around 19:00.

   A. supposed   B. entitled   C. should   D. likely

7. The Huaqing Pool Hot Spring is in _____.

   A. Beijing   B. Luo Yang   C. Xi'an   D. Kaifeng

8. Which of the following four major grottoes constitutes an anthology of Buddhist art with paintings and sculptures spanning a period of a thousand years? _____

   A. Maiji Grottoes   B. Yungang Grottoes

   C. Longmen Grottoes   D. Mogao Grottoes

9. The Buddha is flanked _____ Ananda (阿难) and Kashyapa (迦叶) on each side.

   A. of   B. with   C. about   D. at

10. What's _____ the schedule for tomorrow?

    A. on   B. in   C. with   D. at

Task 2: Answer the following questions concerning the introductions about Mogao Grottoes in Part B.

1. What are the three major grottoes in China? If there are four, then what is the fourth greatest grotto in the country?
2. What are the Mogao Grottoes well-known for?
3. Why are the Mogao Grottoes also called "Caves of a Thousand Buddhas"?
4. When was the art of the Mogao Grottoes at its best?
5. If many of the tourists show interest in Asian history, which cave will you show them?

Task 3: Decide whether each of the following statements is True or False according to the tips for tour guides in Part C.

1. Different places of tourist attractions need different methods of introduction. (　　)
2. When introducing a scenic spot, a good guide should pay much attention to the tourists' interests and reasons for travel rather than their ages and genders. (　　)
3. To arouse the tourists' interests, it's necessary to ask the tourists some questions while showing them around the scenic spots. (　　)
4. Sometimes, it's a good idea to recite many famous poems concerning the scenic spot to a group of retired people who show less interest in the literature. (　　)
5. If the tourists look bored, try to tell them some dirty jokes to cheer them up. (　　)

II. Translation

Task 4: Translate the following sentences into English.

1. 今天早上，我们将坐船游湖，时间为 45 分钟。
2. 颐和园是中国现存规模最大、保存得最完整的皇家园林。
3. 颐和园里的长廊是中国园林中最长的走廊。
4. "上有天堂，下有苏杭。"
5. 自 2011 年起，杭州西湖文化景观已经正式被列入联合国教科文组织的世界文化遗产名录。
6. "天下西湖三十六，此中最美是杭州"。
7. 午饭后我们会在黄浦江上坐船游览，然后在外滩散步。
8. 著名的白堤和苏堤把西湖分成五个部分，外湖最大，有三个人工小岛。
9. 苏州园林是中国园林的杰出典范，闻名全世界。
10. 龙门有两千一百多座洞窟，拥有十万多尊塑像。

Task 5: Translate the following sentences into Chinese.

1. Classical Chinese garden design, which seeks to recreate natural landscapes in miniature, is nowhere better illustrated than in the nine gardens in the historic city of Suzhou.
2. Suzhou's largest garden, Zhuozheng Yuan, the Humble Administrator's Garden is also considered the city's finest. It was established in the 16th century by a retired magistrate

(地方官), Wang Xianchen (王献臣), and developed over the years as subsequent owners made changes according to the fashion of the day.

3. The Canglang Pavilion (沧浪亭) was the Northern Song poet Su Shunqin (苏舜钦)'s private garden, and was first built in the 11th century.

4. The most famous view of the garden, the "borrowed view" of Beisi Ta (北寺塔), the Northern Pagoda reflected in the water, is visible from here.

5. The Mogao Grottoes, covering an area of 1,600 meters from the north to the south, are located within the eastern cliffs of the Mingsha Hill (Singing Sand Mountain), 25 kilometers southeast of Dunhuang city, Gansu Province.

6. The Mogao Grottoes vary in size, with Cave 37 being the smallest with an area of less than one square meter, and Cave 16 the largest covering an area of 268 square meters. Cave 96 presently is as high as 40 meters with a nine-tiered wooden fore.

7. The Grand Vairocana Buddha (卢舍那大佛) is the most beautiful and valuable statue as well as the largest among all the statues in Longmen Grottoes.

8. The Five Caves created by Tan Yao (昙曜), with their strict unity of layout and design, constitute a classical masterpiece of the first peak of Chinese Buddhist art.

9. A monk named Lezun or Yuezun (乐尊) happened to vision thousands of Buddhas bathed in golden rays at the site in 366. Then inspired, he began to build the first cave in this area.

10. In a word, the Mogao Grottoes constitute an anthology (集萃) of Buddhist art with paintings and sculptures spanning a period of a thousand years.

III. Role Play

Task 6: Play a role in any of the following situations with your partner(s).

Situation 1: Role play all the dialogues in both Part A and B with your partner(s).

Situation 2: You're a tour guide for a Canadian family of four. You've made a schedule for the family's tour in Hangzhou. After you explain it to the family, they seem to be dissatisfied with the plan and want to change some of the activities. Then make a discussion with them before both sides reach an agreement.

Situation 3: You're showing a group of British tourists, most of whom are retired teachers and civil officials, around West Lake as a tour guide.

Situation 4: You're showing a group of American tourists around the Summer Palace.

Situation 5: Choose one of the major gardens in China, and imagine yourself as a guide. Now show your partner(s) as a group of tourists around it.

IV. Problem-solving

Task 7: Make an analysis of the following case, and answer the question as required.

Situation: A local guide has just met a group of American tourists. After the guide explains the travel schedule on the coach, some of the group members are not quite happy with the itinerary and they want to make a change.

Question: If you were the guide, how would you respond to the tour group's request for changing the itinerary or schedule?

Answers for Reference

Unit 8 Temple, Pagoda and Historic Mountains

Warm-up

1. How many Buddhist temples and pagodas have you ever visited in China? Can you name the following temples and pagodas?

1) _____   2) _____   3) _____

4) _____   5) _____   6) _____

2. Do you know any of the following pagodas in China?

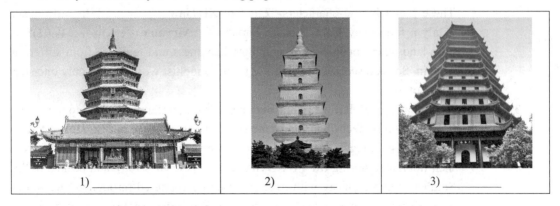

1) _____   2) _____   3) _____

3. How many mountains have you ever been to in China? What are the six famous mountains in China? What about the four sacred Buddhist and Taoist mountains?

Part A   Lingyin Temple

Dialogue 1

Situation: *Chen Yan is showing the American group around Lingyin Temple. Now they are standing in front of the* **screen wall** *(照壁) facing the entrance of Lingyin Temple.*

Questions for comprehension and discussion:
★ When did Buddhism start in Hangzhou?
★ What are the three major schools of Buddhism developed in China?
★ What school of Buddhism does Lingyin Temple belong to?
★ What is Chan?

Chen Yan: We're now at the entrance of Lingyin Temple, the most popular tourist attraction around West Lake. It's at the foot of the Northern Peak and to the northwest of West Lake. This monastery complex covers an area of 36.9 hectares, including the Screen Wall, **Feilai Peak** (Peak Flown from Afar) and the Lingyin Temple proper. It will take us about two hours to look around the whole area.

These four Chinese characters "**Zhi Chi Xi Tian** (咫尺西天)" literally mean "Only a foot away from Western Paradise — **Nirvana** (极乐世界，涅槃)", a pure land where people enjoy complete happiness and feel free from suffering or pain. So, you see, we are so close to the Buddhist world that is only one step ahead of us.

Tourist A: Wow, that's great, but we're not Buddhists. It's an unfamiliar world to us.

Chen Yan: Then it's the perfect opportunity for you to know more about Buddhism today. Buddhism in Hangzhou started in **the Eastern Jin Dynasty** (东晋，317–420), then flourished during **the Five Dynasties** (五代，907–960), and peaked in the Southern Song Dynasty with over 300 temples scattered throughout the whole area. Hangzhou thus earned the name "**A Buddhist Realm in Southeastern China** (东南佛国)". Without a doubt, Lingyin Temple ranks first among all the temples in Hangzhou area. With a history of over 1,600 years, it's not only the oldest temple in Hangzhou but also one of the largest **Chan** (禅) Buddhist monasteries in China.

Tourist B: Sorry to interrupt, do you mean **Zen** (禅)?

Chen Yan: Yes. It's Zen in Japanese, but we call it Chan in Chinese. Chan, developed from **Dhyana** (禅) in **Sanskrit** (梵文) in **Mahayana Buddhism** (大乘佛教), is a large school of homegrown Buddhism in China.

Tourist A: Excuse me, what does Mahayana Buddhism mean?

Chen Yan: There are three major schools of Buddhism in China. One is Mahayana (大乘佛教/汉传佛教) meaning "Greater Vehicle", the second one is **Theravada** (南传上座部佛教) meaning "teachings of the elders" developed from **Hinayana** (小乘佛教) known as "Lesser Vehicle", and the third is **Tibetan Buddhism** (藏传佛教). Mahayana Buddhism emphasizes a common search for **universal salvation** (普度众生) and is quite common in China, Japan and Korea. Theravada Buddhism teaches personal salvation through one's  own efforts and is popular in countries in southeastern Asia such as Thailand, **Myanmar** (缅甸) and **Cambodia** (柬埔寨). Although developed from Mahayana Buddhism, Tibetan Buddhism is now quite independent and dominant in Tibetan region.

Tourist A: I see. Thanks.

Chen Yan: You're welcome. **Bodhidharma** (菩提达摩) from India, the 28th **patriarch** (宗教创始人，鼻祖) of Buddhism, was the first one to **transmit** (传播) the concept of Dhyana to China which later developed into Chan or Zen. Dharma finally settled in Shaolin Temple in the 6th century, which is home to the famous **Shaolin Gongfu** (少林功夫). He's well-known for his nine-year **meditation** (冥想，禅定) while sitting down facing the wall in a cave. Since then, Dharma has been regarded as the first **reverend** (可尊敬的) **originator** (开山祖师) of Chinese Chan.

Tourist A: By the way, which one is older, the Lingyin Temple or the Shaolin Temple?

Chen Yan: The Lingyin Temple, it's over 160 years older.

Tourist B: One of my friends is fascinated by Zen. But what's Zen or Chan, as you call it, mainly about?

Chen Yan: Good question. Chan centers on the attainment of **enlightenment** (启迪，开悟) through meditation and the personal understanding of direct **insight** (领悟) in the Buddhist teachings regardless of any written language. There's a well-known saying among Chan believers, "I'm Buddha (心即是佛)." It means anyone can become a  Buddha oneself through self-cultivation. Therefore, anyone **literate** (识字) or **illiterate** (文盲), male or female, Chinese or non-Chinese, of course also including you, the tourists coming far away from the US, can have the chance of attaining enlightenment and becoming a Buddha. Would you like to try? It's also good for your health.

Tourist B: Great! Let's try then, haha.

Chen Yan: Actually, since it's easy for anyone to practice meditation in any form, it's becoming more and more popular in the West.

Tourist A: That's very interesting.

Chen Yan: Well, do you have any questions now? If not, let's go.

Dialogue 2

Situation: *Chen Yan and the group are walking along the stream up to the Lingyin Temple.*
(In front of Ligong Pagoda, facing Feilai Peak)

Questions for comprehension and discussion:

★ What does Lingyin Temple mean?

★ What is Feilai Peak mainly famous for?

Chen Yan: So, do you know why this small tower was built here?

Tourist A: For the Indian monk?

Chen Yan: Right. It was built in honor of the Indian **monk Huili** (慧理和尚), the founder of Lingyin Temple. His remains are buried beneath it. It was first built in the 13th century and rebuilt in 1590. In 326 AD during the Eastern Jin Dynasty, legend has it that coming far from India, Huili was amazed by the quiet valley surrounded on three sides by woods, especially the **craggy** (陡峭的) hill, which is right in front of us now, with various limestone caves. The small hill looked exactly like the peak **Gridhrakuta** (Vulture Peak, 灵鹫山) in India, a  place where **Buddha Sakyamuni** (佛祖释迦牟尼) used to preach to the crowds. Huili was certain that the peak must have flown over from his hometown because he was able to call out the two monkeys living in a cave on the peak. The peak thus got a strange name "Peak Flown from Afar". Believing it was a **retreat** (静居处) of the soul, Huili settled down, and built a temple up the valley facing the peak and named it Temple of the Soul's Retreat, known as

Lingyin Temple which we'll soon visit.

Tourist A: Sorry, what do you call the flown peak in Chinese again?

Chen Yan: Feilai Feng. Feilai means "has flown here", Feng means "peak".

Tourist A: Thanks. It does look very unusual, strange.

Chen Yan: Yes, it sure does. At a height of 209 meters, Feilai Peak is well-known for  hundreds of Buddhist stone carvings. These carvings date from the 10th to the 14th century, a time when North China saw a decline in grotto art. They're different from those in the Northern grottoes such as the Dunhuang, Yungang and Longmen Grottoes. Before the 10th century, most sculptures were carved into **granite** (花岗岩) in the caves instead of **limestone** (石灰岩) on the cliff. Besides, you'll find the peak has the most **Arhats** (罗汉) figures carved around the 14th century, and most of the sculptures are influenced by Tibetan **Lamaism** (喇嘛教). Therefore, the stone carvings here are regarded as representative of grotto art in Southern China.

Tourist B: I see. By the way, how many carvings are there on the peak?

Chen Yan: Well, there used to be over 470 stone carvings, but now only 335 remain **intact** (完整).

Chen Yan: Now, up the valley we can go to see the most attractive statue on the peak.

(In front of Maitreya Buddha on the Feilai Peak)

Chen Yan: Here we are. Can you see the happy big-bellied statue over there? It's the **Maitreya Buddha** (弥勒佛), **incarnated** (化身) as a **chubby** (圆胖的) monk carrying a sack in Ningbo, Zhejiang Province. The monk is called **Budai Monk** (布袋和尚) in Chinese, and Budai means sack. It's the largest and  the most impressive statue on the peak. Together with the surrounding 18 various arhats, it was carved around 1000 AD. Measuring 9 meters in length and 3.6 meters in height, the sculpture is quite vivid and lifelike. Bare-chested,

 with a big smile on his face, Maitreya Buddha, also known as the Laughing Buddha, is always happy to welcome you and visitors from all over the world. It's so popular among tourists that no one wants to miss it, and it thus earned another name — "**Ambassador Buddha** (大使佛)". Do you like him?

Tourist A: Definitely. But it's so crowded here that it's impossible to take a picture of it without any people in the shot.

Chen Yan: Sorry. That's because he's too popular…Well, if you've finished taking the picture, let's move on.

(In front of Cool Spring Pavilion)

Chen Yan: Well, this is **Cool Spring Pavilion** (冷泉亭). The stream is called this to contrast it with the hot spring. The pavilion was first built in the middle of the stream during the mid-Tang Dynasty (probably in the 8th century) but was later destroyed by the **torrents** (急流). It was rebuilt on the bank here, possibly in the Song Dynasty.

Endowed with beautiful surroundings especially in the summer time, the Cool Spring Pavilion, for over 1,000 years, has been frequented by many famous writers including the best-known poets, Bai Juyi and Su Dongpo. Numerous poems have been dedicated to the pavilion. In the eyes of Bai Juyi, the Cool Spring was second to none among all the pavilions in the entire area.

Now, please look at the couplet hanging on two of the pillars. The first line says: "When did the spring begin to cool, where did the peak fly from?" The second line in response is: "The spring began to cool when it was supposed to cool, the peak flew over from where it was supposed to fly over."

Dialogue 3

Situation: *Chen Yan and the group are visiting the Lingyin Temple.*

Questions for comprehension and discussion:

★ Why is the temple also called Yunlin Temple?

★ Why is the sculpture of Buddha in the Main Hall so popular?

★ Who is Buddha?

★ What are the Buddha's major teachings?

(In front of the Front Hall, the Hall of Heavenly Guardians)

Chen Yan: Well, since the 4th century, Lingyin Temple has developed into a large monastery complex. **In its heyday** (鼎盛时期) in the 10th century when Hangzhou served as the capital of the Kingdom of Wuyue, the temple complex comprised 9 buildings, 18 pavilions, 72 halls and 1,300 rooms for over 3,000 monks.

The temple was so **prestigious** (有声望的) that many emperors throughout history would visit whenever possible. **Emperor Kangxi** (康熙皇帝, 1654−1722) and his grandson **Emperor Qianlong** (乾隆皇帝, 1711−1799) in particular took a fancy to it. Both of them are known as the longest reigning monarchs in China, whose ruling period together is famed as "**the Flourishing Age of Kangxi and Qianlong** (康乾盛世)".

Each of them made a tour of Jiangnan (the southern reaches of the Yangtze River, 江南) at least six times, and their visit to the temple provided an inspiration for many of their poems and **inscriptions** (题词).

Well, can you see the two **plaques** (匾额) hanging above the main entrance of the hall? The upper one bears the name **bestowed** (赏赐) by Emperor Kangxi on the temple. However, it was called "**Yunlin Chan Temple** (云林禅寺)" instead of "Lingyin Temple", because he thought the name "Yunlin" meaning "misty woods" was more suitable. According to another popular folklore, the emperor made such a writing mistake because he had drunk too much. Anyway, "Lingyin Temple" is a much more popular name now. By the way, the inscriptions on the lower plaque tell us that the hill facing the temple was the peak that had flown from the Vulture Peak in ancient India.

Tourist A: Sorry, it's morning, why is the main entrance closed now?

Chen Yan: Good question. According to folklore, Emperor Qianlong was also keen on travelling. Once, together with his followers, the Emperor **in disguise** (乔装),

arrived at the gate of the temple a bit late in the day when the main entrance was already closed. To his great shame, he was refused entrance through the main gate due to the rule that the main gate should be opened and closed only once daily. After returning to the Forbidden City, the Emperor felt so angry that he issued an **edict** (诏令) that the main gate of the Lingyin Temple be closed all the time. Now it's closed except for some special occasions.

Tourist A: Wow, it's an interesting story.

Tourist B: This temple can't be the original one, is it?

Chen Yan: No, it isn't. The temple has undergone multiple reconstructions and renovations. Only the two **Sutra Pillars** (石塔/经幢) in front of the Front Hall here as well as the **Twin Pagodas** (双石塔) **flanking** (两侧) the Main Hall can be traced back to as early as the 10th century. The present temple was rebuilt in the 19th century and renovated in the middle of the 20th century. Besides, it owes its existence to our former **Premier Zhou Enlai** (周恩来总理) who helped prevent it from being destroyed during the Cultural Revolution in the late 1960s.

Now the whole monastery complex, as common in China, is comprised of the major halls on the south-north axis as listed: the **Hall of Heavenly Guardians** (天王殿), the **Grand Buddha Hall** (Mahavira Hall, 大雄宝殿), the **Hall of Medicine Buddha** (Bhaishajyaguru Hall, 药师殿), the **Sutra Hall** (藏经阁/法堂), and **Hall of Avatamsaka** (华严殿). Some other

halls and rooms are on either side: the **Praying Hall** (念佛堂), **Meditation Hall** (禅堂), the **Hall of 500 Arhats** (五百罗汉堂), **Monks' Dorms** (僧寮/房), **Abbot's Room** (方丈室), and so on.

OK, let's go to the Front Hall first. This way, please.

(Inside the Hall of Heavenly Guardians)

Chen Yan: Do you recognize the Buddha now?

Tourist A: The Laughing Buddha.

Chen Yan:

Exactly. The Maitreya Buddha. He is believed to be the successor of **Buddha Sakyamuni** (释迦牟尼佛), the founder of Buddhism. Hence the name of the **Future Buddha** (未来佛) in relation to the **Present Buddha** (现在佛) Sakyamuni. This sculpture of high artistic value is over 200 years old. The Laughing Buddha set in the center of the Front Hall of the temple, greets you like a receptionist. A popular saying is "His belly is big enough to contain all intolerable things in the world; His mouth is ever ready to laugh at all **ridiculous** (荒谬的) **deeds** (行为) under heaven." So if you have any concerns, sadness, and worries, ask him to help you.

Do you see the tall Buddhist guardians in each of the four corners of the hall? They are known as the four Heavenly Guardians, each taking care of one **cardinal** (主要的) direction (north, east, south and west). With the weapons in their hands, they are supposed to bring fair weather, keep the world peaceful and prosperous.

Please look at the statue facing toward the Main Hall. It's the **Guardian of the Law, Skanda** (护法神韦陀), head of the 32 generals under the Four Heavenly

Guardians according to the Buddhist legend. He's known to use the **pestle** (降魔杵) to **dispel** (驱除) the **evil** (邪恶). The sculpture is over 700 years old, carved from the trunk of a single **camphor tree** (樟树) in the Southern Song Dynasty. It's the oldest Buddhist sculpture in the temple, and is regarded as a masterpiece of wood-carving in ancient China.

(In Front of the Main Hall)

Chen Yan: Well, here's the Main Hall, the Grand Buddha Hall. It stands 33.6 meters high, only about 1.5 meters lower than **Taihe Hall** (太和殿) in the Forbidden City. With **triple-eaved roofs** (三叠重檐), it's a typical single-storied structure of the Tang Dynasty style. It was rebuilt in 1910 and renovated in 1953.

Tourist B: Excuse me, are the twin pagodas flanking the hall also old?

Chen Yan: Yes, just as I mentioned in front of the entrance. The **octagonal** (八角形) nine-storied pagodas were built in 960, a perfect example of stone carvings of the Five Dynasties (907–960) almost 1,100 years ago. By the way, do you know why these people are burning the **incense** (香)?

Tourist C: Sorry, no idea.

Chen Yan: Well, not only Buddhists but also many lay people often visit the temple to pray to the Buddha for blessings. It's said that their wishes will be delivered to the Buddha through the smoke from the burning incenses. Nowadays, each person is allowed to burn three **joss sticks** (香) for the sake of environmental protection.

Tourist C: I see. Thanks.

Chen Yan: Have you all taken pictures? If so, let's go inside the hall.

(Inside the Main Hall)

Tourist A: What an **awesome** (令人惊叹的) statue! I've never seen such a huge one.

Chen Yan: That's the imposing Buddha Sakyamuni, the highlight of the temple. The present statue was vividly carved out of 24 pieces of camphor wood and **gilded** (镀金) with about 140 ounces of gold. With a height of 24.8 meters together with the **canopy** (华盖) and **lotus pedestal** (莲花座), it's one of the largest wooden statues of a sitting Buddha in China. Do you know how long the Buddha's ear is?

Tourist A: Maybe one meter?

Chen Yan: It's 1.3 meters long.

Tourist B: And the **earlobes** (耳垂) are huge.

Chen Yan: In China, a person with big earlobes is supposed to be happy.

Tourist B: Really?

Chen Yan: Yes, it's a saying. Many people believe it.

Tourist C: Sorry, why does the Buddha have blue hair knots?

Chen Yan: The hair knot design was one of the male popular hairstyles in ancient India. Artistically, it was painted blue to show that the Buddha is as gorgeous as the blue sky. The lotus pedestal symbolizes the purity of Buddha. The mirror behind his head is the symbol of brightness, while the glass ball on his forehead is believed to be the Eye of Wisdom through which he got enlightened before becoming Buddha.

The Buddha was once called **Siddhartha Gautama** (悉达多·乔达摩). He is said to be the prince of a royal family, a large **clan of Shakya/Sakya** (释迦族) in or near what is **Nepal** (尼泊尔) around 2,500 years ago. At the age of 29, he began to reflect on the four stages of human life: the birth, old age, sickness and death after seeing an aged man, a sick man, a dead body and an **ascetic monk**

(苦行僧) outside the palace. Then he firmly left his family as a wandering monk in search for truth. He then got enlightened under the **Bodhi tree** (菩提树) after six-year meditation and became the Buddha, "the Awakened One," hence the name Sakyamuni, meaning "**Sage of the Sakyas** (释迦族的圣人)". He realized that nothing is lost in the world and there are continuous changes due to the law of cause and effect known as **karma** (因缘). Then he started to **preach** (讲道) his teachings, encouraging people to achieve enlightenment because "Every living being has the Buddha nature and can become Buddha." His famous **Four Noble Truths** (四谛) are: **Suffering** (苦), **Cause of Suffering** (集), **End of Suffering** (灭) and **Path to End Suffering** (道). Finally, he passed away and went into nirvana at the age of 80.

Tourist B: I have heard the law of **cause and effect** (因果报应). It's true that suffering is common to us all. But can you explain the cause of suffering a little bit?

Chen Yan: OK. According to the law of Karma, one's actions in this life affect one's future. One feels pain mainly because of **greed** (贪), **hatred** (恨/嗔) and **ignorance** (愚痴/无知). So if one stops being greedy, angry and ignorant, one will be surely free from suffering and gets ready to be enlightened as Buddha, escaping the turning wheel of life — **Samsara** (六道轮回), the six paths of rebirth.

Tourist A: What are the six paths like?

Chen Yan: One will be born into the paths of gods, humans, and **asuras** (阿修罗道) if doing good deeds, or will fall into the ones of animals, hungry ghosts, or hell-beings if doing evil deeds.

Tourist A: Thanks. It's quite **sensible** (合理的).

Chen Yan: Well, there's a lot to say about Buddhism. If you're interested in it, we can have a further discussion later. Now, on either side of the Buddha are 20 **devas** or **heavenly beings** (天神), and 12 **Pratyeka Buddhas** (缘觉) sit cross-legged behind.

Tourist B: Pardon, what do you call these sitting statues?

Chen Yan: Pratyeka Buddhas. They are hermits who attain enlightenment by self-cultivation.

There are four stages of enlightenment: Buddhas, **Bodhisattvas** (菩萨), Pratyeka Buddhas and Arhats. Buddhas are perfect in enlightenment; Bodhisattvas enlighten both themselves and the others; Pratyeka Buddhas achieve enlightenment after self-cultivation; Arhats are enlightened Buddhists. Do you see my point?

Tourist B: Yeah, I see. Thanks.

Chen Yan: Here on the back wall is a group of colored **relief clay sculptures** (泥塑浮雕) with a number of 156 figures. There are three levels on display. First, in the

middle of the bottom level, is **Guanyin**, or **Bodhisattva of Infinite Compassion** (观音菩萨) standing on the head of a legendary fish. She's supposed to live at sea and carry all the living creatures to the shore of happiness. She's also believed to deliver a boy to a childless family, and that's why you can often see many couples coming to pray to her for a boy. The boy standing beside her is called **Sudhana** (善财童子) or Red Child. He is said to have gone through various **ordeals** (考验) to learn from 53 famous masters before getting enlightened and serving as a **disciple** (徒弟) of Guanyin. Here you can find him visiting the masters in different poses. The maiden statue is the **Dragon Maiden** (龙女), the daughter of the dragon king. She's also the disciple of Guanyin.

Secondly, the Bodhisattva riding a Chinese **unicorn** (独角兽) at the middle level is **Ksitigarbha** (地藏菩萨), the Guardian of the Earth. He used to be Prince of the Kingdom of Silla (present Korea) who was called **Jin Qiaojue** (新罗国王子金乔觉). He finally resided in **Mount Jiuhua** (九华山), one of the four sacred Buddhist mountains.

Now, let's look at the top level. Can you see the skinny old man at the very top in the middle? Do you know who he is?

Tourist B: Is he the Buddha?

Chen Yan:

Right. He's the Prince Siddhartha practising **asceticism** (苦行) in the snow mountains before becoming Buddha. He ate so little that he nearly starved to death. Later, he gave up asceticism and started again to eat nourishing food such as milk from the deer and fruit from the monkey to keep healthy. Finally, he found the middle way between asceticism and the worldly lifestyle, and thus got enlightened under the Bodhi tree.

OK, I think I should stop here. Let's go to the Back Hall, housing the **Buddha of Medicine,** also known as the **Past Buddha** (过去佛). He's said to be dominant in the Eastern World while Sakyamuni in the Central World and **Amitabha** (阿弥陀佛) in the Western World. It is believed that he helps cure people of all diseases, making them healthy and promoting longevity…

Part B   Six Harmonies Pagoda

Dialogue 1

Situation: *Chen Yan is introducing pagodas in Hangzhou to the American tourist group in the coach on the way to Six Harmonies Pagoda standing on* **Yuelun Hill,** *which is also called Moon Disc Hill (月轮山).*

Questions for comprehension and discussion:
★ How did the pagoda come into being?
★ What are the most noteworthy pagodas in Hangzhou?
★ Why was the Six Harmonies Pagoda built?

Chen Yan: Hello, everyone. Now we're heading for Six Harmonies Pagoda on the northern shore of Qiantang River, south of West Lake. Do you know the origin of the pagoda in China?

Tourist A: It must be related with Buddhism, isn't it?

Chen Yan: Yes, the pagoda **evolves** (发展) from the **stupa** (印度塔，浮屠) in ancient India, originally meaning "tomb". It used to house the **Buddhist relics** (佛舍利) and **sutras** or **scriptures** (佛经) in a temple. According to the Buddhist sutra, about 2,500 years ago, the remains of the Buddha Sakyamuni turned into **crystals** (结晶体) including 84,000 shiny pearl-like beads in different colors after the **cremation** (火葬) and thus are known as **Sariras** (舍利) or Buddhist relics.

Tourist B: Pardon? How many beads altogether? You said 84,000?

Chen Yan: Yes. Every part of the Buddha's body is said to have turned into sariras including his bones, teeth and even his hair.

Tourist B: Even his hair? Why? It's unbelievable.

Chen Yan:  Yes, it's really amazing. It is said that his hair finally turned into **fleshy protuberance** (肉凸，肉髻) after becoming the Buddha. It's the consequence of the **cultivation** (修行) of Sakyamuni with **perfect virtue** (功德圆满), for it's not possible for a common person to have the sariras after cremation except for Buddhas, Bodhisattvas, arhats and the **eminent monks** (高僧).

Tourist B: I see. No wonder I see the statue of the Buddha's hair looks like mounds of flesh.

Chen Yan: You got it. So let's continue, the Buddhist relics were then separated into eight parts and kept in eight pagodas respectively by eight kings in India. It's not until about 200 years later that the great king **Ashoka** (阿育王), a **devout Buddhist** (虔诚的佛教徒), had 84,000 pagodas rebuilt to **enshrine** (珍藏) and **venerate** (敬仰) each piece of all the Buddhist relics. With the introduction of Buddhism to China in the 1st century, pagodas were thus introduced to China to preserve some of the Buddhist relics. Nowadays, the Buddhist relics are found in eight places in China including Leifeng Pagoda in Hangzhou.

Leifeng Pagoda towers on **Xizhao Hill** (Sunset Hill, 夕照山) on the south of West Lake. It was first **erected** (建立) in 977 by **Qian Chu** (钱俶, 929−988), the last king of Wuyue Kingdom, to house the **Buddha's hair Sarira** (佛螺髻发舍利) together with Buddhist scriptures and to **commemorate** (纪念) the birth of his son as well. Over almost a thousand years, it barely survived fires, wars and other damage, and was only left to be the tower core made of bricks. It finally fell down in 1924 because many local people had taken away the bricks from the remaining tower core for use as **talismans** (避邪物). The present one was rebuilt in 2002, and you can see it quite closely when passing it by very soon.

Facing Leifeng Pagoda, its twin pagoda stands on the opposite side of West

Lake. Do you know what it is? Actually, you have already seen them at a distance when taking the boat tour of the lake yesterday. Do you remember?

Tourist C: Sure. Is that the one on the precious stone hill as you call it?

Chen Yan: Yes, that's **Baochu Pagoda** (Blessing Chu Pagoda, 保俶塔) on **Baoshi Hill** (Precious Stone Hill, 宝石山), on the lake's north shore. It was built in the hope of blessing King Qian Chu so that he could come back safe and sound after having been **summoned** (召见) by the emperor to **Kaifeng** (开封), the capital of the Northern Song Dynasty.

Both Leifeng Pagoda and Baochu Pagoda are noted as the landmarks of Hangzhou thanks to their unique **silhouette**s (轮廓) in the sunglow. The original **dilapidated** (破败不堪的) Leifeng Pagoda used to be compared to an old monk, while the latter looks like a slender beauty; thus they are considered as twin pagodas overlooking

West Lake. In addition to the twin pagodas, a third one is also a landmark. Its massive silhouette is compared to a stout general. Does anybody know its name?

Tourists: The Six Harmonies Pagoda.

Chen Yan: Right. Well, ahead of us on your right hand is the newly built Leifeng Pagoda. Since we don't have much time, we'll just pass it and go directly to the Six Harmonies Pagoda. OK, now please look to your right. That's Leifeng pagoda…

Dialogue 2

Situation: *After getting off the coach, Chen Yan is showing the group around Six Harmonies Pagoda.*

Questions for comprehension and discussion:

★ Why was Six Harmonies Pagoda built?

★ What were the festivities associated with the pagoda in the Southern Song Dynasty?

Chen Yan: Here's Six Harmonies Pagoda, known as Liuhe Ta in Chinese, overlooking the Qiantang River. First of all, I have a question for you. Do you know why this pagoda was built?

Tourist A: For the purpose of preserving the Buddhist relics.

Chen Yan: Yes, but the main reason was related with the Qiantang River. Can you guess why?

Tourist B: To **tame** (制服) the river?

Chen Yan: Right, you got it. The Qiantang River is world-known for its **gigantic** (排山倒海似的) tidal bores because of the **funnel-shaped** (漏斗状的) **Hangzhou Bay** (杭州湾). The bay is 100 kilometers wide at the mouth and only 3 kilometers at the narrowest point. The highest tides occur on the 18th day of the 8th lunar month every year and reach a height of several meters. Together with the river **Ganges** (恒河) in India and the **Amazon River** (亚马孙河) in **Brazil** (巴西), it's one of the three rivers in the world famous for their most spectacular tidal waves.

However, over a thousand years ago when the river was not properly **dyked** (筑堤坝) to **avert** (防止，避免) the floods, the flooding was not only a disaster to the local people but also a **recurring** (重复发生的) **headache** (令人头疼的事)

to the rulers of Wuyue Kingdom, especially King **Qian Liu** (钱镠, 852–932). Folklore says that King Qian Liu spared no effort to repair the dykes but still failed. Later, having learned that the **God of Tides** (潮神) was the real troublemaker, the king decided to **subdue** (制服) him. So the king ordered 10,000 of his best **archers** (弓箭手) to **release** (释放) 10,000 arrows three times into the tide on the 18th day of the 8th lunar month, the birthday of the God of Tides, who was **galloping** (策马飞奔) on a white horse along the **crest** (浪尖) of the waves. Finally, after the God of Tides was killed, the tide turned to the southwest right at the foot of this hill and soon went out. The **dykes** (堤坝) were then successfully repaired and named "Qian Dykes" or "Qiantang" in Chinese in memory of King Qian Liu for his achievements in **water conservation** (水利). The river was named after him as "Qiantang River".

However, the area near the river was still **liable** (容易遭受) to flood. In order to completely control the **ravaging** (肆虐的) tides, King Qian Chu had a pagoda built in his **South Orchard** (南果园) right in this present site in 970.

As far as the name of the pagoda is concerned, there are many sayings. Two of them sound reasonable. One saying is related to **the Six Codes of Buddhism**^① (六和敬): the harmony of one's body, speech, mind, opinion, wealth and **abstinence** (节欲) from temptation. The other is associated with an intention to restore a balanced relationship among the six directions of the universe: north, south, east, west, heaven and earth. In a word, whatever the saying is, the pagoda was built to control the tide and hopefully bring harmony to the world.

But after the pagoda was built, it had some other functions. Can you guess what they might be?

Tourist C: Serving as a landmark?

Tourist D: Watching the tides?

Chen Yan: Good answer. Both of you are right. This pagoda later also served as the light house, an important **navigational** (航行的) landmark for the ships in the river at night. As a matter of fact, as time went on, pagodas in China became more than just related to Buddhism. Many of them were built to serve as a landmark, an **ornament** (装饰物) to a mountain or a scenic spot, a watchtower to enjoy a distant view. So, from the top of the pagoda, people can have a good view of the Qiantang River and listen to the roar of the tides at night, especially when the full moon is high in the sky.

Watching the tidal bore has been a **spectacle** (奇观) among the local people even since 2,000 years ago. It became more popular in the Southern Song Dynasty when Hangzhou again served as the capital. Every year, people enjoyed weeklong **festivities** (庆祝活动) during the Mid-Autumn Festival when the tides were the highest. Miles of tents and viewing platforms were erected along the banks of the river. Hundreds of expert swimmers with long hair and **tattooed backs** (刺青的背脊) lined up to test their strength against the might of the tide. Those ancient **surfers** (冲浪者) were called **Nong Chao'er** (弄潮儿) in Chinese, meaning Tide Players. Now the term is used to describe those courageous and creative people in the leading position in a very difficult situation, like the **vanguard** (先锋).

OK, please look at the pagoda. It's one of the most significant ancient **octagonal** (八角形的) brick-and-wood structures in China. It's 60 meters high above Yuelun Hill, the **Moon Disc Hill** (月轮山). The **brick structure of the pagoda** (塔心室) is traced back to the original 12th-century Southern Song Dynasty reconstruction, while the existing **wooden galleries** (外廊木檐) are a product of late Qing Dynasty **refurbishment** (整修) at the beginning of the 20th century. By the way, do you know how many stories the pagoda has?

---

① 佛教典籍《璎珞本业经》中之"六和敬"：身和同住，口和无净，意和同悦，戒和同修，见和同解，利和同均。

Tourist A: 13 stories?

Chen Yan: Yes, but not exactly. There are 13 stories of wooden galleries outside, but the inner brick structure has only seven levels with **magnificent caisson ceiling** (华丽的藻井). Now, let's go inside and take the stairs up to the top to have a 360-degree view of the surrounding hills and **sprawling cityscape** (庞大的城市景观) along the Qiantang River.

Part C   Historic Mountains

Questions for comprehension and discussion:

★ What was the legend about the Five Sacred Mountains?

★ What's the aim of the Daoists or Taoists? Where do they prefer to cultivate themselves?

★ Which of the Buddhist or Daoist mountains will you like to visit first? Why?

China boasts many **sacred** (神圣的) mountains with various striking features. These lofty mountains have been **primary** (首要的) **pilgrimage** (朝圣) sites for people throughout the ages, as they are believed to be the closest access point to heaven and the dwelling places of powerful immortals or **deities** (神). Generally speaking, these mountains are grouped into several types. First of all, the group which refers to five of the most renowned mountains is called **Wu Yue** (五岳) in Chinese meaning the Five Sacred Mountains. The group associated with Buddhism is known as the **Four Buddhist Holy Mountains** (四大佛教名山), while the group related with Daoism is noted as the **Four Daoist Holy Mountains** (四大道教名山). Moreover, **Mount Huang** (黄山) is well-known for its unique pines, grotesque rocks, rosy clouds and hot springs, and ranks among the top mountains.

Wu Yue symbolizes the unification of China. Legend has it that the Five Sacred Mountains originated from the body of **Pangu** (盘古), the creator of the world in Chinese mythology. **Mount Tai** (泰山) is believed to be Pangu's head and is thus considered as the most sacred of the Five Great Mountains. **Mount Song** (嵩山) in the middle is his belly, **Mount Heng** (恒山) in the north his right arm, **Mount Heng** (衡山) in the south his left arm and **Mount Hua** (华山) in the west his feet. Besides, Wu Yue stands for the most essential "**Five Elements** (五行)" such as metal, water, wood, fire and earth[①]. The five mountains, especially Mount Tai, have been the

places of worship (祭祀场地) for many emperors offering sacrifices to Heaven and Earth in Chinese history.

Daoism, along with Confucianism, is one of the two great indigenous philosophical systems of China. Originally, it was founded by the great thinker **Laozi** (571−471 BC). Later it was developed into a religion by **Celestial Masters** (天师) lineage founder, **Zhang**

---

① 东方属木，南方属火，西方属金，北方属水，中央属土，因此，东岳泰山属木，南岳衡山属火，西岳华山属金，北岳恒山属水，中岳嵩山属土。

Daoling (张道陵) during the 2nd century. Daoism is about the **indefinable** (难以名状的) Dao, though it is often translated as "Way". Dao is the mother of all things or the ultimate creative principle of the universe. It stresses the **dialectical** (辩证的) unity of opposites, the principle of **Yin** (阴) and **Yang** (阳).

In the eyes of Daoists or hermits, one is inseparable from nature and can finally achieve immortality by living in accordance with Dao. They prefer to cultivate themselves in search for eternal life deep in the grottoes or caves of the mountains where they believe the immortals or deities live. So many mountains in China are also home to many Daoist temples and shrines as well as **alchemy furnaces** (炼丹炉) for making **elixirs** (灵丹妙药). **Mount Wudang** (武当山) in Hubei, **Mount Qingcheng** (青城山) in Sichuan, **Mount Qiyun** (齐云山) in Anhui and **Mount Longhu** (龙虎山) in Jiangxi are the four major Daoist mountains.

The Four Sacred Mountains of Buddhism are **Mount Wutai** (五台山) in Shanxi, **Mount Putuo** (普陀山) in Zhejiang, **Mount Emei** (峨眉山) in Sichuan and **Mount Jiuhua** (九华山) in Anhui. According to Buddhist legend, the patron Bodhisattva in Wutai is believed to be **Wenshu, the Bodhisattva of Wisdom** (文殊菩萨[1]). Mt. Putuo has a strong association with **Guanyin, the Bodhisattva of Infinite Compassion** (观音菩萨[2]). **Puxian, the Bodhisattva of Universal Benevolence** (普贤菩萨[3]), is dominant in Mt. Emei. Mt. Jiuhua is associated with the **Silla** (新罗国，今韩国) monk **Jin Qiaojue** (金乔觉) who is regarded as the reincarnation of **Dizang, the Bodhisattva of Hell Beings** (地藏菩萨[4]). The bodhisattva vowed not to enter Nirvana until the **Hell Realm** (地狱) is empty and is thus noted as the guardian of the earth.

1) Mt. Tai/Taishan

Situated in central Shandong Province, east China, Mt. Tai or Taishan is the most exalted and sacred mountain of historical and cultural significance in China. It's **ascended** (攀登) year-round by millions of travelers and **pilgrims** (香客). There are presently 22 temples and over 1,800 stone tablets and inscriptions on the mountain. It's a World Heritage Site listed by UNESCO in 1987.

Taishan literally means a majestic and peaceful mountain. Due to its supreme eastern location—the symbol of **sovereignty** (君权), Taishan has been an essential imperial climb since the time of Qin Shi Huang (the First Emperor of the Qin Dynasty) 2,000 years ago. In order to show that he had a sovereign power with a **mandate** (授权) from the Jade Emperor or God of Heaven, Qin Shi Huang conducted a grand ceremony of **offering**

---

① 文殊菩萨，梵文 Manjusri，是释迦牟尼佛的左胁侍菩萨，代表聪明智慧。
② 观音菩萨，梵文 Avalokitesvara，是西方极乐世界教主阿弥陀佛左胁侍，同阿弥陀佛、大势至菩萨（Mahasthamaprapta）并称"西方三圣"。观音相貌端庄慈祥，经常手持净瓶杨柳，具有无量的智慧和神通，大慈大悲，普救人间疾苦。
③ 普贤菩萨，梵文 Samantabhadra，是释迦牟尼佛的右胁侍菩萨，代表高尚品德。
④ 地藏菩萨，梵文 Ksitigarbha，以其悲愿"地狱不空，誓不成佛"成为大愿的象征；《地藏王菩萨十轮经》称其"安忍不动，犹如大地，静虑深密，犹如秘藏"，故尊号为"大愿地藏王菩萨"。

sacrifice to Heaven and Earth (封禅) [1] on the top of Taishan. Later as many as 12 emperors followed suit to strengthen their sovereignty, and offering sacrifice to Heaven and Earth became the most important royal sacrifice ceremony. Taishan's outstanding importance is further highlighted by many other notables including Confucius, **Du Fu** (杜甫), the famous poet of the Tang Dynasty, and **Mao Zedong** (毛泽东), the first chairman of the People's Republic of China, who spoke highly of it in their poems.

On the top of the mountain, at a height of 1,545 meters, is **Yuhuang Miao** (Temple of Jade Emperor, 玉皇庙) dedicated to the supreme deity of Daoism. The last and most **strenuous** (费劲的) part of the climb is **Shiba Pan** (十八盘), the steep Path of Eighteen Bends from **Zhong Tian Men** (中天门), the halfway gate to Heaven, to **Nan Tian Men** (南天门), the last gate to Heaven. It symbolizes the utmost hardships one has to bear before reaching Heaven.

2) Mt. Wudang/Wudang Shan

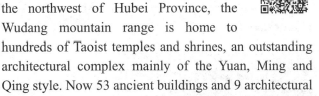

Nestled in the heart of the mainland in the northwest of Hubei Province, the Wudang mountain range is home to hundreds of Taoist temples and shrines, an outstanding architectural complex mainly of the Yuan, Ming and Qing style. Now 53 ancient buildings and 9 architectural sites survive including the **Purple Heaven Palace** (紫霄宫) and the **Golden Hall** (金殿顶). The Purple Heaven Palace rebuilt in the 15th century is the largest and best-preserved building complex in Mt. Wudang. Jindian, also called "**Golden Top** (金顶)", is the ancient bronze shrine built in 1416 at the summit — the ultimate destination for Taoist pilgrims. It houses a statue of the **Heavenly Emperor of North Zhenwu** (真武大帝), incarnation of tortoise and snake.

Mt. Wudang is also believed to be the birthplace of Wudang martial arts, originally created by **Zhang Sanfeng** (张三丰), a legendary Taoist priest in the Ming Dynasty (1368−1644). Inspired by a fight between a crane and a snake, he worked out the basis for **Taiji Quan** (Tai Chi, 太极拳) by combining martial arts with Daoist dialectical concept of Yin and Yang or **the unity of opposites** (对立统一). Wudang style is often depicted using the sword opposite to Shaolin Kungfu using the **cudgel** (棍棒). Now it's the place where many westerners come to learn playing Taiji.

3) Mt. Huang/Huangshan

A World Heritage Site listed by UNESCO in 1990, known as the most

---

[1]　"封"为"祭天","禅"为"祭地",是指中国古代帝王在太平盛世或天降祥瑞之时祭祀天地的大型典礼。远古暨夏商周三代,已有封禅的传说。古人认为群山中泰山最高,为"天下第一山",因此人间的帝王应到最高的泰山去祭过天帝,才算受命于天。

beautiful mountain in China, Huangshan or Mt. Huang is located in the south of Anhui Province, east China. Its core scenic area covers over 160 square kilometers with its peak at a height of 1,864 meters above sea level. Huangshan has been widely **acclaimed** (赞誉) for its scenery of **precipitous** (险峻的) peaks, **jagged** (嶙峋的) rocks, odd-shaped pine trees, **jutting** (突出) out of **cliffs** (悬崖峭壁) emerging out of a sea of clouds. Therefore,

it has been a source of inspiration for Chinese artists, poets and scholars. For example, such magnificent scenery is often illustrated in classic Chinese landscape paintings as well as numerous poems and essays. In addition, it also features hot springs. Huangshan is thus characterized by its "four wonders": the wind-carved pines, jagged rocks, sea of clouds and hot springs. The beauty of the mountains is evidenced by the popular saying that one who has just returned from Huangshan would have no more interest in visiting any of Wu Yue, the Five Sacred Mountains.

It's called Yellow Mountain in memory of **Emperor Huang** (黄帝) or Yellow Emperor, the mythical ancestor of the Chinese. According to folklore, Emperor Huang became immortal here, so to commemorate the legendary emperor, **Emperor Li Longji of the Tang Dynasty** (唐王李隆基) in 747 changed the name from **Yishan** (黟山) — Black Mountain to Yellow Mountain — **Huangshan** (黄山).

With an interesting but complex geological history, Huangshan has over 1,600 plant species and 300 species of **vertebrate fauna** (脊椎动物). Its main attractions include the massive **Feilai Rock** (飞来石), **Greeting Pine** (迎客松), **Refreshing Terrace** (清凉台), **Aoyu Back** (鳌鱼背), **Shixin Peak** (始信峰), etc. Feilai Rock is a rock flown from afar, overlooking **Xihai Area** (Western Sea, 西海), an endless **vista** (全景) of peaks out of fluffy clouds. The Greeting Pine stands on the cliff beside **Yuping Lou Hotel** (玉屏楼宾馆) near the cable car terminal

beckoning the visitors up the mountain. It's said to have a history of over 800 years. The Refreshing Terrace is a popular spot for watching the sunrise. Aoyu Back is a peak that looks like the legendary turtle's backbone. Standing on its top, one can have a good view of **Lotus Peak** (莲花峰) and the **Sunlight Summit** (光明顶). Shixin Peak, "Beginning to Believe Peak" in Chinese, means the peak where one starts to believe the beauty of Huangshan. It's the right place to offer one of the most **spectacular** (壮观的) views at Huangshan.

4) Mt. Wutai/Wutai Shan

Mt. Wutai, meaning "the five terrace mountains", located in northeastern Shanxi Province, north China, rising to a height of 3,061 meters above sea level, is the oldest and the most renowned among the four holy Buddhist mountains. With five flat peaks, the mountain range is believed to be the place where the Bodhisattva of Wisdom,

Manjusri (文殊菩萨) preached Buddhism. Known as the **patron deity** (护法神) of Mt. Wutai, Manjusri is a disciple of Sakyamuni and often portrayed riding a lion or holding a sword which is used to **cleave** (劈开) both ignorance and suffering. Many temples and halls are dedicated to him. The construction of the temples dates back to as early as the 1st century when two visiting Indian eminent monks[①] built here a temple named after the sacred **Lingjiu Peak**

(Vulture Peak, 灵鹫山) back in India. Now the temple is called **Xiantong Temple** (显通寺). It's not only the earliest temple but the largest on Wutai as well. Its highlight is the Bronze Hall

which is made entirely of metal decorated with thousands of small Buddhist figures.

There were over 300 temples during the Tang Dynasty, but now only 47 temples remain including 7 lamaseries. Apart from Xiantong Temple, other hot attractions are **Pusa Ding** (菩萨顶), **Great White Dagoba** (大白塔), **Shuxiang Temple** (殊像寺), **Nanchan Temple** (南禅寺) and **Foguang Temple** (佛光寺). Pusa Ding, meaning the Bodhisattva Summit, is the largest lamasery in Wutai dating back to the **Northern Wei Dynasty**

(北魏，386-534). The distinctive Tibetan-style Great White Dagoba serves as a landmark and symbol of Wutai. The Ming Dynasty Shuxiang Temple or Temple of Manjusri features a series of huge **three-dimensional sculptures** (立体塑像) depicting 500 arhats crossing the river. What's more, one can see the oldest surviving wooden halls of the Tang Dynasty in both Nanchan Temple and Foguang Temple (Buddha's Light Temple).

Part D   Language Checklist

A. Tourist Attractions

Tourist Attractions	中 文 名	城市/省
Baima Temple, White Horse Temple	白马寺	洛阳，河南
Famen Temple	法门寺	宝鸡，陕西

---

① 相传东汉永平十年（67年），两位印度高僧迦叶摩腾（Kasyapa Matanga）和竺法兰（Dharmaratna）随汉使以白马驮经和佛像，来到洛阳弘扬佛法。第二年，汉明帝在洛阳兴建了中国第一座佛教寺院白马寺，以作他们译经场所。白马寺从此就有中国佛教的"祖庭"和"释源"之称。之后，两位高僧从白马寺来到原为道士修行的五峰山（当时的五台山），认为这里是文殊菩萨讲经说法的道场，便想修建佛寺，但遭到道士们的反对。于是，他们通过在和道士们的"约期焚经"比赛中取胜，获取汉明帝的支持，在当地修建了第一座寺，即如今的显通寺（灵鹫寺）。从此，台怀镇一带佛教寺院开始兴盛。

Tourist Attractions	中 文 名	城市/省
Lingyin Temple	灵隐寺	杭州，浙江
Shaolin Temple	少林寺	登封，河南
Wooden Tower	木塔	朔州，山西
Dayan Tower, Greater Wild Goose Tower	大雁塔	西安，陕西
Liuhe Pagoda/Six Harmonies Pagoda	六和塔	杭州，浙江
Mount Tai/Taishan	泰山	泰安，山东
Mount Huang/Huangshan	黄山	黄山，安徽
Mount Emei	峨眉山	峨眉，四川
Mount Putuo	普陀山	舟山，浙江
Mount Wudang	武当山	十堰，湖北
Mount Wutai	五台山	忻州，山西

B. Vocabulary

patriarch 宗教创始人 Sakyamuni 释迦牟尼 Siddhartha Gautama 悉达多·乔达摩 Bodhidharma 菩提达摩	Mahayana Buddhism 大乘佛教 Theravada/Hinayana Buddhism 小乘佛教 Tibetan Buddhism/Lamaism/Vajrayana 藏传佛教/喇嘛教	Buddha 佛 Bodhisattva 菩萨 Pratyeka Buddha 缘觉 Arhat 罗汉
西方三圣： Amitabha 阿弥陀佛 Avalokitesvara 左胁侍观音菩萨 Mahasthamaprapta 右胁侍大势至菩萨	Bodhisattva of Wisdom/Manjusri 文殊菩萨 Bodhisattva of Universal Benevolence/Samantabhadra 普贤菩萨 Goddess of Mercy/Avalokitesvara 观音菩萨 Bodhisattva of Hell Beings/Ksitigarbha 地藏菩萨 Guardian of the Law/Skanda 护法神韦陀	Past Buddha 过去佛 Present Buddha 现在佛 Future Buddha 未来佛 Maitreya Buddha 弥勒佛
Hall of Heavenly Guardians 天王殿 Grand Buddha Hall/Mahavira Hall 大雄宝殿 Hall of Medicine Buddha/ Bhaishajyaguru Hall 药师殿 Hall of Avatamsaka 华严殿 Depository of Buddhist Scriptures/Sutra Hall 藏经阁/法堂	Meditation Hall 禅堂 Praying Hall 念佛堂 Hall of 500 Arhats 五百罗汉堂 Abbot's Room 方丈室 Monks Dorms 僧寮/房	Dhyāna, Zen 禅 Nirvana 极乐世界，涅槃 karma 因缘 meditation 冥想/禅定 enlightenment 启迪/开悟 universal salvation 普度众生
Sanskrit 梵文 scripture/sutra 佛经	dispel the evil 驱除邪恶 talismans 避邪物	relief clay sculptures 泥塑浮雕
stupa 印度塔，浮屠 Sarira 舍利	incarnation 化身	Sudhana 善财童子 Dragon Maiden 龙女

the Six Codes of Buddhism 六和敬	inscriptions 题词 plaques 匾额	canopy 华盖
offer sacrifice to Heaven and Earth 封禅	asceticism 苦行 ascetic monk 苦行僧	Ashoka 阿育王
Heavenly Emperor of North Zhenwu 真武大帝 Celestial Masters 天师	elixirs 灵丹妙药 dialectical 辩证的	patron deity 护法神

C. Key Patterns

Three Major Schools of Buddhism in China 中国的三大佛教派系	• There are three major schools of Buddhism in China. One is Mahayana meaning "Greater Vehicle", the second one is Theravada developed from Hinayana known as "Lesser Vehicle", and the third is Tibetan Buddhism. 中国有三大佛教派系：大乘佛教（汉传）、小乘佛教（南传）和藏传佛教。 • Mahayana Buddhism emphasizes a common search for universal salvation and is quite common in China, Japan and Korea. 大乘佛教强调普度众生，多见于中国、日本和韩国。 • Theravada Buddhism teaches personal salvation through one's own efforts and is popular in countries in southeastern Asia such as Thailand, Myanmar and Cambodia. 小乘佛教教导人们通过自己的努力进行自我解脱，主要流行于泰国、缅甸和柬埔寨。 • Tibetan Buddhism also called Tibetan Lamaism (西藏喇嘛教) is dominant in Tibetan area.
Buddhist Creed 佛教的要义	• Chan centers on the attainment of enlightenment through meditation and the personal understanding of direct insight in the Buddhist teachings regardless of any written language. 禅是通过静思默想直接领会佛理获得开悟的修持方法，无关任何语言，可谓"教外别传，不立文字"。 • According to the law of Karma, one's actions in this life affect one's future.佛教中的因果报应指的是一个人今世的行为会影响其来世的生活。 • Samsara, the six paths of rebirth: One will be born into the path of gods, humans, and Asuras if doing good deeds, or will fall into the one of animals, hungry ghosts, or hell-beings if doing evil deeds. 六道轮回指众生轮回的六大去处：天道、人道、阿修罗道、畜生道、饿鬼道和地狱道。一个人积德行善的话就可以进前三道，作恶多端的话就要进后三道。 • There are four stages of enlightenment: Buddhas, Bodhisattvas, Pratyeka Buddhas and Arhats. 佛教中修行开悟的四个境界：佛、菩萨、缘觉和罗汉。 • Buddhas are perfect in enlightenment; Bodhisattvas enlighten both themselves and the others; Pratyeka Buddhas achieve enlightenment after self-cultivation; Arhats are enlightened Buddhists. 佛觉行圆满，大彻大悟，处于最高境界；菩萨觉行尚未圆满，但已经达到自觉和觉他的境界，即不仅自我开悟而且还使其他众生顿悟；缘觉属于自我修行后顿悟；罗汉是佛教徒修行后达到的最高果位（断除一切烦恼，不再进行生死轮回）。
Characteristics of a Temple 寺庙的特点	• Lingyin Temple ranks the first among all the temples in Hangzhou area. With a history of over 1,700 years, it is not only the oldest temple in Hangzhou but also one of the largest Chan (禅) Buddhist monasteries in China. • Buddhism in Hangzhou started in the Eastern Jin Dynasty (317−420), then flourished during the Five Dynasties (五代, 907−960), and peaked in the Southern Song Dynasty with over 300 temples scattered throughout the whole area.

Characteristics of a Temple 寺庙的特点	• Hangzhou thus earned the name "A Buddhist realm in Southeastern China". • In its heyday (鼎盛时期) in the 10th century when Hangzhou served as the capital of the Kingdom of Wuyue, the temple complex contained 9 buildings, 18 pavilions, 72 halls and 1,300 rooms for over 3,000 monks.
Buddhist Legends 佛教传说	• He then got enlightened under the Bodhi tree (菩提树) after six-year meditation and became the Buddha, "the Awakened One", hence the name Shakyamuni/Sakyamuni, meaning "Sage of the Sakyas (释迦族的圣人)". • The small hill looked exactly like the peak Gridhrakuta (Vulture Peak, 灵鹫山) in India, a place where Buddha Sakyamuni (佛祖释迦牟尼) used to preach to the crowds. The peak thus got a strange name "the Peak Flown From Afar". • It's the Maitreya Buddha (弥勒佛), incarnated (化身) as a chubby (圆胖的) monk carrying a sack in Ningbo, Zhejiang Province. • It's the Guardian of the Law, Skanda (护法神韦陀), head of the 32 generals under the Four Heavenly Guardians according to the Buddhist legend.
Layout of a Temple 寺庙的建筑布局	• The whole monastery complex comprises the major halls in order on the south-north axis as listed: Hall of Heavenly Guardians/Kings (天王殿), Grand Buddha Hall (Mahavira Hall, 大雄宝殿), Hall of Medicine Buddha (Bhaishajyaguru Hall, 药师殿), Sutra Hall/the Depositary of Buddhist Scriptures (藏经阁/法堂), and Hall of Avatamsaka (华严殿). Some other halls and rooms on its either side: the Praying Hall (念佛堂), Meditation Hall (禅堂), the Hall of 500 Arhats (五百罗汉堂), Monks' Dorms (僧房), Abbot's Room (方丈室), and so on.
Legends about Pagodas 有关塔的传说	• According to the Buddhist sutra, about 2,500 years ago, the remains of the Buddha Sakyamuni turned into crystals (结晶体) including 84,000 shiny pearl-like beads in different colors after the cremation (火葬), and thus are known as Sariras (舍利) or Buddhist relics. • It's not until about 200 years later the great king Ashoka (阿育王), a devout Buddhist (虔诚的佛教徒), had 84,000 pagodas rebuilt to enshrine (珍藏) and venerate (敬仰) each piece of all the Buddhist relics. • Leifeng Pagoda was first erected (建立) in 977 by Qian Chu (钱俶, 929–988), the last king of Wuyue Kingdom, to house the Buddha's hair Sarira (佛螺髻发舍利) together with Buddhist scriptures and to commemorate (纪念) the birth of his son as well. • Baochu Pagoda was built in the hope of blessing King Qian Chu (钱俶) so that he could come back safe and sound after having been summoned (召见) by the emperor to Kaifeng (开封), the capital of the Northern Song Dynasty. • In order to completely control the ravaging (肆虐的) tides, King Qian Chu had a pagoda built in his South Orchard (南果园) right in this present site in 970.
Functions of Pagoda 塔的功能	• Pagoda is used to house the Buddhist relics (佛舍利) and sutras or scriptures (佛经) in a temple. • The pagoda was built to control the tide and hopefully bring harmony to the world. • This pagoda later also served as an important navigational (航行的) landmark like the lighthouse for the ships in the river at night. • As a matter of fact, as time went on, pagodas in China became more than just related to Buddhism. Many of them were built to serve as a landmark, an ornament to a mountain or a scenic spot, a watchtower to enjoy a distant view. • 随着时间的推移，中国的塔在功能上有了更多的衍生，不只是和佛教相关。很多塔变成了地域性标志，点缀一座山或者一个景区，也可以作为瞭望塔供人们远眺。

Main Features of Wu Yue **五岳的特点**	• These lofty mountains have been primary (首要的) pilgrimage (朝圣) sites for people throughout the ages, as they are believed to be the closest access point to heaven and the dwelling places of powerful immortals or deities (神). • The five mountains, especially Mt. Tai, have been the places of worship (祭祀场地) for many emperors offering sacrifices to Heaven and Earth in Chinese history. 五岳，尤其是泰山，一直以来是中国历史上许多帝王封禅祭祀的地方。 • Wu Yue stands for the most essential "**Five Elements** (五行)" such as metal, water, wood, fire and earth. 五岳代表五行，即金、木、水、火和土。
Four Buddhist Sacred Mountains and Their Patron Bodhisattvas **四大佛教名山及** **其护法神**	• It is believed that the patron Bodhisattva in Wutai is Wenshu, the Bodhisattva of Wisdom. • Mt. Putuo has strong association with Guanyin, the Bodhisattva of Infinite Compassion. • Puxian, the Bodhisattva of Universal Benevolence, is dominant in Mt. Emei. • Mt. Jiuhua is associated with the Silla monk Jin Qiaojue (金乔觉) who is regarded as the reincarnation of Dizang, the Bodhisattva of Hell Beings (地藏菩萨) who vowed not to enter Nirvana until the Hell Realm (地狱) is empty and thus is noted as the guardian of the earth.
Daoism and Famous Mountains **道教和名山**	• Daoism, along with Confucianism, is one of the two great indigenous philosophical traditions of China. Originally, it was founded by the great thinker Laozi (571–471 BC). Later it was developed into a religion by Celestial Masters (天师) lineage founder, Zhang Daoling (张道陵) during the 2nd century. • In the eyes of Daoists or hermits, one is inseparable from nature and can finally achieve immortality by living in accordance with Dao. They prefer to cultivate themselves in search for eternal life deep in the grottoes or caves of the mountains where they believe the immortals or deities live. 在道士或隐士的眼里，天人合一，人们可以通过遵循自然法则和谐生活获得永生。他们相信山洞里都是神仙居住的地方，于是都喜欢在那里修炼以求长生不老。 • Many mountains in China are home to many Daoist temples and shrines as well as alchemy furnaces (炼丹炉) for making elixirs (灵丹妙药).
Features of Mountains **名山的特点**	• The sacred Mount Tai was the object of an imperial cult for nearly 2,000 years, and the artistic masterpieces found there are in perfect harmony with the natural landscape. It has always been a source of inspiration for Chinese artists and scholars and symbolizes ancient Chinese civilizations and beliefs. (Mt. Tai/Taishan, UNESCO World Heritage Site description) 泰山是近 2,000 年来广受历代帝王顶礼膜拜的地方，各种题刻艺术精品随处可见，浑然天成。泰山也是中国艺术家、学者等文人雅士萌发创作灵感的源泉，彰显中国古代文明和人们的信仰。（泰山，联合国教科文组织世界遗产地说明） • Taishan is the most exalted and sacred mountain of historical and cultural significance in China. • Nestled in the heart of the mainland in the northwest of Hubei Province, the Wudang mountain range is home to hundreds of Taoist temples and shrines, an outstanding architectural complex mainly of the Yuan, Ming and Qing style. • Mt. Wudang is also believed to be the birthplace of Wudang martial arts, originally created by Zhang Sanfeng (张三丰), a legendary Taoist priest in the Ming Dynasty (1368–1644). • The palaces and temples which form the nucleus of this group of secular and religious buildings exemplify the architectural and artistic achievements of China's Yuan, Ming and Qing dynasties. (Mt. Wudang, UNESCO World Heritage Site description) 武当山的主要殿堂、庙宇和道观展示了中国元、明、清时期的建筑艺术成就。（武当山，联合国教科文组织世界遗产地说明）

Features of Mountains 名山的特点	• Huangshan has been widely acclaimed (赞誉) for its scenery of precipitous (险峻的) peaks, odd-shaped pine trees jutting (突出) out of cliffs (悬崖峭壁) emerging out of a sea of clouds. • Huangshan, often described as the "loveliest mountain of China", has played an important role in the history of art and literature in China since the Tang Dynasty around the 8th century. (Mt. Huangshan, UNESCO World Heritage Site description) 黄山是"中国最秀美的名山"，自唐朝（约 8 世纪）以来，在中国的艺术和文学史上起着举足轻重的作用。（黄山，联合国教科文组织世界遗产地说明）

Part E   English in Use

I. Reading Comprehension

Task 1: Choose the best answer to complete each sentence below.

1. A monastery complex usually consists of the Hall of Heavenly Guardians, the Grand Buddha Hall, Hall of Medicine Buddha as well as the _____ arrayed on the north-south axis.
   A. Meditation Hall
   B. Praying Hall
   C. Depositary of Buddhist Scriptures
   D. Hall of 500 Arhats

2. "The Flourishing Age of Kangxi and Qianlong" refers to the period during the _____.
   A. 15th–16th centuries
   B. 16th–17th centuries
   C. 17th–18th centuries
   D. late 17th–18th centuries

3. Bodhidharma, credited as the transmitter of Dhyana from India to China, was regarded as the first patriarch of Chinese Chan. He finally settled down in _____.
   A. Mt. Wudang
   B. Lingyin Temple
   C. Shaolin Temple
   D. Nanchan Temple

4. Lingyin Temple was first built in _____ by an Indian monk named Huili.
   A. 329
   B. 326
   C. the 3rd century
   D. 330

5. Feilai Peak is famous for its Buddhist rock carvings dating back to _____, a period when the grotto art became less prosperous in North China.
   A. the 10th–14th centuries
   B. the 10th–13th centuries
   C. the 9th–14th centuries
   D. the 11th–14th century

6. The largest and the most impressive state on the Feilai Peak is Buddha Maitreya, carved around _____.
   A. the 11th century
   B. 1000
   C. 1004
   D. late 11th century

7. The two Sutra Pillars in front of the _____ and the Twin Pagodas flanking the Main Hall are the oldest surviving stone carvings in Lingyin Temple.
   A. Hall of Heavenly Guardians
   B. Hall of Grand Buddha
   C. Hall of Medicine
   D. Hall of Avatamsaka

8. _____ is known as the Future Buddha, the successor of Buddha Sakyamuni.
   A. Ksitigarbha
   B. Monk Budai

    C. Medicine Buddha   D. The Maitreya Buddha

9. Those childless couples often go to the temple offering sacrifices to _____.
    A. Bodhisattva of Infinite Compassion   B. Bodhisattva of Wisdom
    C. Bodhisattva of Universal Benevolence   D. Ksitigarbha

10. The Buddhists believe that there were _____ pearl-like Sariras left after Buddha Sakyamuni went into nirvana.
    A. 48,000   B. 8,400   C. 480,000   D. 84,000

Task 2: Answer the following questions concerning the introductions about Buddhist temples and pagodas in Part A and Part B.

1. What are the three major schools of Buddhism developed in China?
2. What is the focus of Chinese Chan?
3. What are the Buddha's Four Noble Truths?
4. Why was the Six Harmonies Pagoda built?
5. What was the festivity associated with the pagoda in the Southern Song Dynasty?

Task 3: Decide whether each of the following statements is True or False according to the introduction about the sacred mountains in China in Part C.

1. The Five Sacred Mountains in China are Mount Tai in the east, Mount Song in the middle, Mount Heng in the north, Mt. Huang in the south and Mount Hua in the west. (   )
2. Daoism and Confucianism are the two great homegrown philosophies in China. (   )
3. Laozi was the founder of religious Daoism and later improved by Zhang Daoling (张道陵) during the 2nd century. (   )
4. Daoists or Taoists aim to look for elixirs to enjoy an eternal life in the grottoes or caves of the mountains. (   )
5. The Bodhisattva of Wisdom is dominant in Wutai; Mt. Putuo has a strong association with the Bodhisattva of Infinite Compassion; Bodhisattva of Universal Benevolence is the patron Bodhisattva in Mt. Jiuhua; Ksitigarbha is revered in Mt. Emei. (   )

II. Translation

Task 4: Translate the following sentences into English.

1. 灵隐寺有着 1,600 多年的历史，不仅是杭州最古老的寺庙，也是中国最大的禅宗寺庙之一。
2. 灵隐景区由照壁、飞来峰和灵隐寺等景点组成，要游览完整个景区大约需要 2 个小时。
3. 公元 10 世纪，灵隐寺处于鼎盛时期，当时就有 9 楼、18 阁、72 殿，房舍 1,300 多间，僧徒 3,000 余人。
4. 修禅的方式在西方越来越受欢迎，因为任何人都可以任何形式冥想禅定。
5. 佛教中的因果报应指的是一个人今世的行为会影响其来世的生活。
6. 理公塔是为了纪念灵隐寺的开山祖师印度和尚慧理而修建的。
7. 这是寺里最古老的一尊刻像，被人誉为中国古代的木刻艺术精品。

8. 塔最早用来供奉（consecrate）和安置舍利、经文或各种法物（Buddhist appliances）。

9. 在古印度有一位伟大的国王叫阿育王，是一名虔诚的佛教徒。在释迦牟尼涅槃 200 年后，他命人重建了 84,000 座塔，供奉每一颗佛舍利。

10. 这就是矗立在钱塘江边的六和塔。它是为了镇江潮而建的，人们希望天下从此和谐。

Task 5: Translate the following sentences into Chinese.

1. Buddhism in Hangzhou started in the Eastern Jin Dynasty (317−420), then flourished during the Five Dynasties (907−960), and peaked in the Southern Song Dynasty with over 300 temples scattered throughout the whole area.

2. Siddhartha Gautama is said to be the prince of a royal family, a large clan of Sakya in Kapilavastu (迦毗罗卫国) where present Nepal is around 2,500 years ago. His father was King Suddhodana.

3. Bodhidharma from India, the 28th patriarch of Buddhism, was the first one to transmit the concept of Dhyana to China which later developed into Chan or Zen.

4. According to Buddhist legend, Maitreya Buddha was incarnated as a bare-chested chubby monk carrying a sack in Ningbo, Zhejiang Province.

5. This is one of the largest wooden statues of a sitting Buddha in China. The imposing statue was vividly carved in 1956 out of 24 pieces of camphor wood and gilded with about 140 ounces of gold.

6. One saying is related to the Six Codes of Buddhism: the harmony of one's body, speech, mind, opinion, wealth and abstinence from temptation.

7. Mt. Jiuhua is associated with the Silla monk Jin Qiaojue who is regarded as the reincarnation of Dizang, the Bodhisattva of Hell Beings. The bodhisattva vowed not to enter Nirvana until Hell is empty and is thus noted as the guardian of the earth.

8. Huangshan has been widely acclaimed as the loveliest mountain in China for its scenery of precipitous peaks, jagged rocks, odd-shaped pine trees jutting out of cliffs emerging out of a sea of clouds.

9. The Bodhisattva of Universal Benevolence, Puxian, is said to have ascended Mt. Emei during the 6th century atop a six-tusked elephant.

10. If one stops being greedy, angry and ignorant, one will be surely free from suffering and gets ready to be enlightened as Buddha, escaping the turning wheel of life — Samsara, the six paths of rebirth.

III. Role Play

Task 6: Play a role in any of the following situations with your partner(s).

Situation 1: You work for an Overseas Tourist Company as a tourist guide. You're showing a group of western tourists around Lingyin Temple. Talk briefly about Chan/Zen Buddhism as well as the main halls in the temple, and get ready to answer any questions.

Situation 2: You're showing your western friends or business partner around a Buddhist temple in China. Talk briefly about Chan/Zen Buddhism as well as the main halls in the temple, and get ready to answer any questions.

Situation 3: You're a tourist guide from a China International Travel Service. You're showing a group of Australian tourists around the Six Harmonies Pagoda. Talk briefly about the origin of the Buddhist pagodas as well as the functions of the pagoda, and get ready to answer any questions.

Situation 4: You're showing your western friends or business partner around some of the famous pagodas in China. Talk about the origin of the Buddhist pagodas as well as the main features of the pagoda, and get ready to answer any questions.

Situation 5: You're showing a group of western tourists around some of the four famous Buddhist mountains in China. Give a general introduction to the four mountains as well as the main attractions in the mountain, and get ready to answer any questions.

Situation 6: You're showing a group of western tourists or foreign friends around some of the four sacred Daoist mountains in China. Give a general introduction to the four mountains as well as the main attractions in the mountain, and get ready to answer any questions.

Situation 7: You're showing a group of western tourists or foreign friends around Mt. Huang, or Mt. Tai, or any of other famous mountains in China. First, give a general introduction to the five top mountains, then talk about the main attractions in the mountain, and get ready to answer any questions.

IV. Problem-solving

Task 7: Make an analysis of the following cases, and answer the questions as required.

Case 1

Situation: Bai Yun is giving a brief introduction to Buddhism to a group of tourists, some of the group members show extreme interest in it and keep asking her many further questions which are probably beyond the understanding of the other tourists. Bai Yun doesn't have much time then and some other tourists seem upset.

Question: If you were Bai Yun, how would you handle the problem?

Case 2

Situation: You're required to lead a group of elderly people from the United States. They're quite active in sightseeing though most of them are over sixties.

Question: How would you do the tours for the seniors?

Answers for Reference

Unit 9   Imperial Palace, Mausoleum and Confucius Temple

Warm-up

1. Do you recognize the following world-renowned places? What do they have in common?

1) _____

2) _____

3) _____

4) _____

5) _____

6) _____

7) _____

8) _____

9) _____

2. What's the largest imperial palace now in China? What's the landmark in Tibet?
3. How many imperial mausoleums do you know of in China? Which imperial mausoleums have you ever visited in China? What's the Mausoleum of the First Qin Emperor mainly famous for? Do you recognize the following places?

1) _____   2) _____   3) _____

4. Have you ever visited any of Confucius Temples in China?

Part A   The Forbidden City

Dialogue 1

Situation: *Yuan Lin, the tour guide, is showing Klaus around the Forbidden City, officially known as the Palace Museum. Klaus is a German student from Hamburg University and is very interested in Chinese culture. In awe of the magnificent buildings, Klaus has many questions to ask Yuan Lin.*

Questions for comprehension and discussion:

★ How many names does the imperial palace in Beijing have?

★ What does the Chinese **Zijin Cheng** (紫禁城) mean?

★ What's the unique architectural feature of the Forbidden City in Beijing?

★ Which numbers is the architecture in the Forbidden City closely related to? Why?

★ What's the function of **Wu Gate** (午门)?

★ What does Golden Water Bridge mean?

Yuan Lin: So here in the center of Beijing is the **epic** (宏大的) Forbidden City, off limits to most people for 500 years. It was declared a World Heritage site as early as in 1987. The imperial palace was home to 24 emperors during the Ming and Qing dynasties from 1420 to 1911. It's also known as the **Palace Museum** (故宫博物院), though we usually call it Gugong in Chinese, meaning the "Past Palace".

Klaus:　Excuse me, how long did it take to build the huge palace?

Yuan Lin:　The construction started in 1406 and was completed in 1420 during the reign of **Emperor Zhudi** (朱棣, 1403–1424). So it took fourteen years to be exact. It's said that millions of **artisans** (工匠) and **laborers** (劳工) were involved and various kinds of special materials were collected throughout the country.

Klaus:　Well, it's **incredible** (不可思议). I've heard that it's also called **Zijin Cheng** (紫禁城) in Chinese, literally meaning "Purple Forbidden City". Is this because the wall was painted purple?

Yuan Lin:　Well no, but you are right. The "Zi" in Chinese means the color "purple", but in ancient Chinese **astrology** (星象学), it refers to **the Ziwei Enclosure** (紫微垣) — the **North Star** (北极星) in the center of the universe where the **celestial Emperor** (天帝) **resided** (居住). Since the Emperor claimed to be the "Son of Heaven", the imperial palace was thus believed to be the **counterpart** (对应物) of Heaven on earth.

Klaus:　Aha, I see.

Yuan Lin:　Now, the whole area is **rectangular** (长方形) in shape surrounded by a ten-meter high **curtain wall** (围墙) and a 52-meter wide moat. There's a gate on each side of the wall with a **tower** (角楼) at each of the four corners watching over both the palace and the city outside. Each watchtower has a **triple-eaved roof** (三层檐) in various shapes covered with **yellow glazed tiles** (金黄色琉璃瓦顶). With an area of 720,000 square meters, it's the most magnificent architectural complex in China. Besides, it's also believed to rank first among the four major imperial palaces in the world, the other three being **Versailles Palace** (凡尔赛宫) in France, **Buckingham Palace** in the UK, and the **Kremlin** (克里姆林宫) in Russia. By the way, have you ever been to any of these palaces?

Klaus:　Well, unfortunately, I've only been to Buckingham Palace. Comparatively speaking, I could say yes, Gugong seems much more **massive** (巨大的) and impressive. Actually, I've been looking forward to visiting the world's largest **palace complex** (宫殿群) since I started to learn Chinese two years ago.

Yuan Lin:　Now you're in the right place. But it'll take you at least a whole day to walk through the entire area, as there are nearly 9,000 halls and rooms here.

Klaus:　Wow, there's no way that we can manage all that in a day!

Yuan Lin:　But the legend has it that, at the beginning of its construction, there were supposed to be 9,999.5 rooms, only half a room less than those in Heaven or Paradise, for the number symbolized the mighty power of the Emperor, only slightly less superior to that of **Jade Emperor or Heavenly Emperor** (玉皇大帝).

Klaus:　Fancy that! But what happened to the other 1,000?

Yuan Lin: Well, actually that's just a **rumor** (传闻).

Klaus: I know, but does it have anything to do with the number "Nine"?

Yuan Lin: Oh, yes, you are right. The number "Nine" is the highest **single-digit** (个位数) **odd number** (奇数). Moreover, its pronunciation is similar to that of another Chinese character "**Jiu** (久) " meaning "everlasting". Therefore, it has become the Chinese people's favorite number in daily life, and was particularly important for ancient emperors who had **ultimate sovereignty** (至高无上的权力). For example, the emperors wore robes with the designs of nine dragons, had **Nine Dragon Screen** (九龙壁) built, and lived in palaces concerning the number in **architectural details** (各种建筑细部) in order to showcase their **dignity** (尊贵) and **sovereignty** (王权). And the Forbidden City presents the perfect example of the **embodiment** (体现) of such Chinese **hierarchical culture** (等级制文化) in architecture. So you see, it doesn't matter whether the saying is true or not, as long as we know from the legend that there are **countless** (无数的) halls and rooms in this fantastic **imperial residence** (皇家住地).

Klaus: Now I see. The number of steps here in the building complex must also be connected with the number "Nine", is that right?

Yuan Lin: Exactly, you've got it. Well, if you doubt it, you can count them yourself later. By the way, can you see those **brass studs** (铜钉) on the door? Do you know how many there are altogether?

Klaus: Oh, I've got it! Let me see, nine times nine is 81, so altogether there are 81 studs, aren't there?

Yuan Lin: Absolutely right, you're a quick learner. Actually, there are 81 brass studs on every door at all the gates on the curtain wall except for the eastern gate which only has 72.

Klaus: Why?

Yuan Lin: Well, it's still a **riddle** (迷). One of the sayings is that the coffin of a **deceased** (亡故的) emperor would be carried out through the eastern gate after the last Emperor **Chongzhen** (崇祯皇帝, 1611–1644) of the Ming Dynasty **committed suicide** (自杀) under the force of the **rebel army** (叛军), hence the **even number** (偶数) "72" implies **misfortune** (不幸).

Klaus: Got it. So why is it called the **Meridian Gate** (午门)?

Yuan Lin: Well, we're now at the main entrance. It's called Wu Men in Chinese, meaning the south gate like the **Meridian Line** (子午线) going from south to north through the royal residence. The 37.95-meter high Meridian Gate is the largest and most magnificent of all four gates. It has two **protruding wings** (突出的两侧殿屋) with four watchtowers at the corners. Looking from far away, you can see five **delicate** (精美的) **double-eaved** (重檐的) towers on the top of the gate that look like five golden phoenix flying in the sky, so it's also commonly known as the **Five-Phoenix Towers** (五凤楼). Look at the bell pavilion on the east and the drum pavilion on the west of the middle tower. Whenever a big ceremony was held, the bell and drum would sound to mark the occasion.

Klaus: Mm, very interesting, indeed.

Yuan Lin:

From the balcony, the Emperor would **survey** (检阅) his armies before setting out on an **expedition** (远征). From here, he would also perform the ceremony marking the start of a new calendar[①]. In addition, on the 15th day of the first month of each lunar year during the Ming Dynasty, the Emperor would watch the lanterns and compose poems together with his **courtiers** (廷臣/文武百官) after banqueting with them. Each time an **imperial edict** (圣旨) was delivered, the courtiers would gather here on the square in front of the gate. Besides, some special **pastries** (糕点) would be **bestowed** (赐) by the Emperor on the citizens to celebrate certain festivals such as **the Beginning of the Spring** (立春) and the **Dragon Boat Festival** (端午节/龙舟节), etc. However, it's also the place where some of the guilty courtiers were **punished** (惩罚) by the **hatchet men** (打手) beating them on the **buttocks** (臀部) during the Ming Dynasty[②]. Some were even **flogged** (鞭打) to death.

Klaus: Oh, poor people.

Yuan Lin: Well, there are three doors at the gate. But mind you, no one was allowed to go through the main door except the Emperor and the Empress in the sedan chair during the wedding ceremony. It was not until the Qing Dynasty that the top three candidates from the final imperial examination were allowed to walk through the main door, and only once[③]. The west door was only for the royal family while the east one was for the courtiers. But today every one of us can **swagger** (昂首阔步) over the imperial way just like the Emperor.

Klaus: Great, let's go.

Yuan Lin: Sorry, just a minute. Do you know what you can expect to see after entering the gate?

Klaus: Actually, I have no idea. I've heard that it's a **maze** (迷宫), and I'm afraid I'll get lost if I just go in alone.

---

① 午门是皇帝下诏书、下令出征的地方。每遇宣读皇帝圣旨，颁发年历书，文武百官都要齐集午门前广场听旨。

② 明代午门前是皇帝"廷杖"朝臣之地。明代时，如果大臣触犯了皇家的尊严，便以"逆鳞"之罪，被绑出午门前御道东侧打屁股，名叫"廷杖"。起初只象征性地责打，后来发展到打死人。

③ 殿试考中的前三名（状元、榜眼、探花）才可以从此门走出一次。文武大臣进出东侧门，宗室王公出入西侧门。

Yuan Lin: Well, as a masterpiece in ancient Chinese architecture, Gugong has a **symmetrical** (对称的) design indicating a **hierarchical system** (等级礼制) of the **urban layout** (都城设计)①. With the **Ancestral Temple** (祖庙/太庙) on the east and **Altar of Land and Grain** (presently the Working People's Cultural Palace, 社稷坛) on the west, the whole complex was constructed along the **central north-south axis** (南北中轴线) of the city and was divided into two

parts: the Outer Court and the Inner Court. The former is the place where the Emperor exercised his supreme power over the nation, whereas the latter is the living quarters for the Emperor and his royal family. **Taihe Hall** (the Hall of Supreme Harmony, 太和殿), **Zhonghe Hall** (the Hall of Central Harmony, 中和殿) and **Baohe Hall** (the Hall of Preserving Harmony,

保和殿), flanked by **Wenhua Hall** (the Hall of Literary Glory, 义华殿) on the east and **Wuying Hall** (the Hall of Martial Valor, 武英殿) on the west in the Outer Court, are the most impressive buildings in the palace complex. **Qianqing Gong** (the Hall of Heavenly Purity, 乾清宫), **Jiaotai Hall** (the Hall of Union, 交泰殿) and **Kunning Gong** (the Hall of Earthly Tranquility, 坤宁宫) in the Inner Court are the buildings mirroring those of the Outer Court but on a smaller scale. Well, am I **getting** the message **across** (表达清楚) to you?

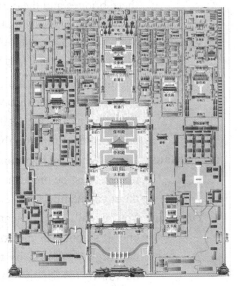

Klaus: **As clear as a bell** (非常清楚). Thank you.

Yuan Lin: You're welcome. OK, now, let's move. First we'll cross the five marble bridges over the **Golden Water River** (金水河).

Klaus: Sorry, why five? Why is it called Golden Water River?

Yuan Lin: That's what I was going to ask you, haha.

Klaus: And these beautiful bridges look much the same as those in front of the gate with the portrait of Mao Zedong.

Yuan Lin: Exactly, that's Tian'an Men in Chinese, **the Gate of Heavenly Peace** (天安门). Now, please look at the water in the river. It's flowing from the northwest to the southeast, right?

---

① 中国古代建筑一般遵循 "前朝后寝，左祖右社" 的宗法等级礼制。

According to **the theory of Yin-yang (阴阳) and Five Essential Elements** (五行) which are metal, wood, water, fire and earth, the west is related to the gold referring to metal, and the north the water, hence the name Golden Water River.

There are two Golden Water Rivers running through Gugong, the inner one here and the outer one in front of Tian'an Men. So, likewise, there are the **Inner and Outer Golden Water Bridges** (内金水桥和外金水桥). The five marble bridges represent the five **virtues** (美德) in **Confucianism** (儒家思想): **goodness** (仁), **righteousness** (义), **ritual** (礼), **wisdom** (智), and **integrity** (信). But the river here is actually a man-made waterway and used to serve as a **reservoir** (水库) in case of fire. By the way, can you guess, together with the large courtyard and the huge gate ahead, what these bridges and the curving river look like?

Klaus: Let me see. The river is like a belt, isn't it?

Yuan Lin: Yes, like a jade belt worn by the officials. The bridges are said to be the **decorative buckles** (装饰搭扣) on the jade belt. The other saying is that the curving river takes the shape of a bow and these bridges are the five arrows drawn by the largest gate — **Gate of Supreme Harmony** (太和门) and the most imposing hall — the Hall of Supreme Harmony, which symbolizes the supreme power of the Emperor, the Son of Heaven.

Klaus: I see. What an **ingenious** (匠心独具) design. Then the largest bridge in the middle must be only for the Emperor, and the other ones on its both sides are for the royal members and courtiers.

Yuan Lin: You're really a quick learner. Let's walk on the middle one. It's about 23 meters long. Now can you see the **carvings** (雕刻) on its **balustrades** (栏杆)? They're the **motifs** (装饰的图案) of dragon and phoenix.

Klaus: They're quite **exquisite** (精美) indeed.

Yuan Lin: Yeah, these bridges are not only the largest but also the most **gorgeous** (华丽的) marble ones in Gugong.

Dialogue 2

Situation: *Yuan Lin and Klaus continue to walk around the Forbidden City. Now they are standing in front of Gate of Supreme Harmony, the largest gate in Gugong.*

Questions for comprehension and discussion:
★ How much do you know about the bronze lions in front of the Gate of Supreme Harmony?
★ Why are there no trees in the Outer Court?
★ What may a tourist see in the Hall of Supreme Harmony?

Yuan Lin: Klaus, please look at the two powerful bronze lions at each side of the gate — Taihe Men, Gate of Supreme Harmony. Of all the six pairs of bronze lions in Gugong, they are the largest ones, but can you guess which is male and which is female?

Klaus: Aha, interesting. Now this one with a ball under its paw must be the male and the other one with a **lion cub** (幼狮) must be the female. Is there also any **significance** (意义)?

Yuan Lin: You're quite smart. The ball is the symbol of the sovereignty and the **unification** (统一) of the country, while the lion cub refers to the **fertility** (繁殖力/子嗣昌盛), the everlasting succession to the imperial throne.

Klaus: Very interesting. Wow, is that the grandest hall ahead of us?

Yuan Lin: Yes, that's Taihe Dian, the Hall of Supreme Harmony, the **highlight** (精华部分) of the whole area. No one would like to miss it.

Klaus: But it's impossible to take a good picture of the hall with so many people.

Yuan Lin: No, you couldn't. Sorry, we're now in the summertime and it's quite normal to have thousands of visitors every day here. But you could never believe the number of the visitors here during the festivals. For example, the **record** (最高记录的) number of the visitors last October reached 182,000. It's hard for one to move even an inch. As a matter of fact, nearly every tourist attraction in China is over-crowded with the tourists during the weeklong national holiday every year. Incredible, isn't it?

Klaus: My God, you have too many people everywhere. The number of the tourists should be controlled to protect the property.

Yuan Lin: Right, I'm with you there. But there's still a continuing dispute concerning the **preservation** (保护) of the cultural relic, as no visitor, especially after a long journey to Beijing, would be happy if they were told it would not be possible to visit Gugong, a must-see place, because the tickets were sold out. Would you be happy then?

Klaus: Well, no, to be honest, I wouldn't be happy either.

Yuan Lin: It's really a big headache. Anyway, online reservation will be available. Shall we move on?

Klaus: Sure. By the way, it's so strange that I cannot see a single tree here in this **vast** (开阔的) **plaza** (广场). Is there a special reason for that?

Yuan Lin: Yes. It's designed to show the **loftiness** (高大) of the three halls in the vast Outer Court. Believe it or not, another saying is related to the **restriction among five elements** (五行相克) in the **theory of Five Elements** (五行学说). According to the theory, the five elements like metal, wood, water, fire and earth are closely **correlated** (相互关联的)  but **restrict** (制约) each other. For example, the earth is restricted by the wood, and the wood **generates** (生成) the fire. As the earth was supposed to be the symbol of the sovereignty and the trees stand for the wood, the earth would be restricted by the wood if there were any trees planted in the yard. What's more, the halls would be easily burned if someone sets the trees on fire. By the way, it had been burned down several times in the Ming Dynasty, and the present hall was rebuilt in the Qing Dynasty.

Klaus: Um, that sounds quite reasonable. And perhaps there's no other place for a **burglar** (盗贼) to hide in.

Yuan Lin: You're right. That has also been said. Wow, you're as smart as the emperor.

Klaus: You bet.

Yuan Lin: By the way, can you see the roof? Like the height and decoration of the terraces and buildings, all the roofs here were also designed hierarchically. As the grandest structure, the hall has a **double-eaved hip roof** (重檐庑殿顶).

Klaus: I see. Are these roof figures just for decoration or do they have any special meanings?

Yuan Lin: Well, both. That's what I'm going to tell you. Altogether there are ten **unique** (独特的) animals[①] standing in line at each of the roof corners. They follow an **immortal** (仙人) riding a **phoenix** (凤凰). It's the **maximum** (最大的) number of the **roof guardians** (脊兽) in ancient Chinese architecture.  In addition to the decoration, each of them has its special meaning or power. For example, the first one following the immortal is **Chiwen** (螭吻), one of the nine sons of the dragon. It's said to stop and **put out** (熄灭) fire, and the phoenix indicates the happiness and good luck to the owner, while the lion stands for the power of the owner, etc. All these animals are **associated** (关联) with either their power or characteristics, but only the emperor and his high officials were allowed to have them on their buildings.

---

① 太和殿的檐角有一个骑凤仙人（an immortal riding a phoenix）和十个走兽（龙/螭吻 Chiwen, a son of the dragon；凤 phoenix；狮子 lion；天马 heavenly horse；海马 sea horse；狻猊 Suanni, a lion-like dragon；押鱼 Yayu, a storm-summoning fish；獬豸 Xiezhi, a unicorn-like beast；斗牛 Douniu, a bull-like fighting dragon；行什 Hangshi, meaning the tenth, the flying monkey），属中国古建筑中最高规格。

The higher one's official rank, the larger the number of the roof figures. Therefore, no other buildings had more roof figures than Taihe Hall.

Klaus: Mm, very interesting. Chinese court culture is really interesting.

Yuan Lin: It certainly is. It's impossible to cover everything. The bronze crane and tortoise,

flanked on both sides of the hall, symbolize the longevity of the emperor. The **Sundial** (日晷) in front of the hall on the east indicates that the Emperor owned the highest power to grant time to all his people, while the **Grain Measure** (嘉量)

on the west shows that only the Emperor set the standard for the weights and measures in the whole country.

Klaus: Then what about the **cauldron** (大缸)?

Yuan Lin: It's used to hold the water in case of fire. Now, let's look at the hall. It has a floor area of 2,377 square meters and a height of 35 meters including the three-tiered white marble **terrace** (台基), and thus is the largest wooden building in the

palace. With 63 meters in width from west to east and 35 meters in length from north to south, the **ratio** (比例) of width to length in the rectangular hall is nine to five. Like the number "Nine", the number "Five" was also the Emperor's favorite number, as it's the middle number among the odd ones, the symbol of the **centrality** (中心). Moreover, such ratio also perfectly **accords with** (符合) the **aesthetical principles** (美学原则) in architecture. So, the ratio stands for the majesty and sovereignty in Chinese culture[①].

Klaus: So do you mean it was also built to the highest standard of architecture?

Yuan Lin: Right. Since no one is allowed to enter and too many people are around here at the main gate of the hall, let me just briefly tell you what you'll see before you're able to **edge in** (挤进) and take a closer look. It's also called the Golden Carriage Hall, the **Throne Hall** (金銮殿), which simply means what you'll see

is a unique golden throne decorated with the motif of dragons set two meters high in the center of the hall. It's the place where the enthronement of the new emperor or queen was held as well as other grand rituals and ceremonies such as the Emperor's wedding ceremony and birthday celebrations, etc.

---

① 太和殿是紫禁城诸殿中最大的一座建筑，且形制规格最高，也最富丽堂皇。大殿高 35.05 米，东西 63 米，南北 35 米，面积约为 2,380 平方米。长宽之比为 9：5，寓意为九五之尊，该比例也非常符合建筑中的美学原则。

Altogether there are 72 pillars in the hall, and among them are six massive golden ones flanking the throne. Decorated with golden dragon design, each of the six pillars is about 12 meters high with a diameter of one meter. Above the throne in the **recessed ceiling** (藻井), is a large coiled golden dragon with a silvery pearl suspended from its mouth. The pearl was supposed to be a mirror made by **Xuanyuan** (轩辕), thus called **Xuanyuan Mirror** (轩辕镜). Xuanyuan, the Yellow Emperor, has been regarded as one of the **legendary** (传说的) **Chinese sovereigns** (华夏部落首领) in ancient times. He's also known as one of the **initiators** (创始者) of Chinese civilization, numerous **inventions** (发明) and thus the **ancestor** (始祖) of all Chinese people, together with **Yandi** (炎帝), the Yan Emperor. Therefore, the mirror indicates the Emperor was the legal **descendant** (后裔) of the Yellow Emperor.

Klaus: I see. The Emperor always knew how to represent his superiority over the people.

(After Klaus comes out of the crowd of people at the gate of Taihe Hall)

Yuan Lin: Interesting, isn't it? Now we're going to visit the other two halls in the Outer Court: Zhonghe Hall and Baohe Hall. Zhonghe Hall is the place where the Emperor took a rest and **rehearsed** (演习) for ceremonies to be held in Taihe Hall. And Baohe Hall is the place where banquets and **final imperial examinations** (殿试) were held. This way, please.

Part B   Mausoleum of the First Qin Emperor

Dialogue 1

Situation: *Bo Bing is showing his American business associate Dan around the **Mausoleum of the First Qin Emperor** (秦始皇陵) in a car.*

Questions for comprehension and discussion:

★ How large is the Mausoleum of the First Qin Emperor?

★ How many laborers and artisans were involved to construct the mausoleum?

★ How old was the emperor when the construction of his mausoleum began?

★ What measures were taken to protect the tomb from being excavated by the tomb robbers?

★ What were the emperor's major achievements and evil deeds?

Bo Bing: Dan, please look to the right. Can you see the mountain range over there? It's called **Mount Li** (骊山), meaning mountains like a **galloping** (飞驰的) black **steed** (骏马). With numerous hot springs and beautiful scenery, it became the imperial resort 3,000 years ago.

Dan: Hmm, I see.

Bo Bing: Do you find anything special in this area? Can you see the grand **mounds** (土丘) there?

Dan: Yes. Are they the tombs?

Bo Bing: Exactly, they're the **grave mounds** (封冢). Now at the foot of Mount Li, we're actually entering the **Mausoleum of Qin Shihuang** (秦始皇陵), the First Emperor of the Qin Dynasty (221–206 BC). It covers a total area of about 56 square kilometers, nearly eight times of the area of the Forbidden City in Beijing. It's the first and largest imperial mausoleum in China in terms of extent and magnificence. The tomb complex was designed to mirror the urban plan of the

Qin capital **Xianyang** (咸阳) with both inner and outer cities. The inner city has a circumference of about 3.8 km while the outer runs around 6.2 km. Historical records show that the tomb construction began after the emperor took the throne at the age of 13 in 246 BC, and over 700,000 people were **enlisted** (征募) in the tomb's construction for nearly 40 years. Now the tomb still houses the coffin of the emperor and the **funerary objects** (殉葬品) underneath the imposing mound.

Dan: Is the tomb of the emperor open to the public?

Bo Bing: No, it isn't. It hasn't been really **excavated** (挖掘) yet, because it was safeguarded by **automatically triggered** (一触即发的) weapons such as **crossbows** (弩弓) and arrows to shoot at anyone entering the tomb according to the historical records. In addition, tons of **mercury** (水银) were used not only to prevent the **tomb robbers** (盗墓者) but to symbolize the rivers and sea on the earth as well.

Dan: The design was really ingenious.

Bo Bing: Yes, indeed. The emperor was named **Ying Zheng** (嬴政). He was the first emperor to unify the whole country after conquering the other six states during the **Warring States Period** (战国时期, 475–221 BC) and set up a strong **autocratic** (专制的) **centralized system** (中央集权制). He called himself as the First

Emperor, claiming that the throne should be handed down from generation to generation. With the help of his **chief minister Li Si** (丞相李斯), he undertook a series of major economic, political and cultural reforms including the establishment of **administrative prefectures and counties** (郡县制), a network of roads with the capital of Xianyang at the **hub** (中心) like ancient Rome, **standardizing the system of currency, weights and measures** (统一货币和度量衡) as well as the **Chinese characters** (汉字), etc. What's more, he had the various sections of the Great Wall, which had been built in each of the warring states, connected at the expense of numerous lives. However, he was a cruel **tyrant** (暴君) as he had many books burned and nearly 500 **Confucian scholars** (儒生) buried alive in order to secure his almighty power.

Dan: Well, horrible **tyranny** (暴行)! How could he have done that!

Bo Bing: What's worse, it's said that all the laborers and **craftsmen** (工匠) were buried alive after the tomb construction in order to keep the location and design of the tomb secret. What's more, the **concubines** (嫔妃) without children were forced to be buried to accompany the dead emperor.

Dan: Wow, it must have been really miserable for these concubines too.

Bo Bing: Definitely. Actually, up to now, over 600 tombs and pits for various people, animals and funerary objects have been discovered in the complex. The terracotta army pits, guarding the Emperor's tomb, are the most imposing **attendant pits** (陪葬坑).

Dan: That's where we are going right now, isn't it?

Bo Bing: Right. It's one mile east of the Emperor's mausoleum.

Dialogue 2

Situation: *Bo Bing and Dan arrive at the **Terracotta Army Museum** (兵马俑博物馆).*

Questions for comprehension and discussion:

★ How many pits of the Terracotta Army Museum are open to the public?

★ Which pit is the most impressive? Why?

Bo Bing: OK, here we are, the Terracotta Army Museum. Altogether there are three pits with over 8,000 life-size pottery figures now open to the public. Pit One is filled with **infantry** (步兵); Pit Two contains **cavalry** (骑兵), soldiers, archers and **chariots** (战车); Pit Three seems to be the command center with 68 high-ranking officers. The whole army is **arrayed** (排列) in **battle formation** (军阵). Here's Pit One, the most impressive one. It was discovered by peasants digging a well in 1974.

Dan: Wow, what a huge place it is! Look at all these figures, they look very real.

Bo Bing: There are almost 6,000 warriors and horses here. All of the figures were originally painted in vivid colors, but most of them **faded** (褪色) after exposure to air. And each figure is different from the others with individual details.

Dan: Yes, you're right. This warrior's hairstyle is not the same as his neighbor's, and his belt is also different. It's really fantastic. I've seen them only in the pictures before, now it's exciting to see the real ones here.

Bo Bing: Please look at this figure which is taller than the pottery infantry figures. He's dressed in a long, double-layered knee-length war robe with a colorful fish-scaled armor. He's remarkable because of the unique clothing and special **headgear** (头饰). Both his appearance and his height show his high rank. Obviously, he's one of the seven "generals or high-ranking officers" found in the pits.

Dan: He appears to be **overseeing** (监督) them.

Bo Bing: Exactly.

Part C　Confucius Temple

Monologue 1

Situation: *Bai Yu, a tour guide from Shandong CITS (China International Travel Service), is introducing Confucius to a group of German tourists on the way to the temple,* ***family mansion and cemetery of Confucius*** *(孔府、孔庙和孔林).*

Questions for comprehension and discussion:

★ What's the focus of Confucius' social philosophy?

★ What's the focus of Confucius' political philosophy?

★ What is Confucius' philosophy of education?

★ What were Confucius' Six Arts?

Hello, good morning, everyone. We're going to visit the temple, family mansion and cemetery of Confucius this morning. It'll take us at least three hours to cover the three places. It's 8:30 now, our coach will arrive at Confucius Temple in about half an hour if the traffic is not heavy. I'll take this opportunity to briefly talk about Confucius, one of the most **revered** (受尊重的) **sages** (圣贤) in China.

Confucius (551−479 BC), or as literally translated "Master Kong (Kongfuzi)", was born here in **Qufu** (曲阜), a capital in the **Lu State** (鲁国) of ancient China, 2,500 years ago before Christ, a time known as the late Spring and Autumn Period (770−476 BC). He was a great philosopher, educator, statesman as well as the founder of Confucianism. The concept of **goodness** (Ren, 仁) is the focus of his social and political philosophy. His teachings made a significant impact on the culture of China as well as other nations, especially many Asian countries like Japan, Korea, Malaysia, Singapore, etc.

1) Personal Life

It was said that Confucius was born in a royal family of the Zhou Dynasty but lived in poverty mainly with his mother. After he grew up, he became as tall as 1.9 meters and took various jobs to make a living. Though he was poor, he started to learn hard at the age of 15. He enjoyed learning from many masters including Lao Zi, the Daoist master, and soon became very **erudite** (博学多才) and **well-informed** (见多识广). He was not only good at music but also expert in many skills like shooting and chariots-riding.

At the age of 30, he set up a private school to teach common people, offering equal opportunity in education, in contrast with the schools only for the **aristocrats** (贵族) and officials then. It was said he had no less than 3,000 followers coming from different states, among which 72 were his favorite disciples.

In the meantime, he was seriously interested in politics, but it was not until he was 51 years old that he began to serve as an **official handling judicial affairs** (中都宰) in his homeland, the state of Lu. Later, he was promoted to be the **Minister of Justice** (大司寇). However, his political career soon ended at the age of 55, due to the king's life of **indulgence** (放纵) and neglect of administration. He was then forced to leave his own home and traveled with some of his followers through the other neighboring states during the following 14 years, still with a wish to publicize his political thoughts. On many occasions was he in life-threatening danger. Despite his efforts, he finally failed and returned home at the age of 68. Then he devoted the rest of his life to teaching and compiling ancient books, and was widely revered as Master Kong, though not officially recognized by the king. He passed away when he was 72. His followers established a mourning period in his honor after the funeral.

2) Social Philosophy

Living in the time of moral decline as well as the economic and political chaos caused by civil wars among **vassal states** (诸侯国) for **primacy** (首要地位), Confucius **felt obliged to** (有义务) reinforce the traditional values. His social philosophy is primarily rooted in the concept of **goodness** (Ren, 仁), especially **kindheartedness** (仁爱). It's actually a kind of **self-cultivation** (自我修养), as shown in his golden rule: "Do not do to others what you would not like done to yourself (己所不欲, 勿施于人)."

3) Political Philosophy

Confucius' political philosophy is likewise based on the concept of exercising **self-discipline**

(克己/自律) and being **subject to** (遵从) Li (ritual, 礼) which emphasizes **ritual activities** (礼仪活动), proper etiquettes, right **ethics** (行为准则) and etc. In his opinion, to have a good government, the ruler should govern his **subjects** (臣民) by practicing what he preaches and treating them with love and compassion. Thus, he should not only cultivate and carry forward his inherent **virtues** (德) but also teach and encourage others to do likewise. Good government consists of the **notion** (观念) that the ruler should be a ruler, the minister be a minister, the father be a father, and the son be a son, as hierarchical relationships should be established and respected in a government as well as in a family.

4) Philosophy of Education

Confucius devoted most of his time to education. He advocated equal opportunity in education, and initially set up a private school expanding access to education so that it was open to all common people, which broke the **monopoly** (垄断) of the schools only for the **aristocrats** (贵族) at that time. His teachings revolved around "**Six Arts**" (六艺) including **ritual, music, archery, chariot-driving, literacy** and **computation** (礼、乐、射、御、书、数), encouraging his disciples to reach perfection by self-cultivation. He emphasized the **moral ethics** (道德原则) of **goodness** (Ren, 仁), **righteousness** (Yi, 义), **ritual** (Li, 礼), **wisdom** (Zhi, 智) and **integrity** (Xin, 信). He stressed **individualized instruction** (个性化教育) according to the needs and aptitude of the learner. Each learner was encouraged to develop his own abilities. He also taught the learners to cultivate the good habit of reviewing and thinking. Many of his disciples later became high officials or famous scholars in their own states, carrying forward his teachings and thoughts. Some of them became businessmen as well.

His teachings, stressing morality, government, learning and education, were later recorded in the **_Analects_** (《论语》) by his disciples and their followers, and laid a sound foundation for the ideology of Confucianism. Since then, Confucianism has been adopted as the **dominant ideology** (主导思想) by successive rulers in China for over 2,000 years. Many **honorific titles** (尊称) were **conferred** (授予) on him by various subsequent emperors.

Due to his great contribution to the education, Confucius was **acclaimed** (拥戴) as the **Sacred Model Teacher for All Generations** (万世师表) by subsequent emperors.

I hope you may have a better idea of Confucius as well as his philosophy now. We'll be arriving at the Temple of Confucius in a minute. Please get ready to get off the coach and remember to take your belongings.

Monologue 2

Situation: *Bai Yu is showing the German tourists around the Confucius Temple.*

Questions for comprehension and discussion:
★ Why is the Temple of Confucius so well-known in the world?
★ What are the main buildings in the temple?
★ What is the temple famous for?

Here's the temple in memory of Confucius, also known as the **Temple of Great Sage** (至圣庙). It was first built as a simple shrine in 478 BC the year after his death. From then on, it has been reconstructed and expanded into an outstanding architectural complex on the model of an imperial palace owing to the support given by successive emperors. Specifically speaking, twelve emperors in history came here to offer sacrifice to him and paid homage to his disciples and 172 great masters of Confucianism as well. The current temple complex, mainly renovated in the Ming and Qing dynasties, covers an area of 140,000 square meters with 460 rooms in over 100 buildings. It's the earliest and largest of all the temples of Confucius not only in China but also worldwide. It's also one of the three largest ancient architectural complexes[①] in China, next

① 北京的故宫、曲阜的孔庙和河北的承德避暑山庄为中国已列入联合国教科文组织世界文化遗产名录的三大古建筑群。
(http://whc.unesco.org/en/list/704，http://whc.unesco.org/en/list/703)

only to the Forbidden City in Beijing.

Besides, the temple houses over 1,000 **stelae** (石碑) with numerous **inscriptions** (碑文) and carvings dating from the Han Dynasty (206 BC–220 AD). Some of these stelae recorded the imperial donations and sacrifices, the **posthumous titles** (加封谥号) conferred on Confucius, and the reconstruction process of the temple, while the others bear the inscriptions of the poems and essays written by various notable people and emperors. All these inscriptions[①] made from the 3rd century BC to the 6th century show the fascinating examples of ancient Chinese calligraphy.

In addition to the distinctive inscriptions, the most valuable ones in the temple also include **the stone reliefs of the Han Dynasty** (汉石画像), **the carved pictures of the Ming Dynasty depicting the life of Confucius** (明刻圣迹图), and **the dragon carvings of the Ming and Qing dynasties on the stone pillars** (明清石柱雕龙).

As the supreme model for all the subsequent temples of Confucius, the temple complex features a symmetrical design with a central axis through nine courtyards. It mainly consists of the main gate **Lingxing Gate** (Ling Star Gate, 棂星门), the main hall **Dacheng Hall** (Great Achievements Hall, 大成殿) housing the statue of Confucius and his 72 disciples, the highlight of the temple, **Kuiwen Pavilion** (奎文阁) for storing books and **Xing Altar** (Apricot Pavilion, 杏坛) where Confucius instructed his disciples.

The first memorial gate we're going through now is Lingxing Gate. Ling Star was believed to be the utmost important star in the sky in charge of agriculture in ancient times, so the ancient emperors often offered sacrifices for a favorable harvest. The gate was thus named to show that Confucius was as great as the star.

Here you can see that the gateway to the main hall is flanked by **cypresses** (柏树) and pines on either side showing **solemnity** (庄重) of the temple as well as the **profundity** (深奥) of Confucianism. The long **row** (一排) of **memorial gateways** (牌坊) leading to the 11th-century Kuiwen Pavilion brings you back to the Confucian period. So let's take our time to enjoy walking into the Sage's world…

---

① 这些碑刻又称汉魏六朝碑刻。

Part D　Language Checklist

A. Tourist Attractions

Tourist Attractions	中 文 名	城　市
Elysée Palace	爱丽舍宫	巴黎
Buckingham Palace	白金汉宫	伦敦
Palace of Versailles	凡尔赛宫	巴黎
The Kremlin	克里姆林宫	莫斯科
Mausoleum of Qin Shihuang	秦始皇陵	西安
Qian Mausoleum	乾陵	咸阳
Eastern Mausoleums of the Qing Emperors	清东陵	唐山
the Terracotta Army Museum	兵马俑博物馆	西安
Temple of Confucius/Confucius Temple	孔庙	曲阜
the Forbidden City	紫禁城，故宫	北京
the Gate of Heavenly Peace	天安门	北京
the Meridian Gate	午门	北京
Ancestral Temple	祖庙/太庙	北京
Altar of Land and Grain	社稷坛	北京
Taihe Hall, the Hall of Supreme Harmony	太和殿	北京
Zhonghe Hall, the Hall of Central Harmony	中和殿	北京
Baohe Hall, the Hall of Preserving Harmony	保和殿	北京
Qianqing Gong, the Hall of Heavenly Purity	乾清宫	北京
Kunning Gong, the Hall of Earthly Tranquility	坤宁宫	北京
Wenhua Hall, the Hall of Literary Glory	文华殿	北京
Wuying Hall, the Hall of Martial Valor	武英殿	北京
Inner Golden Water Bridge	内金水桥	北京
Outer Golden Water Bridge	外金水桥	北京
Golden Carriage Hall, the Throne Hall	金銮殿	北京
Lingxing Gate, Ling Star Gate	棂星门	曲阜
Dacheng Hall, Great Achievements Hall	大成殿	曲阜
Kuiwen Pavilion	奎文阁	曲阜
Xing Altar, Apricot Pavilion	杏坛	曲阜

B. Vocabulary

epic 宏大的 massive 巨大的 imposing 令人难忘的 palace complex 宫殿群 imperial residence 皇家住地 a symmetrical design 对称的设计 central north-south axis 南北中轴线 theory of Yin and Yang 阴阳理论 Five Essential Elements 五行	hierarchical system 等级制 ultimate sovereignty 至高无上的权力 autocratic tyrant 专制的暴君 centralized system 中央集权制 unification 统一 standardize the system of currency, weights and measures 统一货币和度量衡	imperial edict 圣旨 Inner Court 内廷 Outer Court 外朝 courtiers 文武百官 vassal states 诸侯国 administrative prefectures and counties 郡县
triple-eaved roof 三层檐 yellow glazed tiles 金黄色琉璃瓦顶 motifs 装饰的图案 stone relief 石刻画 balustrade 栏杆 stone pillars 石柱 roof guardians 脊兽/immortal 仙人	grave mounds 封冢 funerary objects 殉葬品 attendant pits 陪葬坑 crossbows 弩弓 mercury 水银 excavate 挖掘 enlist craftsmen/artisan 征募工匠	single-digit 个位数 double-digit 双位数 odd number 奇数 even number 偶数
honorific titles 尊称 revered 受尊重的 acclaim 称赞、拥戴 sage 圣贤 erudite 博学多才的 well-informed 见多识广 Confucian scholars 儒生	goodness 仁 righteousness 义 ritual 礼 wisdom 智 integrity 信 self-discipline 克己/自律 self-cultivation 自我修养	Six Arts 六艺： 　ritual 礼 　music 乐 　archery 射 　chariot-driving 御 　literacy 书 　computation 数 individualized instruction 个性化教育

C. Key Patterns

Characteristics of Imperial Palace 皇宫的特点	• The Forbidden City is the largest and best-preserved ancient palace complex in the world. • The Forbidden City presents the perfect example of the embodiment (体现) of such Chinese hierarchical culture (等级制文化) in architecture. 紫禁城完美地展示了中国建筑上的等级制文化。 • The Forbidden City in Beijing, China is a top UNESCO World Heritage Site. • As a masterpiece in ancient Chinese architecture, the Forbidden City has a symmetrical (对称的) design indicating a hierarchical system (等级礼制) of the urban layout (都城设计). 紫禁城是中国古代建筑的典范，整体结构对称，彰显都城设计中的等级礼制。 • Seat of supreme power for over five centuries (1416–1911), the Forbidden City in Beijing, with its landscaped gardens and many buildings (whose nearly 10,000 rooms contain furniture and works of art), constitutes a priceless testimony to Chinese civilization during the Ming and Qing dynasties. (the Forbidden City, UNESCO description) 紫禁城是中国五个多世纪以来的最高权力中心，它以园林景观和庞大的建筑群成为明清时代中国文明无价的历史见证。建筑群内有近万间房屋，里面陈列着各种家具和艺术品。 • The imperial palace was home to 24 emperors during the Ming and Qing dynasties for almost 500 years, from 1420 to 1911.

Outline of Imperial Palace 皇宫的布局	• The whole area is rectangular (长方形) in shape surrounded by a ten-meter high curtain wall (围墙) and a 52-meter wide moat. 整个建筑呈长方形，四周是一堵10 米高的围墙和一条 52 米宽的护城河。 • The whole complex was constructed along a central north-south axis (南北中轴线), which is also the axis of the old Beijing city, and was divided into two parts: the Outer Court (外朝) and the Inner Court (内廷). • Taihe Hall, Zhonghe Hall and Baohe Hall in the Outer Court are the most impressive buildings in the palace complex, while in the Inner Court, Qianqing Gong, Jiaotai Hall and Kunning Gong are the buildings mirroring (再现) those of the Outer Court on a smaller scale. 太和殿、中和殿和保和殿是故宫外朝中最为壮观的建筑，内廷的乾清宫、交泰殿、坤宁宫的建筑形态与前者相同，只不过规模较小。
Architectural Concept of Imperial Palace 皇宫的建筑理念	• According to the theory of Five Essential Elements (metal, wood, water, fire and earth) (五行学说), the west is related with the gold referring to the metal, and the north the water, hence the name Golden Water River. • The five marble bridges represent the five virtues (美德) in Confucianism (儒家思想): goodness (仁), righteousness (义), ritual (礼), wisdom (智) and integrity (信). • The ball is the symbol of the sovereignty and the unification (统一), while the lion cub refers to the fertility (繁殖力/子嗣昌盛), the everlasting succession to the imperial throne. • The Sundial (日晷) in front of the hall on the east indicates that the Emperor owned the highest power to grant time to all his people, while the Grain Measure (嘉量) on the west shows that only the Emperor set the standard for the weights and measures in the whole country.
Characteristics of Imperial Mausoleum 皇陵的特点	• It's the first and largest imperial mausoleum in China with regard to extent and magnificence. • The tomb complex was designed to mirror the urban plan of the Qin capital Xianyang (咸阳) with both inner and outer cities. • It covers a total area of about 56 square kilometers, nearly eight times that of the Forbidden City in Beijing.
Outline of Imperial Mausoleum 皇陵的布局	• The inner city has a circumference of about 3.8 km while the outer runs around 6.2 km. 内城周长 3.8 公里，外城周长 6.2 公里。 • Altogether there are three pits with over 8,000 life-size pottery figures.
Architectural Concept of Imperial Mausoleum 皇陵的建筑理念	• It was safeguarded by automatically triggered (一触即发的) weapons such as crossbows (弩弓) and arrows to shoot at anyone entering the tomb according to the historical records. • Tons of mercury (水银) were used not only to prevent the tomb robbers (盗墓者) but to symbolize the rivers and sea on the earth as well.
Characteristics of Temple of Confucius 孔庙的特点	• It's the earliest and largest of all the temples of Confucius not only in China but also worldwide. • It's also one of the three largest ancient architectural complexes in China, next only to the Forbidden City in Beijing. • The temple houses over 1,000 stelae (石碑) with numerous inscriptions (碑文) and carvings dating from the Han Dynasty (206 BC−220 AD).
Outline of Temple of Confucius 孔庙的布局	• It mainly consists of the main gate Lingxing Gate, the main hall Dacheng Hall housing the statue of Confucius and his 72 disciples, the highlight of the temple, Kuiwen Pavilion for storing books and Xing Altar where Confucius instructed his disciples. 孔庙主要设有大门棂星门、供有孔子像和其 72 位徒弟像的主殿大成殿、藏书楼奎文阁以及孔子讲学之处杏坛。

D. Historic Figures

Emperor Qin Shihuang's Achievements and Devilry 秦始皇的成就和恶行	• Emperor Qin Shihuang undertook a series of major economic, political and cultural reforms including the establishment of administrative prefectures and counties (郡县制), a network of roads with the capital of Xianyang at the hub (中心) like ancient Rome, standardizing the system of currency, weights and measures (统一货币和度量衡) as well as the Chinese characters (汉字), etc. • However, he was a horrible tyrant (暴君) as he had many books burned and nearly 500 Confucian scholars (儒生) buried alive in order to secure his mighty power.
Confucius Main Philosophical Ideas 孔子的主要哲学思想	• His social philosophy is primarily rooted in the concept of goodness (Ren, 仁), especially kindheartedness (仁爱). It's actually a kind of self-cultivation (自我修养), as shown in his golden rule: "Do not do to others what you would not like done to yourself." • He emphasized the moral ethics (道德原则) of goodness (Ren, 仁), righteousness (Yi, 义), ritual (Li, 礼), wisdom (Zhi, 智) and integrity (Xin, 信). • Confucius' political philosophy is likewise based on the concept of exercising self-discipline (克己/自律) and being subject to Li (ritual, 礼) which emphasizes ritual activities (礼制活动), proper etiquettes (礼节/仪), right ethics and etc. 孔子的政治哲学同样基于克己复礼的思想概念。礼重在礼制活动、恰当的礼仪和规范的行为准则等。 • Confucius advocated equal opportunity in education, and initially set up a private school expanding access to education so that it was open to all common people, which broke the monopoly (垄断) of the schools only for the aristocrats (贵族) at that time. 孔子倡导教育平等，首创私学，扩大教育受众，使广大平民都能接受教育，打破了当时奴隶主、贵族垄断教育的局面。

Part E   English in Use

I. Reading Comprehension

Task 1: Choose the best answer to complete each sentence below.

1. Which of the following palaces is the largest in the world now? _____
   A. Versailles Palace   B. Buckingham Palace
   C. the Forbidden City   D. The Kremlin

2. There were _____ emperors in the Ming and Qing dynasties living in the Forbidden City.
   A. 20   B. 24   C. 18   D. 22

3. It took Emperor Zhudi _____ years to have the Forbidden City built in the Ming Dynasty.
   A. 15   B. 14   C. 18   D. 20

4. Which are the three major halls in the Outer Court of the Forbidden City_____.
   A. The Hall of Supreme Harmony, the Hall of Central Harmony and the Hall of Preserving Harmony.
   B. The Hall of Supreme Harmony, the Hall of Union and the Hall of Preserving Harmony.

    C. The Hall of Supreme Harmony, the Hall of Central Harmony and the Hall of Earthly Tranquility.

    D. The Hall of Supreme Harmony, the Hall of Central Harmony and the Hall of Mental Cultivation.

5. _____ is the largest hall and the most dignified building in the Forbidden City, where grand rituals or ceremonies were held.

    A. The Hall of Central Harmony   B. The Hall of Preserving Harmony

    C. The Hall of Mental Cultivation   D. The Hall of Supreme Harmony

6. It's in the _____ that the Emperor conducted routine government affairs and held celebrations like "Banquets for a thousand elders" during the reign of Kangxi and Qianlong in the 17th-18th centuries.

    A. Hall of Preserving Harmony   B. Hall of Union

    C. Hall of Earthly Tranquility   D. Hall of Heavenly Purity

7. The first roof figure following the immortal riding a phoenix at each of the roof corners of the Halls in the Forbidden City is _____.

    A. Chiwen, a son of the dragon   B. a phoenix

    C. Suanni, a lion-like dragon   D. Xiezhi, a unicorn-like beast

8. Confucius was not only good at music but also expert in many skills like shooting and _____.

    A. horse-riding   B. chariots-riding   C. swimming   D. fencing

9. Temple of Confucius houses over 1,000 stelae with numerous inscriptions and carvings dating from the _____ Dynasty.

    A. Tang   B. Qing   C. Han   D. Jin

10. The final imperial examinations were held in the _____.

    A. Hall of Central Harmony   B. Hall of Mental Cultivation

    C. Hall of Preserving Harmony   D. Hall of Supreme Harmony

Task 2: Answer the following questions concerning the Forbidden City and the Mausoleum of Emperor Qin Shihuang in both Part A and Part B.

1. What's the unique architectural feature of the Forbidden City in Beijing?

2. Which numbers is the architecture in the Forbidden City closely related to? Why?

3. What can a tourist see in the Hall of Supreme Harmony?

4. What measures were taken to protect the tomb of Emperor Qin Shihuang from being excavated by the tomb robbers?

5. What were the Emperor Qin Shihuang's major achievements and evil deeds?

Task 3: Decide whether each of the following statements is True or False according to the introduction about Confucius and Confucianism in Part C.

1. Confucius, the founder of Confucianism, was a great philosopher, educator but not a stateman. (   )

2. Ritual, music, archery, chariot-driving, painting and computation were the "Six Arts" which Confucius required his disciples to learn. (   )

3. Confucius was forced to leave his own home and started to take a fourteen-year outbound

travel with his followers because his political ideas were not accepted by the King of Lu State. (   )

4. The saying that one should not do to others what one would not like done to oneself shows the perfect example of Confucius' social philosophy. (   )

5. Confucius attached great importance to individual education and would offer different teaching methods to different learners. (   )

II. Translation

Task 4: Translate the following sentences into English.

1. 紫禁城是世界上最大，保存得最完善的古代宫殿建筑群。
2. 紫禁城完美地体现了中国建筑上的等级制文化。
3. 整个宫殿群沿着北京城的南北中轴线布局建造，分为两大部分：外朝和内廷。
4. 从 1420 年到 1911 年，明清两朝的 24 个皇帝都曾在故宫处理朝政和居住，历时约 500 年。
5. 球象征着君权和国家的统一，幼狮寓意子嗣昌盛，皇位千秋万代。
6. 秦始皇是个可怕的暴君，为了巩固自己的强权，他焚书坑儒，烧毁了大量的书籍，活埋了约五百位儒生。
7. 孔子，儒家思想的创立者，不仅是一位伟大的哲学家和教育家，还是一名政治家。他的社会和政治哲学的中心思想是"仁"。
8. 孔庙有一千多块汉代碑碣，上面有大量的碑文和石刻。
9. 2,500 年前，孔子就出生在古代鲁国曲阜的这个地方，比耶稣基督还要早。
10. 30 岁时，孔子创办私塾，招收平民，为其提供均等的教育机会，当时的学校只有贵族才能就读。

Task 5: Translate the following sentences into Chinese.

1. The Forbidden City, rectangular in shape, covers 720,000 square meters and is the world's largest palace complex. Its curtain wall has a gate on each side and there are four corner towers, watching over both the palace and the city outside.

2. The legend has it that, at the beginning of its construction, there were supposed to be 9,999.5 rooms, only half a room less than those in Heaven or Paradise, for the number symbolized the mighty power of the Emperor slightly less superior to that of Jade Emperor or Heavenly Emperor (玉皇大帝).

3. The Sundial in front of the Hall of Supreme Harmony on the east indicates that the Emperor owned the highest power to grant time to all his people, while the Grain Measure on the west shows that only the Emperor set the standard for the weights and measures in the whole country.

4. Altogether there are ten unique animals standing in line at each of the roof corners following an immortal riding a phoenix. It's the maximum number of the roof guardians in ancient Chinese architecture, showing that it's superior to other buildings.

5. Emperor Qin Shihuang undertook a series of major economic, political and cultural reforms including the establishment of administrative prefectures and counties, a network of roads with the capital of Xianyang at the hub like ancient Rome, standardizing the

system of currency, weights and measures as well as the Chinese characters, etc.

6. The tomb complex was designed to mirror the urban plan of the Qin capital Xianyang (咸阳) with both inner and outer cities.

7. Tons of mercury were used not only to prevent the tomb robbers but to symbolize the rivers and sea on the earth as well.

8. Confucius' social philosophy is primarily rooted in the concept of goodness (Ren, 仁), especially kindheartedness (仁爱). It's actually a kind of self-cultivation, as shown in his golden rule: "Do not do to others what you would not like done to yourself."

9. The most impressive pit contains over 6,000 warrior figures, arrayed in battle formation.

10. All of the figures were originally painted in vivid colors. Some retain traces of paint, but most of them faded after exposure to air.

III. Role Play

Task 6: Play a role in any of the following situations with your partner(s).

Situation 1: You work for a China Travel Service as a tour guide. You're showing an American couple around the Forbidden City. Give a brief introduction of the largest imperial palace including its unique architectural feature. And get ready to answer any questions raised by the American couple.

Situation 2: You're showing your foreign friends around the Forbidden City. Now introduce the Hall of Supreme Harmony to them and answer any questions.

Situation 3: You're a guide from a CYTS International Travel Co. Ltd. (中青国际旅游有限公司). You're talking about Emperor Qin Shihuang, the first Chinese emperor to a group of Canadian tourists on the way to the Mausoleum of Qin Shihuang in a coach. And get ready to answer any questions raised by the tourists.

Situation 4: You have a business partner from Germany named Klaus. You're showing him around the Terracotta Army Museum. Make a dialogue with him and get ready to answer any questions.

Situation 5: You're showing your foreign friends or a group of tourists around any of the famous imperial mausoleums in China. Talk briefly about the emperor's main achievements or deeds as well as the major attractions in the mausoleum, and get ready to answer any questions.

Situation 6: You're showing a group of western tourists around the Temple of Confucius in Qufu. Talk briefly about Confucius's personal life as well as his main thoughts. And get ready to answer any questions or have a discussion with anyone interested in Confucianism.

Situation 7: You're showing your foreign friends or business partner around a Temple of Confucius in China. Talk briefly about Confucius's personal life as well as his main thoughts. And get ready to answer any questions or have a discussion with anyone interested in Confucianism.

IV. Problem-solving

Task 7: Make an analysis of the following cases, and answer the questions as required.

Case 1

Situation: Chen Yan is showing a group of tourists around a historic site. Someone in her group seems quite knowledgeable about the information she is telling her group, and disagrees with her explanation.

Question: If you were Chen Yan, what would you do?

Case 2

Situation: You're working as a guide for a tourist group in the peak season. There are crowds of people everywhere and it's impossible for you to give a detailed lecture right on the spot.

Question: What would you do then?

Module IV
Services for Shopping, Leisure and Entertainment Activities

Unit 10 Gifts and Shopping
Unit 11 Leisure and Entertainment Activities
Unit 12 Health and Wellbeing Activities

Unit 10　Gifts and Shopping

Warm-up

1. What do you consider as the representatives of China's traditional arts and crafts? Can you match them with the following pictures?

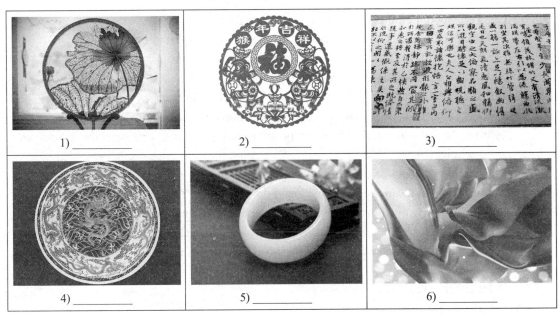

1) _____　　2) _____　　3) _____

4) _____　　5) _____　　6) _____

2. In addition to the above arts and crafts, can you name some other handicrafts?
3. What and how will you recommend a Chinese souvenir to foreign visitors or tourists?
4. What present would you give to a foreign friend or guest as a souvenir? Why?

Part A　Craftwork

Dialogue 1　Jade Bracelet

Situation: *Meng Yu, a shop assistant of a souvenir shop, is serving Adam, a British tourist in Hangzhou.*

Questions for comprehension and discussion:

★ What does Meng Yu say to Adam at first?

★ What does Adam reply?

★ What does she confirm after that?

★ What does she recommend to Adam?

★ How does she introduce it?

Meng Yu: Good morning. Is there anything I can do for you, sir?

Adam: Yes, please. Can you recommend something as a gift to my mother?

Meng Yu: Is it for her birthday?

Adam: Yes, it's going to be her birthday soon.

Meng Yu: In this case, I'd recommend you some jewels such as rings, necklaces, and **bracelets** (镯子), etc. They're all very popular among female customers.

Adam: That's wonderful. She's really interested in jewels. I'm sure she would love them.

Meng Yu: How about this bracelet? Do you like it?

Adam: Do you mean the jade one? Yes, I do. I like jade. There's lots of jade here.

Meng Yu: Exactly. In Chinese culture, jade stands for beauty, grace and purity, and people believe that wearing jade can bring good luck and keep evil away. So it's a very meaningful gift indeed.

Adam: Oh, I see. How much is it?

Meng Yu: 3,000 yuan.

Adam: It's quite expensive.

Meng Yu: That's because it's made of high-quality jade and is really elaborately made.

Adam: Well, I will take it.

Meng Yu: OK, I'll wrap it up for you.

Adam: Thanks.

Dialogue 2   Sandalwood Fan

Situation: *Lu Min, a shop assistant of **Wangxingji** (王星记), a famous fan store which was founded in 1875, is serving Linda, an American visitor in Hangzhou.*

Questions for comprehension and discussion:

★ Is Linda looking for anything in particular?

★ How does Lu Min recommend a sandalwood fan?

★ What does Linda buy?

Lu Min: Good afternoon, ma'am. Are you being served?

Linda: No. I don't know much about Chinese fans. Could you explain them a bit to me?

Lu Min: Sure. There are many kinds of fans in our shop. Our fans, namely **Wangxingji fans** (干星记扇子), have been famous as one of the three matchless products in Hangzhou in addition to silk and **Longjing** (龙井) tea since the Qing Dynasty (1636–1912). If you like, I'll be very glad to show you around our shop and explain some of the items.

Linda: Oh, that would be very nice. What's this? It's so pretty.

Lu Min: It's a **sandalwood** (檀香木) fan.

Linda: Mm, it looks quite **exquisite** (精致) and smells kind of sweet.

Lu Min: Right. The sandalwood fan is one of the four famous ones in China, the others being the **silk fan (绫绢扇)** also here in Zhejiang Province, the **bamboo-knitted fan** (竹丝扇) in Sichuan Province and the **fire painting fan** (火画扇) in Canton or Guangdong Province. The fan got its name because its **ribs** (扇架) are made out of sandalwood. The wood is famous for its pleasant **fragrance** (芳香) and often used to make perfume and incense (香). If you burn it, you can get a stronger **scent** (香味). The smell is quite **soothing** (舒心的), isn't it? So it's also used to make various kinds of Buddhist articles such as **Buddhist rosaries** (佛珠). Besides, many people use the wood as a natural **insect repellent** (驱虫剂) to keep their clothes or quilts free of **moths** (蛾子) and **bugs** (臭虫) and keep them **scented** (芳香的) at the same time.

Linda: Wow, amazing. It's made by hand, isn't it?

Lu Min: Yes, it is. The manufacturing process is rather complex, and it usually takes 45 days for an **artisan** (技工) to make just three quality fans, so it's a little bit expensive. It would be much easier and faster to produce by machine, but the patterns wouldn't be so fine and smooth.

Linda: Yes, I think it's worth every penny of its price. Well, is that West Lake on the fan?

Lu Min: Exactly. It's a **panoramic (全景的)** view of West Lake. Have you been to West Lake?

Linda: Oh yes, my hotel is just near the lake. I can take a nice walk around the lake at any time. It's beautiful. The three isles are fantastic. I love this fan.

Lu Min: Good. By the way, would you like to have a look at other paper-folding fans?

Linda: Well, who's the girl drawn on that fan?

Lu Min: Her name is **Chang'e** (嫦娥), the beautiful goddess of the Moon in Chinese legend.

Linda: Interesting, but I think I like the West Lake view better. How much is it?

Lu Min: It's 980 yuan.

Linda: Here's the credit card for 1,000 yuan. Keep the change, please.

Lu Min: Thank you, but we don't accept tips. Enjoy your time in China.

Linda: Thank you very much. Bye.

Lu Min: Bye.

Part B　Silk and Tea

Dialogue 1: Silk

Situation: *The tour guide Chen Yan is introducing the China National Silk Museum to the American group on the coach on the way to the museum.*

Questions for comprehension and discussion:

★ What does Chen Yan say to the tourists at first?

★ Where is the China National Silk Museum located?

★ How many exhibition halls are there in the museum?

★ Do you know how to choose real quality silk? What is Chen Yan's method?

Chen Yan: Good morning, everyone! Today we're going to visit a national museum in Hangzhou. Do you know what it is?

Tourist A: A silk museum?

Chen Yan: Right, the China National Silk Museum. China boasts silk, and Hangzhou was already known as "home of silk" in China about 1,300 years ago. So, the museum is a must-see place for those interested in silk. It's the first national museum dedicated to silk culture and the biggest silk museum in the world.

Tourist A: Great! That's what I am looking forward to visiting.

Chen Yan: The museum is located at the foot of **Yuhuang Hill** (Jade Emperor Hill, 玉皇山) south of West Lake. It was open to the public in 1992 with an area of about 8,000 square meters. Now covering 42,286 square meters since 2016, the museum has mainly contained five exhibition halls. You can explore the origin and development of Chinese silk through 5,000 years with the **ingenious** (设计精巧的) silk **garments** (服装) and **accessories** (配饰) from the Warring States (475–221BC) to 1949 on display. In 2009, **the Sericulture** (蚕桑业) and **Silk Craftsmanship** (丝织技艺) in **China** (中国蚕桑丝织技艺) was added to the **Representative List of Intangible Cultural Heritage of Humanity** (人类非物质文化遗产代表作名录). In the **Silkworm and Mulberry Hall** (蚕桑馆) and **Weaving Hall** (织造馆), you can see the whole process of silk production from **mulberry planting** (栽桑), **silkworm breeding** (养蚕), **silk reeling** (缫丝), **dyeing** (染色) to **weaving** (丝织). **The Silk Road Hall** (丝路馆) shows you a series of cross-cultural trade routes from China to the Mediterranean through regions of the Asian continent. And if you want to see how those precious textile relics have been restored, then go to the hall of **Textile Relics Conservation** (修复馆). What's more, you can get to know what fashion is like in the **Fashion Hall** (时装馆).

Tourist B: Sounds wonderful, I can't wait to see it. By the way, is there a souvenir shop? I want to buy some souvenirs for my friends.

Chen Yan: Yes, the souvenir shop is down at the basement of the main hall of the Silk Road Hall.

Tourist B: What kinds of silk products are there?

Chen Yan: Well, there's a wide variety of silk products, such as scarves, ties, shirts, garments, fans, umbrellas, even paintings, etc. You can make your own choice as you like.

Tourist B: Last year, my husband bought a silk shirt during his visit to China and it's great. But do you know how to choose real quality silk?

Chen Yan: Well, with the development of advanced processing techniques, it's really hard to tell which fabric is real silk or a fake one although silk has its natural **luster** (光泽). However, one quick test may be helpful to you. You can put a **flame** (火焰) to the threads of the sample fabric with a lighter. If the flame goes out immediately and the burned threads turn into ashes quickly,

then you can tell it's real. Otherwise, it's fake.

Tourist B: Why?

Chen Yan: Because silk is natural **protein fibre** (蛋白纤维) and can burn easily. In the meantime, it smells of burning hair, whereas the fake one will continue to burn and smell awful.

Tourist B: Thank you. This really helps.

Chen Yan: My pleasure. Please remember to ask for the **invoice** (发票) for quality guarantee.

Tourist B: Thanks. We'll keep your advice in mind.

Chen Yan: Great. Now here we're at the museum. We'll stay here for two hours. First, I'll show you the main halls, and then you'll have free time for yourselves. This way, please.

Dialogue 2: Tea

Situation: *Jia Su, a shop assistant of a tea-culture shop located inside the China National Tea Museum, is serving Linda, an American visitor in Hangzhou.*

Questions for comprehension and discussion:

★ What are the major categories of Chinese tea?

★ How are they divided up?

★ What are the top 10 Chinese teas?

Jia Su: Good afternoon, ma'am. What can I do for you?

Linda: I'd like to buy some good Chinese tea.

Jia Su: We have various kinds of tea, such as green tea, black tea, white tea, yellow tea, **Oolong tea** (乌龙茶), **dark tea** (黑茶), and **scented tea** (花茶) or herbal tea (药草茶). May I recommend some to you?

Linda: Yes, please.

Jia Su: The famous brands for green tea are Longjing from here West Lake Zhejiang, **Biluochun** (Green Spiral Shell, 碧螺春) from **Mt. Dongting** (洞庭山) Jiangsu province, **Maofeng** (毛峰) from Huangshan (Mt. Huang or Yellow Mountain) Anhui province, **Yunwu** (Cloud and Mist, 云雾) from Lushan (Mt. Lu) Jiangxi province, **Guapian** (Melon Seeds, 瓜片) from **Lu'an** (六安) Anhui province**,** and **Maojian** (Silvery Tip, 毛尖) from **Xinyang** (信阳) Henan province. The yellow tea is **Yinzhen** (Silvery Needles, 银针) from **Junshan Island** (君山) Hunan. The brands for **Oolong** tea are **Yancha** (Rocky tea, 岩茶) from **Mt. Wuyi** (武夷山) Fujian and **Tie Guanyin** (Ferrous Goddess of Mercy, 铁观音) from **Anxi** (安溪) Fujian. The **Qihong** (祁红) from **Qimen** (祁门) Anhui is a famous black tea brand. In a word, these are the top ten teas in China. So, which one would you like?

Linda: Oh, my goodness, so many types of tea. But I'm wondering what the differences between the various teas are.

Jia Su: Actually, they are divided according to the different ways of processing, or rather the process of **fermentation** (发酵). For example, the green tea is **unfermented** (不发酵); the white and yellow teas are slightly fermented; Oolong tea is half fermented; the black tea is totally fermented; the dark tea is **post-fermented** (后发酵的). But the scented tea or herbal tea refers to the tea reprocessed with different kinds of flowers such as jasmine, rose, **chrysanthemum** (菊花), and other herbs, etc.

Linda: Oh, I see.

Jia Su: By the way, have you visited our museum? The exhibition halls not only tell you the history of tea but also show you the enormous variety of teas grown in China.

Linda: Oh, yes, but just a quick walk around. It's a pity that I don't have enough time this time as I'll fly back home soon this evening. It's such a huge place that I couldn't take in everything within one hour, but the museum is fantastic.

Jia Su: I'm sorry that you don't have enough time to take a closer look at the exhibition of the tea. This is the right place for you to learn about some tea in China, anyway.

Linda: Yeah, I know. It's quite a pity. One of my friends asked me to buy some good Chinese tea, and I think it must be the right place to buy the **authentic** (正宗的) one. It's said that Longjing tea is the most famous Chinese green tea, isn't it?

Jia Su: Yes, right. Longjing tea is listed as No.1 in Chinese green tea, well-known for its four features — **green color** (色绿), **delicate fragrance** (香郁), **sweet flavor** (味甘) and **beautiful appearance** (形美). Here's the Longjing tea, please take a look at it.

Linda: So it's grown here in Hangzhou, isn't it?

Jia Su: Definitely. Longjing tea is grown in the mountainous area near West Lake including **Meijiawu** (梅家坞) and **Shifeng** (狮峰). This tea grown in Shifeng is the best among all the Longjing tea.

Linda: OK, I'll take it. But a moment please, is it the best quality?

Jia Su: Yes. The tea was picked before Qingming Festival around the end of March.

Linda: How much is it?

Jia Su: It's 1,000 yuan per 250 grams as it's **superfine** (特级).

Linda: Well, that's rather expensive. Do you have some other less expensive tea but still with good quality?

Jia Su: Sure. The price of the tea depends on the picking time. We have six grades of the tea: two superfine grades and four other grades. This is Grade I. These leaves were picked during the Qingming Festival in early April. They have a stronger flavor than those picked earlier but with lower price. It's only 800 yuan half kilo.

Linda: Good. Then I'll take this one. One kilo in four cans, please. Here's the VISA card.

Jia Su: OK, madam. I'll be ready in a few minutes.

Linda: Thank you very much. You've been so helpful that I've learned a lot about tea.

Jia Su: My pleasure. You're welcome to visit our museum next time.

Linda: Oh, sure. Bye-bye.

Jia Su: Bye-bye.

Monologue: Longjing Village

Situation: *The tour guide Chen Yan is introducing **Longjing Village** (龙井村) to the tourists. It's one of the major production areas of Longjing tea.*

Questions for comprehension and discussion:

★ What's the origin of tea according to some legends?

★ What does Longjing mean? Why did the name come into being?

★ Why are the 18 bushes so famous?

Now we're on the way to Longjing Village. This **time-honored** (历史悠久的) village is famous for being the source of Longjing tea which is one of the top ten teas in China. Longjing Village is located in the west of the West Lake Scenic Area, 2.5 kilometers from West Lake. It'll take us about 40 minutes to go there if traffic is smooth. Now I would like to take some time to talk about tea.

China is the origin of the numerous tea cultures throughout Asia and many other countries in the world. Tea has played an important role in our daily life. We drink tea every day and serve tea to welcome our guests as you do with coffee. But do you know how the tea came into our life?

There are several legends about the origin of the tea. According to Chinese **lore** (传说), it was **Shennong** (神农氏) who discovered tea over 5,000 years ago. Shennong, known as **Emperor Yan** (炎帝), was regarded as one of the Chinese **forefathers** (祖先) together with **Emperor Huang** (黄帝). He was believed to have invented many tools in farming and **practiced medicine** (行医) by testing over various kinds of **herbs** (植物). One day, while he was boiling water in a pot, some leaves fell from a nearby tree. To his surprise, the **brew** (煮过的水) tasted good, and he soon felt **refreshed** (清醒的) after trying some **poisonous** (有毒的) plants. After studying the tree leaves, he found that one could **digest** (消化) better, think quicker, sleep less, move lighter, and see clearer by drinking the brew which is now known as tea.

Another saying is related with the Indian monk **Bodhidharma** (菩提达摩), the founder of Chinese Chan. Bodhidharma came to China during the 5th and 6th centuries, and finally settled down in Shaolin Temple on **Mount Song** (嵩山) in Henan Province. He spent nine years **sitting in meditation** (坐禅) without sleeping, facing the wall in a cave. One day, he was so sleepy that he cut off his eyelids and threw them to the ground near him to be able to continue the meditation. Then a plant grew out of the place where his eyelids were. When feeling **drowsy** (瞌睡的) again, he happened to chew the tree leaves to keep himself awake. This plant was later called tea. From then on, all his **disciples** (弟子) and other monks **followed suit** (学样) to keep refreshed while meditating by drinking tea. Since the ultimate goal of practicing Chan is to achieve Buddha nature which is pure, peaceful, quite similar to the soothing, refreshing features of tea, it's believed that **drinking tea is practicing Chan** (禅茶一味). Therefore, tea has become an **indispensable** (不可缺少的) part of daily life for Buddhists who have played a major role in the spread of tea across China and the other parts of the world as well. By the way, it was from the then largest Chan temple **Jingshan Temple** (径山寺) which was to the southwest of Hangzhou proper about 700 years ago that the Japanese Buddhists brought tea leaves back to Japan, hence the famous Japanese Tea Ceremony — **Cha Dao** (茶道).

No matter what the legends are, the first historical records of tea date back 3,000 years when tea was drunk as a **tonic** (补药) or medicine. By the Tang Dynasty, tea culture was popular throughout the country. **Lu Yu** (陆羽, 733–804), known as the **Tea Master** (茶圣), wrote the world's first book about tea *The Classics of Tea* (《茶经》) which systemized its production and traditions. The golden era for tea production in China was the Song Dynasty (960–1279), especially the Southern Song Dynasty when

Hangzhou served as the capital. The green tea which was produced near West Lake like the

present Longjing Village was a **tribute** (贡品) to the emperors, hence the custom of sending top quality Longjing Tea to the authorities every year. Now you've made the right choice to come to see how the green tea is produced. Generally speaking, in terms of the process of fermentation, Chinese tea can be divided into six varieties — green, white, yellow, Oolong, black and dark tea. The scented tea is the tea reprocessed with various kinds of flowers such as jasmine, rose, **chrysanthemum** (菊花), **osmanthus** (桂花), etc. The green and white teas are non-fermented; the yellow one is lightly fermented; Oolong tea is half-fermented; the black one is totally fermented; the dark is post-fermented.

Longjing tea is known as the best green tea in China for its unique features — green color, delicate fragrance, sweet flavor and beautiful appearance. It's named after the well-known **Dragon Well** (Longjing, 龙井) in the temple in the village. The well was believed to lead to the sea where the dragon lived for it never dried up even during the **drought** (干旱). The dragon was regarded as the god of rain who could **bless** (保佑) people against the drought. As

a matter of fact, regardless of the folklore, the well is located in an irregular **limestone** (石灰岩) region which is rich in water with perfect weather and is surely the right place for growing quality tea. So now the word "Longjing (Dragon Well)" refers more to the tea than to the well itself.

In addition to the Dragon Well, the other must-see attraction in the village is the famous **18 Imperial Tea Bushes** (18 棵御茶树) which is closely associated with Emperor Qianlong. Emperor Qianlong loved tea so much that he once said he could not live a day without drinking tea. The emperor had been to Hangzhou at least six times. According to folklore, during his third visit, one day he came to the **Hugong Temple** (胡公庙) at the foot of **Mount Shifeng** (狮峰山). The monk from the temple presented him a cup of Longjing tea. Fascinated by the green tea, the emperor started to pick the tea leaves in front of the temple. Just then, he

received a message that his mother was ill and requested him to return to Beijing. Putting the tea leaves in his sleeves, he quickly went back to the palace in Beijing. Later, it was not until the **Empress Dowager** (皇太后) asked about the smell from his sleeves that he remembered the tea leaves and had them brewed for her. After drinking the tea, the dowager felt much better because it was very **conducive to her digestion** (有助消食). The emperor was so delighted

that he issued an order that the tea from the 18 bushes in front of the Hugong Temple should be sent to the palace as a yearly tribute. Since then, no common people have had the chance to try the special tea from the 18 tea bushes.

Now we're in the area of Longjing Village. You can see the rows of tea bushes line up the hillside and the villagers picking up tea leaves and **buds** (幼芽) in their straw hats. It usually takes an experienced picker one day to pick about two kilos of fresh tea leaves which can only be made half a kilo of dry tea. Longjing tea falls into different grades mainly according to the picking time. The best tea picking time is from late March to April, the earlier, the better. The

best quality tea, picked in late March, contains one tea leaf and one tea bud. As the leave looks like a flag and the bud a gun, this kind of tea is known as **Qiqiang** (Flag and Gun, 旗枪) type. Half a kilo of this superfine dry tea contains around 40,000 leaves and buds. Another typical type of quality tea with two leaves and one bud, usually picked during the mid-April, is known as **Queshe** (Bird's Tongue, 雀舌). What's more, the 10 special handmade tea-making skills were inscribed in 2008 on the list of China National Intangible Cultural Heritage of Humanity.

Well, in front of us is the Dragon Well, we'll first stop there to see what the well is like, and then go to see the 18 bushes. Finally, we will try our hands at picking some tea leaves and enjoy a cup of tea in a tea farmer's home. If you like, you can also buy some Longjing tea directly from any of the villagers. OK, here we are. This way, please…

Part C Traditional Chinese Painting and Calligraphy

Part of *Dwelling in the Fuchun Mountains* (《富春山居图》局部) by *Huang Gongwang* (黄公望, 1269−1354)

Questions for comprehension and discussion:
★ What are the two main styles of Chinese painting?
★ What are the most popular subjects in Chinese landscape painting?
★ What are the five major **scripts** (书写体) of Chinese calligraphy?

Painting and **calligraphy** (书法) are regarded as the highest art forms in China. Together with **Qin** (Chinese zither, 古琴/筝) and **Weiqi** (Chinese go/chess, 围棋), they were regarded as two of the four kinds of **artistry** (技艺) for the **literati** and **scholars** (文人雅士) to achieve for self-cultivation in ancient times.

1. Traditional Chinese painting

Traditional Chinese painting is famous for its original style and distinctive national features in the world. It's done with a soft brush, ink or **pigments** (颜料) on **absorbent** (吸水的) **Xuan paper** (宣纸) or silk, and is also known as ink-and-wash painting. With a history of over 2,000 years, Chinese painting has developed into two major styles in terms of technique — Gongbi, **meticulous** (工笔) style and Xieyi, **freestyle** (写意).

Meticulous style features close attention to detail and fine brushwork. Freestyle is a fundamental approach to Chinese painting. It stresses **Yijing,** the **artistic conception** (意境) created by the artist who, with his or her **perception** (洞察力) or understanding of the subject, freely used various lines and **strokes** (笔画) together with brush and ink techniques.

1) Subjects in paintings

In terms of subject matter, Chinese painting can be mainly classified as **figure or portrait** (人物肖像) painting, **landscape** (风景画) painting, and flower-and-bird painting.

The figure painting has a long history which can be traced back to the Shang and Zhou period (商周, 1600–256 BC) or even earlier the **Neolithic Period** (新石器时代). It began to develop during the **Wei, Jin and the Northern and Southern Dynasties** (魏晋和南北朝, 220–589) and **flourished** (兴盛) in the Tang Dynasty (618–907). With the introduction and development of Buddhism as well as the **burgeoning** (快速发展) of Daoism (Taoism), the figure paintings at that time were mainly characterized by religious themes such as **Jataka** (佛本生经) which has various stories about Buddha in his previous lives; portraits of Buddha, **Bodhisattvas** (菩萨), **arhats** (罗汉), Daoist gods and different immortals were thus quite common. The range of subject matter in portrait painting was extended far beyond religious themes during the Song Dynasty (960–1279). The royal family members and nobles were often portrayed in the paintings at that time. More common people were found in the paintings too.

Landscape painting and flower-and-bird painting started to develop in the 4th century and **boomed** (繁荣) during the 6th and 9th centuries. The Song Dynasty saw the peak of landscape painting, influenced by Chinese philosophy—harmony of human and nature. Flower-and-bird painting is derived from decorative art. It already became an independent **genre** (类型) in the Tang Dynasty and reached its zenith during the Song Dynasty. The subject matter in this genre covers a variety of flowers, plants, fruits, birds, animals, insects, fish, etc.

2) Aesthetic values (审美观)

The traditional Chinese ink-and-wash painting differs from that of Western oil painting because of different philosophies and aesthetic values. Characterized by scientific representation, the traditional Western painting tended to **depict** (描画) the real world or reality with fine natural details and exact **proportion** (比例). However, the traditional Chinese painting stressed the **harmonious** (物我融化的) artistic conception which is the **spiritual quality** (精神表现) or the **symbolism** (象征意义) of the object appreciated by the artist who was deeply influenced by the philosophy of the **harmony of human and nature** (天人合一).

Symbolism is often seen in Chinese painting. In the eyes of the artist, all the subjects could be associated with certain human personalities. For example, the **bamboo** (竹), **orchid** (兰), **plum** (梅) and **chrysanthemum** (菊) are regarded as the **Four Noble Ones** (四君子), as they represent the four **virtues** (美德) of an ideal gentleman respectively. The bamboo symbolizes **uprightness** (刚直) and **modesty** (谦虚); the plum blooming in the winter is acclaimed for its **dignity** (高贵) and grace; the orchid stands for an **elegant** (幽雅的) and modest character; the chrysanthemum indicates graceful and unyielding quality. Besides, the pine, bamboo and plum are known for their **indomitable** (坚忍不拔的) spirit in the winter and are thus regarded as "**the**

three friends in winter (岁寒三友)".

It was **Gu Kaizhi** (顾恺之，约 348−409), a noted artist in the Eastern Jin Dynasty (317−420), who first put forward the **esthetic** (美学的) **viewpoint** of **presenting the spiritual quality of the object** (以形写神) instead of just copying the exact one. Gu's notion of **resemblance in spirit** (神似) laid a good foundation for the development of traditional Chinese painting.

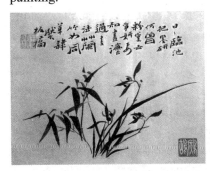

Therefore, the subject in a traditional Chinese painting doesn't look exactly the same as the original object; it goes beyond the real one and comes to life, and is characterized by the artist's individual perception. Thus, the presentation of the same subject in the paintings portrayed by different painters varies greatly. For instance, the bamboo in the paintings of **Zheng Banqiao** (郑板桥，1693−1765), an outstanding artist in the Qing Dynasty, is greatly different from the one in the other painters' paintings.

3) **Composition** (构图) and brush and ink techniques

The traditional Chinese artists' painting techniques and composition varied from those of Western **counterparts** (同时期的艺术家) in terms of composition and use of the painting tools. In Chinese painting, lines were not **merely** (仅仅) used to depict the appearance of the object but its spiritual quality as well. In order to represent the subject in mind, a Chinese artist preferred to make full use of various kinds of lines and strokes together with brush and ink techniques without concern for the light source and the setting from one **focal point perspective** (焦点透视)

as a Western painter would do. The artist also used different **shades** (阴暗层次) of ink and types of strokes rather than the degree of light and shades to show the liveliness of the object, and sometimes the proportion of the object might not be as exact as it should be. And the contrast of white and black is most common seen in the painting with the black subject in the white background. In addition, many Chinese artists favored a technique which is currently said to be similar to "**multi-point perspective** (散点透视) " to achieve a **panoramic view** (全景) of a place. A typical example is the **genre painting** (风俗画) *Riverside Scene at Qingming Festival* (《清明上河图》) painted by **Zhang Zeduan** (张择端，1085−1145), a famous royal artist in the Northern Song Dynasty. Besides, the absorbent Xuan paper or silk adds a flavor to the uniqueness of Chinese painting.

Another **distinctive** (独特的) feature of Chinese painting is the perfect combination of poetry, calligraphy, **seal engraving** (印章篆刻) and painting. The four elements complement each other and are thus **indispensable** (不可或缺的) for the painting. The achievement of "painting in poetry and poetry in painting" has been regarded as one of the **criterion** (标准) for excellent works. The **stamp** (印记) in red is not only the artist's **signature** (签字) but also an essential **touch** (修饰) to liven it up. The **inscription** (题词) or poem on the painting indicates the inspiration for the artist or the background information for the artwork. It's

characterized by the artist's individual calligraphy in the **blank** (空白) and makes a perfect composition for the whole painting.

In short, deeply influenced by traditional philosophy, traditional Chinese painters enjoyed a good reputation for their unique brush and ink techniques to express their **conception** of the subject.

2. Chinese Calligraphy

As beautiful and artistic handwriting, calligraphy is one of the ancient visual art forms in China. Its development lies in the **evolution** (演变) of Chinese characters which is the process of **simplification** (简化) from the inscriptions on the **oracle bones** (甲骨), bronzes or stones to the five core scripts such as the **seal script** (篆书), **clerical script** (隶书), **regular script** (楷书), **cursive script** (草书), and **semi-cursive script** (行书).

1) Origin of Chinese script

Legend has it that the inventor of Chinese script was **Cang Jie** (仓颉), the **official historian** (史官) of the Yellow Emperor. With four eyes, he was **inspired** (受启发的) to create the **pictographic** (象形文字的) script after observing birds and other animals' tracks in the snow, the **textures** (纹理) of **tortoise shell** (龟壳) on the back, the landform, the sky, human **palm print** (掌纹), etc. The **divine revelation** (神圣启示) of his invention was so extraordinary and **startling** (令人吃惊的) that all the **ghosts** (鬼) and gods were frightened.

No matter what the legend is, Chinese calligraphy was originally not different from painting as both are derived from **pictograph** (象形文字) at least 3,000 years ago. Historical records show that Chinese characters can be traced back to the **oracle bone inscriptions** (甲骨文) during the Shang Dynasty (1600−1100 BC), a popular script containing pictograph. During that time, the bones or tortoise shells were often used for **divination** (占卦) by the rulers. Most oracle inscriptions show the **records of divination** (卜辞). Currently, about 4,000 **graphs** (图形) have been found on the remaining oracle bones, among which over 2,500 can be recognized.

2) Main features of Chinese calligraphy

Like painting, calligraphy employs the same tools — writing brush, ink, **ink slab** (砚台) and paper, known as **Four Treasures of the Study** (文房四宝). It not only emphasizes brush and ink techniques but also the **revelation** (启示) and **self-expression** (个性表现) of the artist as painting features. No one's calligraphy is exactly the same as another's. Thus, there's a saying that one's personality can be seen from his or her calligraphy.

Chinese characters may be made of pictographic, **ideographic** (表意的) and **phonetic** (语音的) elements. Each character consists of a group of strokes arranged in a set order. Another unique feature of calligraphy is that each of the strokes can be mentally **retraced** (回想), stroke by stroke. That is to say, the viewer is able to observe the subtle **nuances** (细微差别) of **execution** (创作): whether a stroke was made swiftly or slowly, and whether the brush was handled with great **delicacy** (精美) or force, and so on.

3) Five scripts of Chinese calligraphy

The seal script evolved from the inscriptions on oracle bones and brass, and can be divided into the **great seal script** (大篆) and the **small seal script** (小篆). The former one with more pictographic characters was common during the Zhou period (周朝，1046−256 BC). The latter one was **transformed** (改变) from the former one in the Qin era (秦朝，221−206 BC) under the requirement of the standardization of the writing system given by the Emperor Qin, the first unifier and emperor of China. The characters are less pictographic, and their forms are still slightly round but **vertical rectangular** (竖直矩形的). All the characters are well structured and balanced.

The clerical script is said to have been improved by a **clerical official** (文书官员) in the late Qin period, and reached its mature state during the Han Dynasty (汉朝，207 BC−220 AD). The curving characters in the seal script were changed to be square but slightly flat, which made the writing more easily, especially on the stones, **wooden or bamboo slips** (木牍或竹简). Moreover, the characters became more abstract (抽象) than the previous ones. As a great reformation of Chinese script, the clerical script is another turning point in the development of calligraphy in China, from which the regular, cursive and semi-cursive scripts have mainly developed almost at the same time.

The regular script reached its peak during the Tang Dynasty. Unlike the clerical script, the horizontal strokes of every character extend slightly upwards instead of **tilting** (倾斜) at the end,

and the character looks square but less heavy. Now it's the standard script for all the learners to copy.

The cursive script and semi-cursive script are actually the simplified clerical scripts for hasty writing. They were **modified** (改进的) to make the writing easier and quicker. Many strokes have been reduced, **distorted** (变形) and joined together to offer more freedom and **fluidity** (流畅) in writing. The semi-cursive script is also known as "walking" or "running" script. Since it's not as **dramatic** (夸张，狂放) as the cursive script, nor as regular as the standard script or clerical script, its nature falls between the rectangular scripts (regular script and clerical script) and the cursive script. It can well developed during the Jin Dynasty (265−420) while the cursive script matured in the Tang Dynasty about 400 years later.

Part D　Language Checklist

A. Vocabulary

embroidery 刺绣 hand embroidery 手工绣 double-sided embroidery 双面绣 tapestry 挂毯 satin 缎子	folding fan 折扇 mandarin fan 宫扇 silk fan 绢扇 paper-cutting 剪纸 dough figurine 面人	meticulous style 工笔 freestyle 写意 ink-and-wash painting 水墨画 figure/portrait painting 人物/肖像画 landscape painting 山水画 flower-bird painting 花鸟画
stone carving 石雕 wood figurine 木雕 jade carving 玉雕 color modeling 彩塑	Cloisonné (vase) 景泰蓝 (花瓶) porcelain 瓷器 lacquerware 漆器	bamboo 竹 orchid 兰 plum 梅 chrysanthemum 菊
fermented tea 发酵茶 half-fermented tea 半发酵茶 unfermented tea 非发酵茶	oracle bone inscriptions 甲骨文 seal script 篆书 clerical script 隶书 regular/standard script 楷书 cursive script 草书 semi-cursive script 行书	pictograph 象形文字 wooden slips 木牍 bamboo slips 竹简 divination 占卜 inscription 题词
antique 古董 national treasure 国宝	genuine 真的 fake 仿制的	nonrefundable 概不退换 refundable 可退换

B. Key Patterns

Greeting 问候	• Is there anything I can do for you?/Anything I can do for you? • Are you being served? • Are you being attended to? • Have you been taken care of? • Can I help you? • May I help you? • What can I do for you?
Inquiring Preference 询问喜好	• Which shirt (fan) do you like? • What size (color, kind…) do you want? • Do you like this size (color, kind…)? • What about these (those)? • What else would you like? • There's a wide variety of silk products here, such as scarves, ties, shirts, garments, even paintings, etc. You can make your own choice as you like.
Introducing Silk 介绍丝绸	• China boasts silk, and Hangzhou was already known as "home of silk" in China about 1,300 years ago. • According to legend, Leizu (嫘祖), wife of the mythical Yellow Emperor about 5,000 years ago, first introduced silkworm breeding (养蚕) and invented the loom (织布机).

Introducing Silk 介绍丝绸	<ul><li>The Sericulture (蚕桑业) and Silk Craftsmanship (丝织技艺) in China was inscribed in 2009 on the Representative List of Intangible Cultural Heritage of Humanity. 中国蚕桑丝织技艺于 2009 年被列入人类非物质文化遗产代表名录。</li><li>The Four Famous Embroideries of China refer to the Xiang embroidery in central China's Hunan Province, Shu embroidery in western China's Sichuan Province, Yue embroidery in southern China's Guangdong Province, and Su embroidery in eastern China's Jiangsu Province. 中国"四大名绣"是指产于中国中部湖南省的"湘绣",中国西部四川省的"蜀绣",中国南部广东省的"粤绣"和中国东部江苏省的"苏绣"。</li><li>Xiang embroidery is well known for its time-honored history, excellent craftsmanship and unique style. The earliest piece of Xiang embroidery was unearthed at the No. 1 Tomb of Mawangdui, Changsha City of the Han Dynasty. 湘绣向来以历史悠久,工艺精湛,风格独特而闻名海内外。迄今为止发现的最早的湘绣制品,是长沙马王堆一号汉墓出土的一件丝织品。</li><li>Xiang embroidery uses pure silk, hard satin, soft satin and nylon as its material, which is connected with colorful silk threads. With the spirit of Chinese paintings, the embroidery reaches a high artistic level. 湘绣主要以纯丝、硬缎、软缎、透明纱、尼龙等为原料,配以各色的丝线、绒线绣制而成。它以中国画为神,达到很高的艺术境界。</li><li>You can test the silk by putting a flame (火焰) to the threads of the sample material with a lighter. If the flame goes out immediately and the burned threads turn into ashes quickly, then you can tell it's real. Otherwise, it's fake.</li></ul>
Introducing Tea 介绍茶	<ul><li>According to Chinese lore, it was Shennong (神农氏) who discovered tea over 5,000 years ago.</li><li>Lu Yu (陆羽, 733–804), known as the Tea Master (茶圣), wrote the world's first book about tea *The Classics of Tea* (《茶经》) which systemized its production and traditions.</li><li>We have various kinds of tea, such as green tea, black tea, white tea, Oolong tea (乌龙茶), yellow tea, dark tea (黑茶) and scented tea (花茶).</li><li>The top 10 teas in China: Green tea: West Lake Longjing, Zhejiang; Biluochun (Green Spiral Shell, 碧螺春), Jiangsu; Maofeng (毛峰) and Guapian (Melon Seeds, 瓜片), Anhui; Yunwu (Cloud and Mist, 云雾), Jiangxi; Maojian (Silvery Tip, 毛尖), Henan Yellow tea: Yinzhen (Silvery Needles, 银针), Hunan Oolong tea: Yancha (Rocky tea, 岩茶) and Tieguanyin (Ferrous Goddess of Mercy, 铁观音), Fujian Black tea: Qihong (祁红), Anhui</li><li>Longjing tea is listed as one of the top 10 teas in China. 龙井茶是中国十大名茶之一。</li><li>Longjing tea is the best green tea in China for its unique features — green color, delicate fragrance, sweet flavor and beautiful appearance.</li><li>Green tea is good for one's digestion. And it can also help one dispel the heat and quench (解渴) his or her thirst in summer. 绿茶有助于消化,夏天喝绿茶还能消暑解渴。</li><li>Green tea can also help one lose weight. 绿茶也能帮人减肥。</li><li>Longjing tea falls into different grades according to the picking time. The best tea picking time is from late March to April.</li><li>The special handmade tea-making skills for Longjing tea was included in 2008 on the list of China National Intangible Cultural Heritage of Humanity. 西湖龙井茶炒制技艺于 2008 年荣获中国国家非物质文化遗产称号。</li></ul>

Introducing Tea 介绍茶	• **The steps for making Kung Fu tea** (泡功夫茶的步骤)： （1）Smell: Smell the tea with a deep breath. Good tea should have a strong fragrance. 闻：深呼吸闻茶叶香。上等的茶叶应该有浓浓的茶香。 （2）Tea pot warming: Fill the empty tea pot with boiled water, and then pour the water into the tea-washing tray. 暖茶壶：把开水倒入空茶壶，再将水倒入洗茶具的托盘。 （3）Fill with tea leaves: Use a tea spoon to fill the teapot two thirds full with leaves. 放茶叶：用茶匙将茶叶放进茶壶，达到其容量的三分之二。 （4）Tea warming: Fill the pot to the brim with boiled water, shave the tea bubble with a bamboo stick, then decant the tea into each cup for cup-warming. 暖茶：用开水倒满茶壶，用竹筷撇去泡沫，然后轻轻地把茶水倒进每只杯中暖杯。 （5）Making tea: Fill with hot water, instead of boiled water. 泡茶：注入热水而不是开水。 （6）Watering teapot: Cover the tea pot, and then pour the boiled water over it to keep the same temperature both inside and out. 淋茶壶：盖上壶盖，然后用开水倾泻壶身以保证壶内外的温度一致。 （7）Tea cup warming: Wash the cups with the water used for tea-warming. 暖杯：用暖茶水清洗杯子。 • China is home to tea. Before the Tang Dynasty, Chinese tea was exported by land and sea, first to Japan and Korea, and then to India and Central Asia and to the Arabian Peninsula in the Ming and Qing dynasties. In the early period of the 17th century, Chinese tea was exported to Europe, where the upper class adopted the fashion of drinking tea. 中国是茶的故乡。早在唐代以前，中国生产的茶叶便通过陆运及海运的方式远销各地。首先到达日本和韩国，然后传到印度和中亚地区，明清时期，又传到了阿拉伯半岛。17世纪初期，中国茶叶又远销至欧洲各国，很多上层社会的贵族、绅士因此都养成了喝茶的习惯。
Introducing Painting 介绍绘画	• With a history of over 3,000 years, Chinese painting has developed into two major styles in terms of different techniques — Gongbi, meticulous (工笔) style and Xieyi, freestyle (写意). • In Chinese painting, lines were not merely (仅仅) used to depict the appearance of the object but its spiritual quality as well. • Meticulous style features close attention to detail and fine brushwork. Freestyle stresses the harmonious (物我融化的) artistic conception (意境). • In terms of subject matter, Chinese painting can be mainly classified as figure or portrait (人物肖像) painting, landscape (风景画) painting, and flower-and-bird painting. • Gu Kaizhi (顾恺之，约 348−409) first put forward the esthetic (美学的) viewpoint of presenting the spiritual quality of the object (以形写神) instead of just copying the exact one. • Gu's notion of resemblance in spirit (神似) laid a good foundation for the development of traditional Chinese painting. • Symbolism is often seen in Chinese painting. The bamboo (竹), orchid (兰), plum (梅), and chrysanthemum (菊) are regarded as the Four Noble Ones (四君子), as they represent the four virtues (美德) of an ideal gentleman respectively. • The presentation of the same subject in the paintings portrayed by different painters varies greatly.
Introducing Calligraphy 介绍书法	• As the beautiful and artistic handwriting, calligraphy is one of the ancient visual art forms in China. • The development of Chinese calligraphy lies in the evolution (演变) of Chinese characters which is the process of simplification (简化). • Legend has it that the inventor of Chinese script was Cang Jie (仓颉) with four eyes, the official historian (史官) of the Yellow Emperor.

Introducing Calligraphy 介绍书法	• Historical records show that Chinese characters can be traced back to the oracle bone inscriptions (甲骨文) during the Shang Dynasty (1600–1046 BC), a popular script containing pictograph. • The five core scripts are the seal script (篆书), clerical script (隶书), regular script (楷书), cursive script (草书), and semi-cursive script (行书). • Like painting, calligraphy employs the same tools — writing brush, ink, ink slab (砚台) and paper, known as Four Treasures of the Study (文房四宝). • It not only emphasizes brush and ink techniques but also the revelation (启示) and self-expression (个性表现) of the artist as painting features. • Another unique feature of calligraphy is that each of the strokes can be mentally retraced (回想), stroke by stroke.
Introducing Other Handicrafts 介绍其他手工艺品	• It is said that wearing precious jade ornaments brings good luck. 据说佩戴宝玉饰品可以得到好运。 • Fujian bodiless lacquerware, Beijing cloisonné and Jingdezhen porcelain are known as the "three treasures" of traditional Chinese handicrafts. 福建脱胎漆器、北京景泰蓝和景德镇瓷器被称为中国传统工艺品中的"三大珍器"。 • Cloisonné is well-known traditional enamelware with a history that dates back more than 500 years. It's often called the "Blue of Jingtai" for two reasons. First, blue is the most commonly used color in enameling, and secondly, cloisonné became prevalent during the reign of Jingtai (1450–1456) in the Ming Dynasty. 景泰蓝是著名的传统珐琅工艺品，有五百多年的历史。得名"景泰蓝"的原因有两个：一是其釉料颜色以蓝色为主，二是这项工艺兴盛于明朝景泰年间。 • Kite-making has a history of over two thousand years in China. The earliest kites were made of wood in the shape of a hawk, thus being called wooden hawks. 风筝制作在中国有两千多年的历史。最早的风筝是木制的，形状像鹰，叫木鹰。 • Paper cutting is a traditional Chinese decorative art. The earliest known paper cuts in China date back to the Tang Dynasty (618–907). 剪纸是中国传统装饰工艺。有史记载的最早剪纸出现在唐朝（618–907）。 • Seal plays an important role in Chinese culture, and has been for official and private use in the last 3,000 years. The earliest example of seal comes from the Shang Dynasty (1600–1046 BC) ruins at Anyang. 印章在中国文化发展中起着重要的作用，三千年来一直被官方和私人所使用。最早的印章实物发现于安阳殷墟，是商代（公元前1600—公元前1046年）物品。

Part E   English in Use

I. Reading Comprehension

Task 1: Choose the best answer to complete each sentence below.

1. —Is there anything I can do _____ you?

   —Yes. I am looking for something as a gift to my wife.

   A. to   B. by   C. for   D. with

2. _____ from Anhui is a famous black tea brand.

   A. Qihong (祁红)   B. Yunwu (Cloud and Mist)

   C. Yancha (Rocky tea, 岩茶)   D. Maofeng (毛峰)

3. Cloth made with silk is _____ for its lightness and beauty.

    A. name   B. famous   C. interesting   D. free

4. The famous brand for yellow tea from Hunan is _____.

    A. Yinzhen (Silvery Needles, 银针)

    B. Guapian (Melon Seeds, 瓜片)

    C. Biluochun (green spiral shell, 碧螺春)

    D. Tieguanyin (Ferrous Goddess of Mercy, 铁观音)

5. Sericulture and Silk Craftsmanship in China was ascribed in _____ on the Representative List of UNESCO Intangible Cultural Heritage of Humanity.

    A. 2008   B. 2009   C. 2010   D. 2011

6. Chinese tea can be divided into different _____ according to different ways of processing.

    A. tastes   B. colors   C. categories   D. names

7. There's a wide _____ of silk products in our shop.

    A. kind   B. variety   C. number   D. many

8. The whole process of silk production includes _____, silkworm breeding, silk reeling, dyeing and weaving.

    A. mulberry planting B. pine planting   C. cypress planting   D. silk planting

9. China is an original _____ of tea and is renowned for its skills in planting and making tea.

    A. producer   B. master   C. writer   D. teacher

10. The Four Famous Embroideries of China refer to Xiang embroidery, Yue embroidery, Shu embroidery and _____.

    A. Hu embroidery B. Jing embroidery C. Zhe embroidery D. Su embroidery

Task 2: Answer the questions concerning the introduction of Longjing Village delivered by Chen Yan in Part B.

1. According to Chinese lore, how did Shennong (神农氏) find the tea?
2. What was Lu Yu (陆羽) famous for?
3. How is Longjing tea graded?
4. Why are the 18 tea bushes called the imperial ones?
5. What are the main functions of Longjing tea?

Task 3: Decide whether each of the following statements is True or False according to the passage in Part C.

1. Traditional Chinese painting mainly falls into two schools in terms of different subjects. (   )

2. Wang Xizhi, a noted artist in the Eastern Jin Dynasty, first put forward the esthetic viewpoint of resemblance in spirit in Chinese painting. (   )

3. Like Western painting, traditional Chinese painting also stressed the scientific representation of the real world with fine natural details and exact proportion. (   )

4. One of the distinctive features of Chinese painting is the perfect combination of poetry, calligraphy, seal engraving and painting. (   )

5. The seal script, clerical script, regular script, cursive script, and semi-cursive script are regarded as the five core scripts of Chinese characters. (   )

II. Translation

Task 4: Translate the following sentences into English.

1. 中国丝绸博物馆是那些对丝绸感兴趣的人必去的地方。
2. 这里有各种丝绸产品，如丝巾、领带、衬衫、服装、扇子、伞、丝绸画等。您可以挑选自己喜欢的。
3. 我们店里还有檀香扇，很受顾客欢迎。
4. 我们有各种茶，如绿茶、红茶、白茶和乌龙茶。您想要哪种？
5. 龙井茶是中国最好的绿茶，以其色绿、香郁、味甘和形美而著称。
6. 杭州以出产丝绸而闻名。
7. 这只风筝产自"风筝之都"潍坊。
8. 让我向您推荐这块石雕吧。
9. 这只镯子由上好的玉制成，并且做工精细。
10. 要是您愿意，我很乐意带您参观我们店。

Task 5: Translate the following sentences into Chinese.

1. This sandalwood fan is quite exquisite, and smells pleasant and soothing.
2. It's a lacquer screen with traditional Chinese painting.
3. This sandalwood fan will surely satisfy you.
4. The jade ring is more expensive than the silver ring and the gold ring.
5. We also have some silk scarves. There are many colors for you to choose from. It's thirty yuan a piece.
6. I recommend you to buy some Chinese artwear, such as embroidery, silk painting, silk figurine, carved work, porcelain, and hand painted work, etc.
7. With a history of over 3,000 years, Chinese painting has developed into two major styles in terms of different techniques — Gongbi, meticulous style and Xieyi, freestyle.
8. Like painting, calligraphy employs the same tools — writing brush, ink, ink slab and paper, known as Four Treasures of the Study.
9. It's said that wearing precious jade ornaments can bring good luck.
10. The Xuan paper is a kind of high-quality white paper and is especially good for traditional Chinese painting and calligraphy.

III. Role Play

Task 6: Play a role in the following situation with your partner(s).

Situation 1: Your western friend wants to buy some special local products. Make a recommendation.

Situation 2: You're a shop assistant in an arts and crafts shop in your local area. A foreign visitor comes in and asks for some souvenirs. Recommend him or her some of the articles in your shop.

Situation 3: You're a tour guide introducing silk to your tourist group.

Situation 4: You're a tour guide showing a foreign group around the China National Silk Museum.

Situation 5: You're a tour guide showing an American couple around Longjing village.

IV. Problem-solving

Task 7: Make an analysis of the following cases, and answer the questions as required.

Case 1

Situation: A foreign tourist comes in a silk shop and complains that the silk scarf she has bought here is not made of pure silk. The fact is that the silk scarf is real, but the foreigner doesn't believe so.

Question: What would you do if you were the shop assistant?

Case 2

Situation: Liu Hen, a shop assistant at a tea shop. A foreign tourist comes in and wants to return several cans of Longjing tea he has just bought here because there are shops selling some similar kinds of tea at a much lower price. You know the fact that your price is very reasonable and that the foreigner doesn't really understand how to select good Chinese tea.

Question: Suppose you were Liu Hen, what would you do then?

Answers for Reference

Unit 11 Leisure and Entertainment Activities

Warm-up

1. Have you ever been to any theme parks in your hometown or in China? What do you think of them? Are they interesting? Will you take foreign tourists there? Why or why not?
2. What are the famous ancient towns in China? How many towns have you been to? Which town would you like to show your foreign tourists first? Why?
3. Do you like Peking Opera? What about Shaoxing Opera? How will you introduce Peking Opera or Shaoxing Opera briefly to your foreign tourists?

Part A Theme Parks

*The following introduction is adapted from the article "**Eight Most Popular Theme Parks in China**," Global Focus on Travel, People's Daily Online, March 7, 2010, retrieved on Oct. 25, 2012[①].*

Question for comprehension and discussion:

★ Do you know the following theme parks both in Chinese and English? Where are they located in China?

1) _____   5) _____   3) _____

4) _____   5) _____   6) _____

---

① from http://english.peopledaily.com.cn/90001/90782/92900/6911240.html

7) _____

8) _____

9) _____

In the last few decades, China has opened a dizzying array of theme parks. People can enjoy themselves no matter how old they are. The followings are eight of the most popular theme parks in China.

1) Xishuangbanna Dai Ethnic Garden (西双版纳傣族园)

The Dai Ethnic Garden is in **Ganlan basin of Xishuangbanna area** (西双版纳橄榄坝), 30 kilometers away from **Jinghong** (景洪) city. Located in Yunnan Province in the southwestern part of China, Xishuangbanna is famous for its mysterious tropical **rainforests** (热带雨林), wild animals, and ethnic minorities.

In the garden, there's an original Dai village. The villagers are all hospitable and friendly. Tourists are welcome to stay overnight with a Dai family and join them in their daily work.

2) Hong Kong & Shanghai Disneyland (香港/上海迪士尼)

Located on **Lantau Island** (大屿山), Hong Kong Disneyland opened on 12th September, 2005. It's Disney's fifth "Magic Kingdom" park, and the first theme park in China. It consists of four themed lands similar to other Disneyland parks: **Main Street, U.S.A.** (美国大街), **Fantasyland** (奇幻世界), **Adventure Land** (冒险世界), and **Tomorrow Land** (明日世界).

Shanghai Disney Resort, opened on June 16, 2016, is the first Disney Resort in mainland China and the second in China after Hong Kong Disneyland. Based on the hub-and-spoke (轴辐式) design pioneered by the original Disneyland in California, this "Magic Kingdom" park also ranks third in Asia and sixth in the world featuring some major differences.

As the main part of the resort, Shanghai Disneyland Park covering an area of 116 hectares is divided into six areas with different themes, characters and activities. They are **Mickey Avenue** (米奇大街), **Gardens of Imagination** (奇想花园), **Fantasyland** (梦幻世界), **Adventure Isle** (探险岛), **Treasure Cove** (宝藏湾), **Tomorrowland** (明日世界).

Everyone can have fun in this park and enjoy the various Disney characters and the spectacular shows, or take part in exciting activities like a **rafting ride** (漂流) at Roaring Mountain (雷鸣山), an exciting **voyage to the Crystal Grotto** (晶彩奇航) that goes underneath **Enchanted Storybook Castle** (奇幻童话城堡), or a heroic battle with pirates in **Treasure Cove** (宝藏湾), or even flying a **jet pack** (喷气背包飞行器) high above the skies of Tomorrowland, etc.

3) Beijing Happy Valley (北京欢乐谷)

Occupying an area of 560,000 square meters, Beijing Happy Valley is a large theme park in China. It consists of seven zones: **Wild Fjord** (峡湾森林), **Atlantis** (亚特兰蒂斯), **the Lost**

Maya Kingdom (失落的玛雅), **Aegean Harbor** (爱琴港), **Shangri-La** (香格里拉), **Desserts World** (甜品王国) and **Happy Time** (欢乐时光). Depicting selected mysterious cultures of the world, it covers a wide range of topics in addition to various kinds of recreational facilities. Full of fantasy and spectacle, Happy Valley is a great place for the youngsters and those young at heart.

4) Window of the World (世界之窗)

Window of the World, featuring a wide variety of replicas, is situated at Shenzhen. Here you can see stunning replicas of the world's wonders, historical heritages and famous scenic sites. Shenzhen Window of the World has a lot more to offer. You'll have a good time in this miniature world.

5) Qingming Shanghe Park (清明上河园)

The park is modeled after a famous Chinese scroll painting entitled "***Qingming Shanghe Tu*** (*Riverside Scene at Qingming Festival*,《清明上河图》)". The painting is one of the most renowned paintings in Chinese history. This long watercolor silk landscape scroll was created by the royal artist Zhang Zeduan to depict the daily life of people in the Northern Song period (960−1127) in the capital, **Bianjing** (汴京), today's **Kaifeng** (开封).

In honor of the famous painting, the city Kaifeng has built a modern theme park containing reproduced traditional restaurants, shops, and bridges. Besides, the theme park hosts a large live show featuring Song Dynasty **rituals (仪式)**, attracting thousands of tourists each year. The Theme park has been ranked as a National AAAAA Class Scenic Spot.

6) Tang Paradise Lotus Park (大唐芙蓉园)

Near the Big Wild Goose Pagoda, Tang Paradise Lotus Park is located in the **Qujiang Resort** (曲江新区), southeast of Xi'an, Shaanxi Province (陕西省).

Divided into 12 scenic regions with respective themes, this park covers approximately 66.7 hectares (667, 000 square meters), about one-third of which is water. It claims to be the biggest cultural theme park in northwestern China and the first imperial garden with a full display of the **heyday** (全盛时期) of the Tang Dynasty (618−907).

7) Horticulture Expo Garden (世界园艺博览园)

Although **the International Horticultural Expo** (国际园艺博览会) ended in 1999 in Kunming, the capital city of Yunnan Province, the Horticulture Expo Garden has become a scenic spot with many exotic flowers and plants.

The Horticulture Expo Garden is a first-class garden with typical Chinese features of architecture. In the garden, there are five large exhibition halls: China Hall, the Man and Nature Hall, the Green House, the Science and Technology Hall, and the International Hall.

8) Hengdian World Studios (横店影视城)

Located in the town of **Hengdian** (横店), **Dongyang** (东阳) City in central Zhejiang Province, Hengdian World Studios is often called "Chinese Hollywood".

There are 13 **movie sets** (影视拍摄基地) and two ultra-large modern **studios** (摄影棚) in the total area of more than 30 square kilometers. All of the studio settings are open to the public as theme parks. Visitors can view the movie sets, watch movie stunt projects, or even shoot their own films.

Monologue: Song (Dynasty) Town

Situation: *The tour guide Chen Yan is introducing the Song (Dynasty) Town to a group of Canadian tourists on the coach on the way to the theme park in Hangzhou.*

Questions for comprehension and discussion:
★ Where is Song Town?
★ Is it the largest theme park of Song culture in China?
★ What kind of life can the tourists experience in this town?

We're now on the way to the Song Town in the southwestern part of the West Lake scenic area, near the Qiantang River. Song Town or **Songcheng** (宋城) in Chinese is actually a large theme park in Hangzhou. It's presently the second largest theme park of Song culture in China next only to the **Qingming Shanghe Park** (清明上河园) in Kaifeng, Henan Province with similar design.

Since Hangzhou once served as the capital of the Southern Song Dynasty (1127–1279) for about 150 years, this town, in addition to those historical sites such as the **site of the Imperial City of the Southern Song** (南宋皇城遗址), is also the right place for you to get an idea of what the life was like almost a thousand years ago. So a unique **slogan** (口号) has been created for the town as: Give us one day and we'll give you one thousand years. That's a fascinating thought, isn't it?

Covering an area of over 5 hectares, the town presents an interesting display of people's life in the Song Dynasty as shown in the well-known painting *"Riverside Scene at Qingming Festival* (《清明上河图》)" by **Zhang Zeduan** (张

择端，1085–1145), a noted royal artist of the Northern Song Dynasty.

The town has many streets lined with various shops, stores and restaurants with traditional colorful **banners** (旗幡). Strolling through the town and seeing all the people working there in traditional Song costumes, you might feel as if you were in an ancient world. And if you would like to, you can also wear costumes for free or rent some fancy ones. You can enjoy watching the **street juggling** (街头杂耍) and **acrobatics** (杂技) and, if you're lucky, you might also be chosen as the fiancé of **Landlord Wang** (王员外)'s daughter. That is, if you're single.

Well, this part of a popular custom in some areas of old China. It was customary then for the daughter of a rich family to choose **Mr Right** (意中人) by casting down from her own room upstairs an **embroidered ball** (绣球) to the right person among all the **wooers** (求婚者). The lucky one who caught the ball would be the fiancé. So if you're single, just go there and give it a try.

What's more, there are dozens of grand live shows, the highlight of which is called "***Romantic Show of Songcheng*** (《宋城千古情》)" in the Grand Theatre. It presents not only the history of Hangzhou such as the hardships of **Liangzhu ancestors** (良渚先民), the splendor of Song Palace, the tragedy of **Yue Army (岳家军)** and modern charming Hangzhou, but two beautiful love stories as well. One is about the love between **Lady White** (白蛇娘子) **transformed** (变身) from a white snake and a **mortal man** (凡人) called **Xu Xian** (许仙); the other is known as the Chinese story of Romeo and Juliet — the story about the butterfly lovers.

With hundreds of actors and actresses, the show now attracts an audience of more than 10 million every year, from home and abroad. Since its **debut** (首场演出) in 1997, over 78 million have seen the show.

With modern techniques, it's one of the three great shows in the world, together with the "***Moulin Rouge*** (《红磨坊》)" in Paris and the "*O Show*" in **Las Vegas** (拉斯维加斯). You'll watch the show soon. Hope you'll have fun.

OK, here's Song Town. Please take your personal belongings and follow me.

Part B   Ancient Towns

Questions for comprehension and discussion:

★ Can you name the following ancient towns both in Chinese and English according to the following introductions?

1) _____   2) _____   3) _____

4) _____   5) _____   6) _____

7) _____   8) _____   9) _____

Ancient towns and villages in China are the places where traditional Chinese culture is well preserved. You can see the earliest bank in **Pingyao** (平遥) in northern China, and see **Hakka Tulou** (客家土楼), the unique round houses in southeastern China, as well as the **Hui-style buildings** (徽派建筑) at **Hongcun** (宏村) and **Xidi** (西递) near Mount Huang, Anhui Province. In addition, you can also experience the traditional lifestyle of ethnic minorities, such as that of **Naxi ethnic group** (纳西族) in Lijiang in Yunnan. The following offers a brief introduction to the most well-known ancient towns in China.

Pingyao: "Pingyao is an exceptionally well-preserved example of a traditional Han Chinese city, founded in the 14th century. Its **urban fabric** (城镇格局) shows the **evolution** (演变) of architectural styles and town planning in imperial China over five centuries. Of special interest are the imposing buildings associated with banking, for which Pingyao was the major centre for the whole of China in the 19th and early 20th centuries." (*Ancient City of Pingyao*, UNESCO description)

Lijiang (丽江): With a history of about 1,000 years, Lijiang Old Town in **Dayan** (大研) is an **exceptional** (独特的) ancient town in China. Together with **Pingyao Ancient City** (平遥古城) in Shanxi, **Langzhong** (阆中) in Sichuan, and **Shexian** (歙县) in Anhui, it's one of the four best preserved ancient cities in China. Renowned for its outstanding ancient urban landscape, it has been a UNESCO's World Heritage Site since 1997.

Wandering along the **Square Street** (四方街) or any other **cobbled** (铺鹅卵石的) alleys lined with historical wooden houses, unique cafés, and **souvenir shops** (纪念品店) of traditional ethnic minorities, you'll be deeply impressed by the **harmonious fusion** (完美融合) of different cultural traditions as well as the magnificent ancient **water-supply system** (供水系统). In addition, **Mufu** (Mu's Palace, 木府) is also a must-see place.

Xidi & Hongcun Ancient Villages (西递和宏村): Lying at the southern foot of the Mount Huang, Xidi and Hongcun are **graphic illustrations of a typical Hui-style settlement** (徽派古民居建筑的典型代表) founded in the Ming and Qing dynasties in China. They are on the list of UNESCO World Heritage Sites as the "Ancient Villages in Southern Anhui". "Their street plan, their architecture and decoration, and the **integration** (融合) of houses with **comprehensive water systems** (完备的供水系统) are **unique** (独特的) surviving examples." (*Ancient Villages in Southern Anhui — Xidi and Hongcun*, UNESCO description)

Fujian Tulou: Fujian Province is noted for its unusual **dwellings** (住处) called **Tulou** (土楼, Earthen Fortress-like Buildings). These large round buildings, capable of housing several hundred people, were built as a **fortress** (堡垒) against the outsiders by the **Hakka** (客家人), a branch of Han nationality. The famous Fujian Tulou buildings including those in **Yongding** (永定) and **Nanjing** (南靖) were designated as a UNESCO World Heritage Site in 2008 and enjoy international prestige.

Dialogue: Wuzhen

Situation: *A tour guide named Tong Li is showing a small group of international tourists around Wuzhen, an old town in the north of Zhejiang Province.*

Questions for comprehension and discussion:

★ Where is Wuzhen? How old is Wuzhen?

★ What is Wuzhen mainly famous for?

★ How many celebrities did Tong Li mention? Who are they?

Tong Li: Well, we're now in Wuzhen, an old town in the north of Zhejiang Province, with a history of 1,300 years. There are many old river towns like Wuzhen here in the south of the **Yangtze River Delta** (长江三角洲) known as "**Jiangnan** (江南)". All of them have old bridges, streets, lanes and houses built on the river. But among them, Wuzhen is one of the six best-preserved ancient towns① in Jiangnan and is thus one of the first ten famous historical and cultural towns as well as one of the ten most charming towns in China.

Besides, Wuzhen is renowned for the **International Internet Exhibition & Convention Center** (互联网国际会展中心) and the **International Theatre Festivals** (国际戏剧节). At the entrance, you can find the **Sixth World Internet Conference** (第六届世界互联网大会) and **Light of the Internet Expo** (互联网之光博览会) have just been held here.

Luckily, the 10-day 7th International Theatre Festival is still going on now. The festival consists of the **Specially Invited Plays** (特邀剧目), the **Young Theatre Artists Competition** (青年竞演),

and the **Outdoor Carnival** (古镇嘉年华) etc. Drama lovers from near and far have been coming to enjoy the **festivities** (节庆活动) here. So, in addition to many theaters, the whole area now is a large outdoor stage for people to enjoy themselves during the theatre festival.

Barbara: That's a feast for the eyes! We're here at the right time, aren't we?

Tong Li: Yes, definitely. But we have to stick together so that we don't get lost among the crowds. Let's go in. Follow me, please.

(*After entering the gate*)

The whole town is **crisscrossed** (纵横交错) by the network of rivers and is divided into four zones in four directions. The main river runs through the whole town from west to east. Both the **Eastern Zone** (东栅) **and Western Zone** (西栅) are the tourist attractions and boast the original style of a typical river town in **Jiangnan** (江南) with rich cultural

---

① Six best-preserved ancient river towns in the south of the Yangtze River Delta (Jiangnan,江南) are Zhouzhuang (周庄), Tongli (同里), Luzhi (角直), Xitang (西塘), Wuzhen (乌镇) and Nanxun (南浔).

background. The **Western Zone** (西栅), covering an area of three square kilometers, is the most attractive place, and that's where we're staying.

Now we're passing the remarkable **Wuzhen Grand Theatre** (乌镇大剧院) where many world-known plays are performed in turn, day and night. Well, here's good news for you, we'll come back and see the Russian play "**The Karamazovs** (卡拉马佐夫兄弟)" there this evening at 6:00 pm.

Barbara: Wow, that's cool! Can't wait!

Tong Li:

Yeah, we'll have a lot to see today. Well, next to the grand theatre on the right is **Muxin Art Museum** (木心美术馆) in memory of Muxin (木心，原名孙璞，1927–2011), a celebrated artist, writer and poet who was born here in Wuzhen. But Muxin suffered a lot after being imprisoned during the

Cultural Revolution ("文化大革命"). Despite the imprisonment, he continued to write. Later, he moved to New York and became a Chinese American in 1980s. In 2001，he held his successful large-scale solo exhibition in the **Yale University Art Gallery** (耶鲁大学美术馆), the **Art Institute of Chicago** (芝加哥艺术博物馆), **New York Asian Association Art Museum** (纽约亚洲协会美术馆) and etc. This simplistically modern museum was designed by the disciples of **Ieoh Ming Pei** (贝聿铭)，the designer of the Louvre in Paris.

Actually, Wuzhen is home to many other celebrities like **Maodun** (茅盾，原名沈德鸿，1896–1981), another noted contemporary writer in China. He's best known for his masterpiece "*Midnight*" (《子夜》). But his other best seller "***The Lin's Shop***" (《林家铺子》) depicts the life of people in Wuzhen, which helps make the old town well-known. **Maodun's**

Memorial Hall (茅盾纪念堂) is just opposite the river. But his former residence is in the Eastern Zone, so is Muxin's former residence.

Since there's a nonstop international carnival going on here today, let's first walk through the ancient streets to enjoy the festivities including street plays and

contemporary performance (当代表演) as well as some traditional Chinese operas. Then if we have some time, we can come back to visit Muxin's Art Museum and Maodun's Memorial Hall.

(Half an hour later when the dancing parade is past and the street is less crowded, they stop at a bridge.)

Tong Li: Thank goodness, it's a bit quieter here. Now, please look at those old houses along the street. Do you know how old these houses might be?

Jim: About a hundred years old?

Tong Li:

Well, not exactly. Most of them are still in the original style of the Ming and Qing dynasties (1368–1911) from the 14th century to 20th century. So, many of them may be at least over 100 years old. The interior decoration of some houses is magnificent, and the carvings of stone, brick and wood on the beams, columns, doors and windows are very **exquisite** (精美).

Walking along the street, you may find it's a living museum displaying unique scenery, historic sites, handicraft workshops, classical exhibition halls, religious buildings as well as folk customs. However, unlike the other old towns, the whole area now is equipped with modern, convenient facilities for tourists such as sightseeing boats, water buses, direct drinking water, star-rated public restrooms, Wi-Fi system and smart parking management, etc. Moreover, it offers living space for vacationers. There's a wide range of furnished accommodations including various resort hotels together with a number of fully equipped conference or business centers. All the accommodations have been reconstructed from the folk houses and now are operated by the same tourist company.

Jim: That's rather convenient. I wish I could stay here for a couple of days and just relax.

Tong Li: Yes, you could. We'll stay at a resort hotel here tonight and enjoy ourselves. Now here's the highest bridge with a very interesting name. Can you guess what it might be? Well, it's called **Promotion Bridge** (定升桥) which means anyone crossing it may surely have the chance of getting promoted, isn't that cool?

Jim: Yes, it is. Let's cross it. I do wish I could get promoted in the near future.

Tong Li: Yeah, you should. And, you may have a nice view of the river with houses while standing on the highest point on the bridge.

Barbara: Thanks. The bridges are beautiful. By the way, how many bridges are there in this town?

Tong Li: It's said there used to be over 120, but now there are 72 in this area. Of all the ancient towns in China, there are the most bridges and rivers here. Many of them were built in the Ming or Qing Dynasty with the earliest existing one rebuilt in 1518 and 1718. Now we're heading for the most beautiful bridges in this area.

(After a while)

OK, here we are. Please look at the two bridges. Can you tell the differences between these two bridges?

John: Let me see. This bridge crosses the river from west to east, and the other bridge runs from north to south. Is that right?

Tong Li: Right. The two bridges almost join at a right angle, being only 10 meters apart at one end. Each of the two bridges can be seen through the arch of the other, so the place here is called "Bridge within a Bridge".

Barbara: This is the right place to take a picture.

Tong Li:

Sure. The one crossing the river from south to north is called **Renji Bridge** (仁济桥) which means a bridge of goodness while the other one from west to east is named **Tongji Bridge** (通济桥) meaning a bridge of convenience. Both names, as well as those of other bridges here, express the local people's good wishes.

Barbara: I see. By the way, how long is the waterway between the two old streets here?

Tong Li: It's about 1.8 kilometers long, and it joins the Grand Canal (京杭大运河) just about one or two hundred meters ahead of us. We're standing here on the **wharf** (码头) and opposite us is the **Water Theatre** (水剧场).

Well, we're approaching the end of the old streets where **Wenchang Pavilion** (文昌阁) and **Guandi Temple** (关帝庙) are located. Wenchang Pavilion is an academic venue for scholars to **enshrine** (奉祀) and worship **Wenchang God (文昌帝君)**, a god in charge of scholarly honor and official rank.

In feudal times, before the competitive imperial examination, the candidates would come to Wenchang Pavilion to pray for successful academic achievements and career. Guandi Temple was built in honor of a **deified** (神化的) former general of **Shu Kingdom** (蜀国) named **Guang Yu** (关羽) who was noted for his **loyalty** (忠义) together with virtue and **valor** (勇猛). He lived in the Three Kingdoms period nearly 1,800 years ago. Therefore, both Wenchang Pavilion and Guandi Temple are called

Wenwu Temple (Civil and Military Temple, 文武庙) which can be seen almost everywhere in China, not just here in Wuzhen.

Well, now let's turn back and go down the street westward to the Lotus Square with the tower. This tributary stream also joins the Grand Canal …

Part C   Chinese Operas

Dialogue: Shaoxing Opera/Yue Opera (绍兴/越剧)

Situation: *The tour guide Chen Yan is recommending a famous Shaoxing Opera called "Liang Shanbo and Zhu Yingtai" to an American couple.*

Questions for comprehension and discussion:

★ Why does Chen Yan recommend Shaoxing Opera to the couple?

★ What's the story of Liang Shanbo and Zhu Yingtai?

Chen Yan: Do you have any plan for tomorrow evening?

Mark: Not really. Do you have any suggestion?

Chen Yan: Well, there's a wonderful traditional Chinese play in the Grand Theatre tomorrow evening. I'm wondering whether you would be interested in it.

Sue: Really? Is it Peking Opera?

Chen Yan: No, it's Shaoxing Opera. It's a local Chinese opera quite popular in the southern regions of the Yangtze River. It originated in the current area of Shaoxing, an old well-known tourist town in the south of Zhejiang Province. Since ancient time, Zhejiang belonged to the **Yue State** (越国), and the local opera was popularly known as **Yue Opera** (越剧). Yue Opera has a history of about 80 years.

Sue: Well, that's very interesting. We've never seen a local opera other than the Peking Opera. I can't wait to see it.

Chen Yan: So, we can go tomorrow.

Mark: Will we be able to understand it since it's all in Chinese?

Chen Yan: No, I'm afraid not. It's sung in local **dialect** (方言) and may not be understood by people from other areas of the country. But it's very popular in Zhejiang, especially in the countryside during the festivals such as Spring Festival. Many people love to enjoy the open-air performances whether there's a place to sit or not.

Sue: Interesting. By the way, I've heard that the Chinese opera was performed only by males like Peking Opera, is that true?

Chen Yan: Originally Yue Opera was only performed by males and then changed to all female performances. Since 1949, male and females have worked together.

Mark: What is tomorrow's play about then?

Chen Yan: It's a Chinese love story of Romeo and Juliet. The couple are named **Liang Shanbo** (梁山伯) and **Zhu Yingtai** (祝英台). They're called the Butterfly lovers because they died for love and then turned into a pair of butterflies.

Sue: That's beautiful!

Chen Yan: In the story, Liang Shanbo and Zhu Yingtai are three-year classmates in a  private school in Hangzhou, which you can still visit in the south of our city. Since it was not easy for a girl to study at school at that time, Zhu Yingtai, the girl, disguises herself as a male student. Later, the two become very good friends, and Zhu Yingtai falls in love with Liang Shanbo. However, when Liang learns the truth and hurries to Zhu's family to make an offer of marriage, he finds Zhu's father has promised to marry her to Ma Wencai, the son of a rich family. With grief and indignation, Liang, **lovesick** (相思的), dies. As Zhu **kneels** (跪着) crying in front of Liang's tomb, the tomb opens, and Zhu jumps into it, and then the two lovers turn into a pair of fluttering butterflies.

Monologue: Peking Opera

The following monologue is adapted from the brief introduction of Chinese Opera (http://www.travelchinaguide.com/intro/arts/chinese-opera.htm) combined with an excerpt from the introduction of Peking Opera (http://www.shme.com/culture/opera/peking.htm, retrieved on Oct. 20, 2011).

Questions for comprehension and discussion:
★ When did Peking Opera start?
★ Which opera is Peking Opera derived from?
★ Why is it known as China's national opera?
★ What are the main features of Peking Opera?

It's said that Chinese Opera, together with **Greek tragic-comedy** (希腊悲喜剧) and **Indian Sanskrit Opera** (印度梵剧), is one of the three oldest dramatic art forms in the world. According to the historical record, **Tang Xuanzong** (唐玄宗, 685−762), the emperor of the Tang Dynasty (618−907), once had an opera school established with the poetic name Liyuan (Pear Garden). From then on, performers of Chinese opera have been referred to as "**disciples of the Pear Garden** (梨园弟子)". Since the Yuan Dynasty (1271−1368), Chinese opera, known as **Zaju** or **Varieties** (杂剧) then, has been encouraged by court officials and emperors of different generations and has thus become a traditional art form.

There are dozens of famous traditional operas among hundreds of local ones, such as Peking Opera, **Kun Opera** (昆曲), **Shaoxing Opera** (绍兴越剧), **Huangmei Opera** (黄梅戏), **Yue Opera** (粤剧), **Chuan Opera** (川剧), **Ping Opera** (评剧), etc.

Known as China's national opera, Peking Opera or Beijing Opera, which began in the late 18th century, is one of the most **influential** (有影响力的) operas in China and is thus usually considered as the **representative** (代表) of Chinese opera overseas.

Based upon traditional Anhui Opera, Peking Opera has its own **distinct** (鲜明的) dramatic style by adopting **repertoire** (保留剧目), music and performing techniques from Kun Opera and **Qin Opera** (秦腔), as well as some traditional **folk tunes** (民间曲调) in its development. Its repertoire includes historical plays, comedies, tragedies, and **farce**s (滑稽剧). Many historical events are adapted into Peking Opera plays.

Peking Opera is unique with **singing, speaking, acting, acrobatic fighting** (唱、念、做、打), and symbolic **visual effects** (视觉效果). It can be divided into "**civil**" pieces (文戏), which are characterized by singing and speaking, and "**martial**" **ones** (武戏), which feature acrobatics and **stunts** (特技). Some operas are the combination of both.

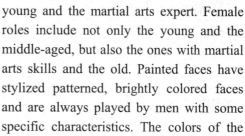

There are four main role types in Peking Opera: the **male** (Sheng, 生), the **female** (Dan, 旦), the **painted face** (Jing, 净), and the **clown** (Chou, 丑), which are further classified by age and profession.

Male roles can be divided into three categories: the old, the

young and the martial arts expert. Female roles include not only the young and the middle-aged, but also the ones with martial arts skills and the old. Painted faces have stylized patterned, brightly colored faces and are always played by men with some specific characteristics. The colors of the painted faces symbolize the individual character's personalities. For example, red represents loyalty and **righteousness** (正义); white suggests a **crafty** (狡猾的) and **suspicious** (多疑的) character; black shows a courageous, **upright** (正直的) and **rough** (粗鲁的) **disposition** (性格); green indicates a brave and **irascible** (暴躁的) nature; blue means uprightness and an **unyielding** (不屈的) character;

brown is often the symbol of a stubborn and **obstinate** (固执的) character. Clown roles are marked by a **dab** (一点) of white on the ridge of the nose. This character is sometimes positive, kind-hearted and humorous, but sometimes negative, **crafty** (狡猾的), **malicious** (恶毒的) or silly. Each role has its fixed singing and acting styles.

The **orchestra** (乐队), playing **stringed** and **percussion instruments** (弦乐器和打击乐器), accompanies the singing, which follows a fixed pattern with a variety of **melodies** (旋律) and **rhythms** (节奏). The **Jinghu** (京胡), a small two-strings bowed instrument, is the backbone of the orchestra.

In addition to singing, the actors and actresses use **well-established** (固定下来的) movements, such as smoothing a beard, adjusting a hat, **jerking a sleeve** (甩袖) or raising a foot, to express certain emotions and meaning.

In a word, as an important part of Chinese culture, Peking Opera is the **fruit** (成果) of the hard work of numerous artists over the past two centuries.

Part D   Language Checklist

A. Tourist Attractions

Tourist Attractions	中 文 名	所在地
Xishuangbanna Dai Ethnic Garden	西双版纳傣族园	景洪，云南
Hong Kong Disneyland	香港迪斯尼乐园	香港
Beijing Happy Valley	北京欢乐谷	北京
Window of the World	世界之窗	深圳，广东
Qingming Shanghe Park	清明上河园	开封，河南
Tang Paradise Lotus Park	大唐芙蓉园	西安，陕西
International Horticultural Expo Garden	世界园艺博览园	昆明，云南
Hengdian World Studios	横店影视城	东阳，浙江
Song Town	宋城	杭州，浙江
Lijiang Ancient Town	丽江古镇	云南
Pingyao Ancient Town	平遥古镇	山西
Tongli Ancient Town	同里古镇	江苏
Yongding, Nanjing Round House	永定、南靖土楼	福建
Hongcun & Xidi Ancient Villages	宏村、西递村	安徽
Wuzhen	乌镇	浙江
Zhouzhuang	周庄	江苏
Luzhi Ancient Town	角直古镇	江苏

B. Vocabulary

theme park 主题公园 well-preserved 保存完好的 well-established 固定下来的 tourist attraction 旅游热点 tourist destination 旅游目的地	renowned 有名望的 well-known 闻名的 masterpiece 杰作 representative 代表性的 unique 独特的 influential 有影响的	repertoire 全部剧目 folk tune 民间曲调 live show 现场表演秀 street juggling 街头杂耍 stunt 特技 acrobatics 杂技 farce 滑稽戏
Greek tragic-comedy 希腊悲喜剧 Peking Opera 京剧 Kun Opera 昆曲 Qin Opera 秦剧 Shaoxing/Yue Opera 绍兴/越剧	orchestra 乐队 stringed instrument 弦乐器 percussion instrument 打击乐器	facial makeup 脸谱 the male 生 the female 旦 the painted face 净/花脸 the clown 丑

personality 个性 characteristics 性格特征 introverted 内向的 extroverted 外向的	uprightness 正直 loyalty 忠诚 courageous 勇敢的 innocent 无辜的 honest 诚实的	crafty 狡猾的 malicious 恶毒的 dissolute 放荡的 stubborn 固执的 obstinate 倔强的

C. Key Patterns

Introducing a Theme Park 介绍主题公园	• Shanghai Disneyland Park covering an area of 116 hectares is divided into six areas with different themes, characters and activities. They are Mickey Avenue (米奇大街), Gardens of Imagination (奇想花园), Fantasyland (梦幻世界), Adventure Isle (探险岛), Treasure Cove (宝藏湾), Tomorrowland (明日世界). • Epcot theme park (未来世界主题公园), one of four Theme Parks at Walt Disney World Resort, sprawls across 300 acres — twice the size of Magic Kingdom theme park — and is divided into Future World and World Showcase. 未来世界主题公园是沃尔特·迪斯尼世界中四个主题公园之一，占地面积 300 英亩，是魔幻王国主题公园的两倍。该主题公园分成未来世界和世界各国陈列馆两部分。 • Disney Epcot Center: Attractions and entertainment dedicated to technological innovation and the culture and cuisine of 11 nations. 迪斯尼——未来世界的游览点和娱乐项目都是技术创新的结晶，展示了 11 个国家的文化和烹饪文化。 • In addition to the attractions, Disneyland provides live entertainment throughout the park. 除了各个游览点，迪斯尼园区还提供现场表演秀。 • "*The Romance of the Song Dynasty*" is one of the three great shows in the world, together with the "*Moulin Rouge*" in Paris and the "*O Show*" in Las Vegas. 《宋城千古情》与法国巴黎的《红磨坊》、美国拉斯维加斯的《O 秀》并称世界三大名秀。 • West Lake is a place for many beautiful legends and romances. 西湖有着很多美丽的传说和浪漫的爱情故事。 • Hangzhou and West Lake are often remembered by many poets and artists for drawing inspiration. 杭州和西湖经常赋予了诗人和艺术家创作的灵感。 • The town is designed to offer an interesting display of people's life in the Song Dynasty as shown in the well-known painting "*Riverside Scene at Qingming Festival*" by Zhang Zeduan, a noted royal artist of Northern Song Dynasty. 该城生动地展示了著名北宋皇室画家张择端在其闻名遐迩的《清明上河图》上表现的宋朝人的生活景象。 • Another highlight of the Song Town is a magnificent live song-and-dance show called "*The Romance of the Song Dynasty*" in the Grand Theatre. 宋城还有一个值得一看的就是在大剧院上演的大型歌舞剧 "宋城千古情"。 • In February 1127, the disaster of Jingkang (靖康) happened that Jin Army invaded Bianjing (汴京/梁), the capital of the Northern Song Dynasty. And the two emperors Song Huizong (宋徽宗) and Song Qinzong (宋钦宗) together with their followers were all captured. As a result, in order to keep safe, the capital was transferred to Hangzhou, naming it as "Lin'an", meaning a temporary place to settle. Thus, a new dynasty was called the Southern Song Dynasty with Zhao Gou (赵构) as its first emperor. From then on, the famous general Yue Fei led his army against the northern Jin invaders. 公元 1127 年 2 月，金兵攻破汴梁城，俘虏了北宋的徽宗和钦宗两位皇帝及后宫、百官，这就是 "靖康之耻"。为了保住宋朝江南半壁江山，宋朝宗室迁都杭州，改称临安，意为 "暂时安顿的地方"。自此，南宋开始，赵构为开国皇帝。此后，著名将军岳飞走上了抗击金兵侵略的道路。

Introducing an Ancient Town 介绍古镇	• Captured by the **Visigoths** (西哥特人), and conquered by the **Moors** (摩尔人), this UNESCO World Heritage site has seen plenty of historical action. 这个被联合国教科文组织列为世界遗产地的小镇经历了很多历史事件。该镇曾经被西哥特人夺取，后来又被摩尔人占领。 • The town has many streets lined with various shops, snack bars and restaurants. 小镇有很多街道，两旁商店林立，到处都是小吃店和餐馆。 • Lijiang is still crisscrossed by an ancient water supply system of ingenuity that functions effectively today. 丽江还拥有古老的供水系统，这一系统纵横交错、精巧独特，至今仍在有效地发挥着作用。 • Their street plan, their architecture and decoration, and the integration (融合) of houses with comprehensive water systems (完备的供水系统) are unique (独特的) surviving examples. (Ancient Villages in Southern Anhui – Xidi and Hongcun, UNESCO World Heritage Site description) 其街道的风格、古建筑和装饰物，以及供水系统完备的民居都是非常独特的文化遗存。(安徽南部古镇——西递和宏村，联合国教科文组织世界遗产地说明) • Pingyao's treasure trove (宝库) of Ming and Qing architecture is a legacy (遗产) of the town's affluent (富足的) days as a banking center. • During the Qing Dynasty, Pingyao was a financial center of China. It's now renowned for its well-preserved ancient city wall and is a UNESCO World Heritage Site. 清朝时期，平遥是中国的金融中心。该镇以其保存完好的古城墙而闻名，是联合国教科文组织认定的世界文化遗产地。
Introducing Operas 介绍戏剧	• Chinese opera, together with Greece tragic-comedy and Indian Sanskrit Opera, is one of the three oldest dramatic art forms in the world. 中国戏剧与希腊悲喜剧和印度梵剧并称为世界最古老的三大戏剧形式。 • Peking Opera is a national treasure in China with a history of over 200 years. 京剧是中国的国粹，有着 200 多年的历史。 • There are four roles in general: the male, the female, the painted face, and the clown, which are further classified by age and profession. 京剧主要有生、旦、净、丑四大行当，这些行当还可以根据年龄和职业进行细分。 • There's a love story about White Snake and her lover Xu Xian who fell into love at the first sight on the Broken Bridge. 有一则白蛇和许仙断桥相会的动人爱情故事。 • Another is a Chinese "Romeo and Juliet" story that the lovers Liang Shanbo (梁山伯) and Zhu Yingtai (祝英台) died for love.

Part E   English in Use

I. Reading Comprehension

Task 1: Select the best answer to complete each sentence below.

1. Which park has the theme of Song Culture in China? _____
   A. Song Dynasty Town.　　　　　　　B. Qingming Shanghe Park.
   C. Tang Paradise Lotus Park.　　　　 D. Both A and B.

2. Zhang Zeduan, the painter of the painting "*Riverside Scene at Qingming Festival*," is a _____.
   A. Song artist
   B. Northern Song writer

    C. royal artist of Northern Song Dynasty

    D. Southern Song artist

3. Tang Paradise Lotus Park is located in _____.

    A. the northwestern of Xi'an, Shaanxi Province

    B. the northeast of Xi'an, Shaanxi Province

    C. the northwestern China

    D. the southeast of Xi'an, Shaanxi Province

4. If the tourists are interested in Tang culture, which park would you suggest them to visit?

    _____

    A. Qingming Shanghe Park.   B. Tang Paradise Lotus Park.

    C. Song Dynasty Town.   D. Beijing Happy Valley.

5. Which of the following ancient towns once served as a trade confluence on the old tea horse road? _____

    A. Pingle Ancient Town.

    B. Lijiang.

    C. Tongli Ancient Town.

    D. Pingyao Ancient Town.

6. Which of the following ancient towns are on the list of UNESCO's World Cultural Heritage? _____

    A. Lijiang and Pingle.

    B. Pingyao and Pingle.

    C. Wuzhen and Yongding.

    D. Xidi, Hongcun, Lijiang, Pingyao and Yongding.

7. What are the six ancient towns in the south of Yangtze River? _____

    A. Pingyao, Pingle, Tongli, Zhouzhuang, Wuzhen, Xidi.

    B. Tongli, Zhouzhuang, Wuzhen, Xitang, Nanxun, Luzhi.

    C. Wuzhen, Xidi, Yongding, Pingle, Wuzhen, Xidi.

    D. Wuzhen, Xidi, Hongcun, Luzhi, zhouzhuang, Shaoxing.

8. In which town does the modern writer Mao Dun's novel "*Lin's Shop*" describes people's life? _____

    A. Wuzhen.   B. Zhouzhuang.   C. Tongli.   D. Xidi.

9. Tulou is a type of Chinese rural dwellings built by _____, a branch of Han nationality in China.

    A. the Hakka   B. the Dai   C. the Han   D. the Bai

10. How many bridges were there in Wuzhen? _____

    A. 120.   B. 30.   C. Over 120.   D. Over 30.

Task 2: Answer the following questions concerning the Chinese opera in Part C.

1. What are the three oldest dramatic art forms in the world?

2. Why are those performing Chinese opera called "disciples of the Pear Garden"?

3. When did Chinese opera start to be welcome by the court officials and emperors?

4. When did Peking Opera start? And why is it known as China's national opera?

5. Which opera is Peking Opera derived from?

Task 3: Decide whether each of the following five statements is True or False according to the introduction of Peking Opera in Part C.

1. In all the "civil" pieces of Peking Opera, the performers only sing, while in the "martial" ones, they often play acrobatics and stunts. (　　)

2. Peking Opera's repertoire includes historical plays and tragedies. (　　)

3. There are usually two orchestras, playing string and percussion instruments, accompanying the singing in Peking Opera but without Jinghu, the two-stringed instrument. (　　)

4. The female roles in Peking Opera usually are those young innocent women. (　　)

5. The color of the painted face can be an indication of the characters or personality of those painted face roles. (　　)

II. Translation

Task 4: Translate the following sentences into English.

1. 乌镇是中国长江三角洲南部（俗称江南）保护得最好的六个古镇之一。
2. 今晚你们将观看根据 2016 年 G20 峰会文艺晚会改编的大型表演《最忆是杭州》。希望你们到时会喜欢。
3. 今晚在东坡剧院上演一出很精彩的绍兴越剧，名叫《白蛇传》，你有没有兴趣去看？
4. 宋城打出了一个非常独特的宣传口号：给我一天，还你千年。
5. 纵横交错的河道把整个小镇主要分成四个不同方向的区域。
6. 请看这条街两旁的旧房子。你们知道这些房子的年代有多久吗？
7. 在这里的小街漫步，会让你感觉真的来到了古镇，因为除了游客，镇里所有的人都穿着传统的宋朝服饰。
8. 中国也有一则像罗密欧和朱丽叶一样的爱情故事。故事中的恋人就是同样殉情的梁山伯和祝英台。
9. 明晚大剧院有一场精彩的中国传统戏剧，不知道你们对此是否有兴趣。
10. 这个古镇出了很多名人。例如，中国著名的现代作家茅盾就出生在这里。

Task 5: Translate the following sentences into Chinese.

1. The town has a history dating back more than 800 years and used to be confluence for trade along the old tea horse road. The Lijiang Ancient town is famous for its orderly system of waterways and bridges.

2. Lijiang also possesses an ancient water-supply system of great complexity and ingenuity that still functions effectively today.

3. During the Qing Dynasty, Pingyao was a financial center of China. It is now renowned for its well-preserved ancient city wall and is a UNESCO World Heritage Site.

4. Red represents loyalty and righteousness; white suggests a crafty and suspicious character; black shows a courageous, upright and rough disposition; green indicates a brave and irascible nature; blue means uprightness and unyieldingness.

5. Epcot theme park (未来世界主题公园), one of four Theme Parks at Walt Disney World Resort, sprawls across 300 acres — twice the size of Magic Kingdom theme park —

and is divided into Future World and World Showcase.

6. In old times in many places in China, it was customary for the only daughter of a rich family to choose Mr Right by casting downstairs from her house an embroidered ball (绣球) to the right person among all the wooers (求婚者).

7. The two bridges almost join at a right angle, being only 10 meters apart at one end. Either of the two bridges can be seen through the arch of the other, so the place here is called "Bridge within a Bridge".

8. Surrounded by one of China's few intact Ming city walls, Pingyao's streets are lined with a wealth of traditional Chinese buildings, including courtyard houses, temples, and more than 3,000 historic ships.

9. Pingyao's treasure trove (宝库) of Ming and Qing architecture is a legacy (遗产) of the town's affluent (富裕的) days as a banking center.

10. Lying in the northeast of Yixian (黟县), Anhui Province and picturesquely ringed by mountains, Hongcun is known as "a village in a Chinese painting". It is laid out in the shape of water-buffalo and is watered by a network of ditches (沟渠). The Moon Pond is regarded as the buffalo's stomach, the ditches the intestines (牛肠) and South Lake the abdomen (牛肚).

III. Role Play

Task 6: Play a role in any of the following situations with your partner(s).

Situation 1: Please role play all the dialogues in both part A, B and C with your partner(s).

Situation 2: You're a tour guide for a group of French people in Hangzhou. Now you're trying to arouse the group's interest in watching the great show "*Most Memorable is Hangzhou* (《最忆是杭州》)" tomorrow evening by telling them the moving love story of White Snake and Xu Xian.

Situation 3: Choose any of the tourist destinations in China and find the most popular entertainment program in the local area, such as "*Impression of Lijiang*" also directed by Zhang Yimou (张艺谋), etc., and try to introduce this program to the tourists.

Situation 4: You're a local guide showing a group of foreign tourists around any of the well-known ancient towns mentioned above in Part B, or any one in your hometown.

Situation 5: You're working as a guide. Some of your guests seem to be interested in Peking Opera, give them a brief introduction of the opera.

Situation 6: You're working as a guide. Some of your guests seem to be interested in Shaoxing Opera or any of other Chinese local operas, give them a brief introduction of the opera.

IV. Problem-solving

Task 7: Make an analysis of the following cases, and answer the questions as required.

Case

Situation: The tour group from the UK is scheduled to watch the show "*Most Memorable is West Lake*" in the evening, but two of them who are the football fans would rather watch the World Cup Soccer Game between the England and the Argentina at the hotel.

Question: As a tour guide, how would you attend to this matter?

Unit 12   Health and Wellness Activities

Warm-up

1. Have you tried traditional Chinese massage and sauna before? How will you introduce them to your foreign visitors?
2. What are the common fitness activities in China? Can you identify them from the following pictures?

1) _____

2) _____

3) _____

4) _____

3. How much do you know about Taiji?
4. Have you ever tried traditional Chinese acupuncture? How will you introduce it to your foreign visitors?

Part A   Sauna and Massage

Dialogue 1: Sauna

Situation: *Adam is tired after a long day of traveling and wants to get some relaxation in a sauna. Lu Cheng, a clerk of the sauna room, is serving him.*

Questions for comprehension and discussion:

★ What is a dry sauna?

★ What is a wet sauna?

★ What is a steam bath?

Lu Cheng: May I help you?

   Adam: Yes. I'd like to have a sauna.

Lu Cheng: OK. What kind of sauna do you like? We have **dry sauna** (汗/干蒸), **wet sauna** (湿蒸) and **steam bath** (蒸汽浴).

   Adam: Sorry, this is the first time for me to try a sauna. What is a dry sauna?

Lu Cheng: The temperature is usually around 80° Celsius or 176° **Fahrenheit** (华氏) or even higher, and the **humidity** (湿度) is 5%–20%.

   Adam: I'm afraid that's too high for me.

Lu Cheng: Sorry, that's why it's called dry sauna. With this high temperature, one's body may sweat a lot, and the skin will also dry fast. but it helps open the **pores** (毛孔) and get rid of **toxins** (毒素). So it's good for those with **arthritis** (关节炎) or skin disease but may not be suitable for those with heart disease or high **blood pressure** (血压).

   Adam: I see. Then perhaps the temperature in a wet sauna may be lower.

Lu Cheng: Exactly. The temperature in this kind of sauna is around 50°C or 122°F, and the humidity rises to 20%–40%.

   Adam: The temperature sounds comfortable for me. But where does the humidity come from?

Lu Cheng: Well, it comes from the **steam** (蒸汽) produced when hot stones are poured with water.

   Adam: It's easier to be in a wet sauna than in a dry sauna. Then what about the steam bath? Isn't it also a wet sauna?

Lu Cheng: They're similar, but the humidity is 65%–100%, and the temperature is around

40°C. It's more relaxing to stay in a steam bath than in a sauna. It's like **Turkish bath** (土耳其浴) which has lower heat, and one may sweat less. It's not only good for the skin but also helps **relieve** (缓解) one's **upper respiratory disorders** (上呼吸道疾病). Now, which one do you like?

Adam: I think I'll take wet sauna because I like to sweat although I cannot bear high temperature.

Lu Cheng: OK. What kind of room do you prefer? We have **wood stove room** (木炉房), **electric stove room** (电炉房), and **infrared room** (远红外线房) with regard to the different devices for heating.

Adam: Which one do you recommend?

Lu Cheng: As far as wood and electricity are concerned, burning wood is the traditional type and it's considered to be healthier, but the electric room is more convenient and can be switched on and off. The **infrared room** (远红外线热) is like a **heat therapy** (热疗) room. The radiating heat goes deeper into the skin and warms the body fast, so one may sweat more in this type of sauna. By the way, there's no water used in the room. The room temperature is usually around 50°C.

Adam: Mm, it's hard to make a choice. OK, let me try the traditional one, the wood stove room.

Lu Cheng: Fine. This way, please.

(After a while)

Here's the room. Please don't stay there for too long time. Usually 10–15 minutes for the first round is enough. Then get out of the sauna, take a shower and take a brisk walk. The shower room is next to it. After a rest of at least 20 minutes, reenter the sauna room. In short, you can do three sauna cycles complete with walks, cold shower and rest. By the way, you can turn on the green switch on the wall if you'd like to enjoy some traditional Chinese music. Here's your locker key, bathrobe and towel. If you need any help, please press the call button. Enjoy yourself then.

Adam: Perfect. Thanks!

Lu Cheng: Pleasure.

Dialogue 2: Massage

Situation: *Cai Ming, a **massage therapist** (按摩师) of a Chinese massage shop in Hangzhou, is serving Alex who is an Australian tourist.*

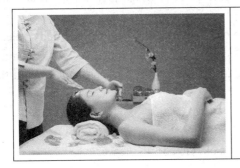

Questions for comprehension and discussion:

★ Where does this massage start?

★ How was massage described in *Yellow Emperor's Classic of Internal Medicine* (《黄帝内经》)?

★ What's **Qi** (气)?

★ What is Chinese massage mainly used for?

Cai Ming: Good evening, sir. I'm Cai Ming, No.5, your massage therapist this evening.

Alex: Fine. Shall I lie on the bed?

Cai Ming: Yes. Please lie on your back and relax. You're taking a body massage, right?

Alex: Right. Where shall we start?

Cai Ming: At the head. Usually, the order is from head to toe. Is this your first time to try Chinese massage?

Alex: You're right. I learned that Chinese massage is very conducive to one's health. Is it true?

Cai Ming: Yes. In ***Yellow Emperor's Classic of Internal Medicine*** (《黄帝内经》), one of the oldest extant medical **treatises** (专著) in China, it's said that if the body is **benumbed** (使麻木) due to a **blockage** (堵塞) in **Jingluo**, **meridians** (经络), it may be cured by massage.

Alex: Sounds interesting. Is the massage safe then?

Cai Ming: Yes, of course. It's safe, effective, comfortable, and free of side effects. It's concerned with the **circulation** (循环) of Qi energy and blood.

Alex: What's Qi?

Cai Ming: Qi in Chinese means "vital force or energy". It's **invisible** (看不见) flowing in the meridians but is reflected in the functions of body **organs** (器官) or **tissues** (组织). Any break in the flow is an indication of **imbalance** (失调) of the body functions, which may lead to diseases. Chinese massage can help **regulate** (调整) Qi and promote blood circulation to keep healthy.

Alex: So you can cure diseases by Chinese massage without having to take medicine or having an **injection** (打针)?

Cai Ming: Not exactly. The massage here can help ease the pain in your body, release your **muscular tension** (肌肉的紧张感), make you relax, as well as treat some illness resulted from the blockage of Qi. However, it may not cure all the other diseases.

Alex: Oh. I see.

Cai Ming: Does it hurt?

Alex: The spot is a bit sensitive, but it's ok. Go ahead, please.

Cai Ming: Ok, By the way, it's normal for you to feel **pain** (痛), **numbness** (麻) or a **tingling sensation** (刺痛感) while taking the massage, especially when this is your first time. So, don't worry, and I'll continue using this pressure. You can close your eyes and take a nap.

Part B　Chinese Martial Arts

Dialogue: Taiji

Situation: *Chen Yan, the tour guide, is introducing Chinese martial arts to the American tourists on the coach when passing a square.*

Questions for comprehension and discussion:

★ What is Taiji?

★ Who created Taiji Quan?

★ What is the aim of Taiji?

★ Is Taiji Quan easy to learn?

Chen Yan: Well, do you know what these people are doing?

Tourist A: Taiji?

Chen Yan: Right. You can find people practicing Taiji Quan or Taiji Sword either in a group or individually everywhere in China. It's one of the most common **fitness activities** (健身活动) in China.

Tourist B: I often see some Chinese people practicing Taiji back in the States. It's intriguing, but I'm wondering what Taiji is.

Chen Yan: Taiji means "**Great Ultimate**" or "**Supreme Polarity**" (太极) and is a typical Chinese philosophical concept. According to *I Ching*, **the Book of Changes** (《易经》), it refers to the **Great Primal Beginning** (宇宙的初始状态) generating the **two primary forces or two polarities** (两仪或两极) which are known as Yin and Yang. While Yin represents **tranquility** (静), Yang stands for **movement** (动). The two polarities **alternately** (交替地) turn to each other and thus generate **Si Xiang, four identities** (四象). The four identities may refer to the four elements known as fire, water, wood and metal in four directions in addition to earth in the middle. Then with the continuous **alternation** (交替) of Yin and Yang, the four identities generate **eight trigrams** (八卦) which continue to create all other things in the world. In other words, Taiji indicates that all things **interact** (相互作用) and are **opposites** (相互对立), for example, day and night, sun and moon, male and female or **masculinity** (阳性) and **femininity** (阴性), movement and tranquility, **positivity** (积极性) and **negativity** (消极), etc. Therefore, Taiji concept is actually the **principle** (原理) of Yin and Yang, which has been applied in Chinese philosophy such as Daoism, Chinese traditional medicine, and **martial arts** (武术), and so on. Today, when we talk about Taiji, we usually refer to the martial art on the basis of the **dialectical** (辩证的) concept of Yin and Yang.

Tourist B: I see. No wonder it looks so different from the other martial arts. Is that because the movements look slow and less aggressive?

Chen Yan:  Yes. Taiji, as a martial art, was created by Zhang Sanfeng (张三丰), a Daoist around the 15th century in Mount Wudang. It's an **internal martial art** (内功) and is also called shadow boxing in slow motion. It aims at **wellbeing** (康乐), so it stresses the smooth flow of Qi, the vital energy, and the **attainment** (获得) of peaceful mind and body, a perfect balance of Yin and Yang. Even when facing **attack** (攻击), the **practitioner** (练功者) does not **exert physical energy** (用尽体力) but makes full use of his or her vital energy to **counteract** (抵消) the **attacking force** (攻击力) peacefully. Now people widely practice it for fitness exercises to stay free of illness like **hypertension** (高血压), **insomnia** (失眠), **depression** (抑郁), and so on.

Tourist B: So fascinating. I want to try it. Is it easy to learn?

Chen Yan: Well, it depends on your **comprehension** (理解). If you try to understand its **essence** (要义) — creating and keeping balance of **shifting** (调整) the **motions** (动作), then it's easy to learn. All you can do is practice and perfect the movement. However, if you ignore the idea of balance, then these movements seem to be strange to you.

Tourist B: OK. I think I can try it. Thank you very much for your introduction.

Chen Yan: You're welcome.

Part C　Traditional Chinese Acupuncture

*The following essay is adapted from the article "**Acupuncture**" retrieved online, Aug. 12, 2012 with the link http://www.tcmpage.com/acupuncture.html.*

Questions for comprehension and discussion:

★ What are the four main diagnostic methods in traditional Chinese medicine?

★   What do you know about acupuncture points? Can you name some of them?

★   Do you think that acupuncture is effective in curing diseases? Why?

Chinese acupuncture is an important element in the heritage and development of traditional Chinese medicine. It dates back at least 3,000 years. The practice of **acupuncture** (针刺) and **moxibustion** (艾灸) is based on the theory of **meridians** (经络). According to this theory, Qi (vital energy) circulates in the body through a system of channels called

meridians, connecting internal organs with external organs or tissues. With certain points of the body surface along the meridians stimulated via needling or moxibustion, the flow of Qi is regulated, blood circulation is increased, and diseases are thus treated. These stimulation points are called acupuncture points, or **acupoints** (穴位).

Acupoints are located along more than dozens of major meridians. It is believed that 12 pairs of **regular meridians** (正经) that are systematically distributed over both sides of the body, and two major extra meridians run along the midlines of the **abdomen** (腹部) and back, known as **Ren vein** (任脉) and **Du vein** (督脉).

Along these meridians more than 300 acupoints can be identified, each having its own therapeutic effect. For example, the **point Hegu** (合谷穴), located between the first and second **metacarpal** (掌部的) bones, can reduce pain in the head and mouth. The **point Shenmen** (神门穴), located on the medial end of the **transverse crease of the wrist** (腕横纹), can help **tranquility** (安静).

In an acupuncture clinic, the practitioner first selects appropriate acupoints along different meridians based on identified health problems. Then they insert very fine and thin needles into these acupoints. The needles are made of stainless steel and vary in length from half an inch to 3 inches. The choice of needle is usually determined by the location of the acupoint and the effects being sought. If the point is correctly located and the required depth reached, the patient will usually experience a feeling of slight **pain** (酸痛), **numbness** (麻木) or **tingling** (刺痛).

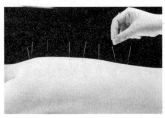

The needles usually stay **in situ** (在原位) for 15−30 minutes. They may be **manipulated** (操作) to **nourish** (滋养) the Qi. Needling skills involve **lifting** (提), **thrusting** (戳), **twisting** (搓) and **rotating** (旋转). Needling may also be activated by electrical stimulation, a procedure usually called **electro-acupuncture** (电针), in which manipulations are attained through varying **frequencies** (频率) and **voltages** (电压).

A professional practitioner will always warn the patient of the possibility of **exacerbation** (恶化) at the start of a course of treatment. The patients may find that in the short term after treatment, the **symptoms** (症状) may get worse before improvement sets in, and this is quite a common feature of acupuncture treatment.

On the whole, the effectiveness of acupuncture treatment lies in the practitioner's accurate medical **diagnosis** (诊断) and professional needling skills and techniques.

Part D   Language Checklist

A. Vocabulary

dry sauna 干蒸 wet sauna 湿蒸 steam bath 蒸汽浴 wood stove room 木炉房 electric stove room 电炉房 infrared room 远红外线房	blood circulation 血液循环 meridian 经络 Chinese medical herb 中草药 free of side effect 无副作用的 imbalance 失调	Great Ultimate/Supreme Polarity 太极 two polarities 两极 four identities 四象 eight trigrams 八卦 principle of Yin and Yang 阴阳原理 masculinity 阳性 femininity 阴性
acupuncture 针刺 moxibustion 艾灸 cupping 拔火罐 acupoint 穴位	a slight pain 轻微酸痛 numbness 麻 a tingling sensation 刺痛感	Taiji Quan 太极拳 Taiji Sword 太极剑 martial arts 武术 self-defense 自卫
rotate the needle 捻转 handle the needle 运针 twist the needle 搓针 insert the needle 扎针 deep insertion 深针 shallow insertion 浅针	manipulations 手法 grasping 拿 rolling 滚 pressing 按 rubbing 摩 pushing 推 tapping 拍	feeling the pulse 切脉 potential diseases 潜在的疾病 diagnosis 诊断

B. Key Patterns

Introducing Sauna Service **介绍桑拿服务**	• We have dry sauna and wet sauna. 我们有干蒸和湿蒸。 • It's about 80°C in the dry sauna room, and the humidity is 5% – 20%. 干蒸桑拿房的温度大概有 80°C，湿度在 5% ～ 20%。 • The temperature in wet sauna is around 50°C or 122°F, and the humidity rises to 20% – 40%. • The high temperature helps open the pores (毛孔) and get rid of toxins (毒素), so it's good for those with arthritis (关节炎) or skin disease. • Sauna helps relieve (缓解) one's upper respiratory disorders (上呼吸道疾病). • Sauna is to step up the blood circulation and produce vigorous perspiration. 桑拿的目的在于加速血液循环和大量出汗。 • We've two well-equipped sauna rooms. 我们有两个配置设备较好的桑拿房。 • Hotel guests will receive a 20% discount for the sauna. 住店客人桑拿享受八折优惠。 • Here's your locker key. Please carry it with you. 这是您的手牌，请随身携带。

Introducing Massage 介绍推拿按摩	• Would you like to take a foot massage or a body massage? • This is the introduction to the massages. 这里是按摩项目的介绍。 • This is the bathrobe for massage. 这是按摩时穿的浴衣。 • There are six stimulus-input regions on the sole, which are related to the heart, brain, liver, lungs, spleen and kidneys. So if there's a strong aching sensation in one part of your sole, it can indicate the potential disease. 足底有六个刺激反应区，它们分别对应心脏、大脑、肝脏、肺、脾和肾脏。因此，如果你的足底的某个部分有很强的痛感，这就表明你可能有疾病。 • It's normal for you to feel a slight pain, numbness or tingling while taking a massage. 在按摩中，你会有点痛、麻或刺痛的感觉，这都是正常的。 • A massage should not be performed within two hours after a meal. 不应在饭后两小时内做按摩。 • Chinese massage helps you regulate Qi and promote blood circulation to keep healthy. 中国推拿按摩有助于调节气血，促进血液循环，使你保持健康。 • Chinese massage treatment is extremely good for aching joints. 中医按摩对疼痛的关节很有好处。 • Massage is very good for relaxing and balancing functions of the body organs. 按摩对放松和平衡身体各器官的机能来说很有帮助。 • The massage can help ease the pain in your body, release your muscular tension (肌肉的紧张感), make you relax. • Whether the location of a point is right or not may directly affect the effect of massage treatment. 取穴正确与否直接影响推拿治疗的效果。
Introducing Martial Arts 介绍武术	• Chinese culture is deeply intertwined with martial arts. So it's a good way to learn Chinese culture through martial arts. 武术与中国文化有着千丝万缕的联系，所以学习武术就是学习中国文化的一个好方式。 • Taiji Quan is an important part of Chinese martial arts. Regular practice can increase balance, flexibility, and strength. 太极拳是中国武术的重要组成部分，可以提高平衡能力，改善关节柔韧性，增强肌肉力量。 • Taiji, as a martial art, was created by Zhang Sanfeng (张三丰), a Daoist around the 15th century in Mount Wudang. • Taiji aims at wellbeing, so it stresses the smooth flow of Qi, the vital energy, and the attainment (获得) of peaceful mind and body, a perfect balance of Yin and Yang. • Practising Taiji helps improve memory, concentration, digestion, balance and flexibility. It's especially helpful for the elderly people, as well as those with serious medical or psychological problems, such as depression, anxiety or stress. • Shaolin Wushu (Shaolin Martial Art) is one of the most influential genres of Chinese martial art, and it's named after the Shaolin Temple. 少林武术是中国最有影响的一个武术流派，因形成于少林寺而得名。
Introducing Acupuncture 介绍针刺	• Acupuncture is a heritage and development of traditional Chinese medicine. It can date back at least 3,000 years. 针刺是中国传统医学的一个继承和发展，它至少有三千多年的历史了。 • Acupuncture is based on the theory of "Jingluo (meridians, or a network of channels and collaterals, 经络)". 针刺的理论基础就是经络学说。 • The needles are very thin. As long as the therapist's technique is good, and the patient is relaxed, it won't hurt while having the acupuncture; on the contrary, it'll actually alleviate pain. 针非常细小。只要治疗师的手艺好，病人也很放松，针刺时就不会感到疼痛。相反，它可以缓解疼痛。 • Acupuncture is very effective especially for some chronic diseases. 针刺对一些慢性病特别有效。

Introducing Acupuncture 介绍针刺	• Briefly, meridians are the passages through which Qi circulates. In an extensive network, they cover the entire body. 简单来说，经络就是人体的气流经的通道。它们是一个巨大的网络，遍布全身各处。 • Along meridians are points called acupoints. They are the connecting points across the whole body, each of which affects a specific organ or another part of the body. 沿着经络有很多的点，叫穴位。它们是整个身体的连接点。每个穴位与不同的人体器官或部位相关联。

Part E   English in Use

I. Reading Comprehension

Task 1: Choose the best answer to complete each sentence below.

1. Our sauna room _____ of three parts.
   A. consist   B. consists   C. consisted   D. is consisted

2. You can _____ a sauna bath there.
   A. take   B. make   C. go   D. give

3. Taking a massage can help _____ pressure from daily work.
   A. kill   B. relieve   C. rest   D. return

4. Good evening, sir. Please lie _____ your back, and relax.
   A. in   B. at   C. to   D. on

5. Sometimes, sole massage can help you to _____ if you have any diseases.
   A. judge   B. choose   C. think   D. believe

6. — Does it _____?
   — Yes, the force is too heavy. I can't bear it.
   A. hurt   B. matter   C. work   D. go

7. Massage must not be _____ to pregnant women.
   A. formed   B. given   C. followed   D. put

8. — Can I _____ an appointment for an acupuncture treatment for tomorrow?
   — Of course, madam.
   A. ask   B. write   C. make   D. list

9. According to legend, Chinese martial arts _____ during the semi-mythical Xia Dynasty more than 4,000 years ago.
   A. originated   B. made   C. remembered   D. practiced

10. Acupuncture is a _____ of traditional Chinese medicine. It has a history of more than 3,000 years.
   A. gift   B. good   C. heritage   D. title

Task 2: Answer the questions concerning the passage in Part C.

1. What theory is the practice of acupuncture based on?

2. How is the flow of Qi regulated?

3. Where are the point Hegu and the point Shenmen? What are their therapeutic actions?

4. How will the patient feel if the point is correctly located and the required depth reached?

5. What is the common feature of acupuncture treatment mentioned in this passage?

Task 3: Decide whether each of the following statements is true or false according to the passage in Part C.

1. The needles are made of stainless steel and are of the same length. (   )

2. The choice of needle is often determined by the location of the acupoint and the effects being sought. (   )

3. There are 15 pairs of regular meridians that are systematically distributed over both sides of the body. (   )

4. The patient may find the symptoms get worse in the short term after treatment. (   )

5. The effectiveness of an acupuncture treatment is strongly dependent upon high-quality needles. (   )

II. Translation

Task 4: Translate the following sentences into English.

1. 请问您要做足浴还是全身按摩？

2. 我们有干蒸和湿蒸。您想要哪种？

3. 脚的某些部位与身体一些器官结构相对应。

4. 我们为您提供了免费的浴衣和浴鞋。

5. 简单来说，经络就是人体的气流经的通道。

6. 很多人练太极是为了健身，防止患上如高血压、失眠、抑郁等疾病。

7. 中式按摩有助于通经，促进血液循环，使您保持健康。

8. 针刺一般使用非常纤细的针，扎入人体的特殊穴位，产生刺激。

9. 针刺穴位沿经络分布。

10. 现在排舞在中国越来越流行。到处都可以看见中国大妈集体跳舞。

Task 5: Translate the following sentences into Chinese.

1. We have a big swimming pool, a sauna room, a gym, a water bar, a beauty salon, and provide a Chinese massage service.

2. The goals of massage therapy are to relieve the pressure from daily work and enhance the harmony between body and mind.

3. Our therapists are high skilled and diversely trained.

4. Manipulations used in this massage can be varied to treat different people and parts of human body.

5. Taiji Quan aims at wellbeing, so it stresses the smooth flow of Qi, the vital energy, and the attainment of peaceful mind and body, a perfect balance of Yin and Yang.

6. According to *I Ching*, the Book of Changes (《易经》), it refers to the Great Primal Beginning generating the two primary forces or two polarities which are known as Yin and Yang.

7. Yin and Yang are the two fundamental forces in the universe, ever opposing and complementing each other.

8. Acupuncture may cause a slight pain and a certain feeling of numbness or a tingling sensation.

9. How do you feel when I rotate the needle?

10. Practising Taiji helps improve memory, concentration, digestion, balance and flexibility.

III. Role Play

Task 6: Play a role in the following situation with your partner(s).

Situation 1: You're working as a service staff member in a gym. A foreign guest comes in and wants to take a sauna. Greet him or her and try to answer any questions concerning sauna.

Situation 2: As a massage therapist, you're giving an English-speaking guest a massage. Please make a conversation with the guest and try to explain anything concerning massage.

Situation 3: You're showing your foreign friends or a group of tourists around your city. Tell them about Taiji when seeing some local people practicing Taiji Quan and try to make yourself understood.

Situation 4: You're showing your foreign friends around your city. Tell them about Chinese people's fitness activities such as line dance when seeing a group of Chinese Da Ma dancing in a group.

Situation 5: You're giving an English-speaking guest acupuncture. Please make a dialogue with him or her and try to make yourself understood concerning acupuncture.

IV. Problem-solving

Task 7: Make an analysis of the following cases, and answer the questions as required.

Case 1

Situation: Mr Grey has just had a massage in a Chinese massage centre, but he doesn't like it because the massage therapist's force is so heavy that he feels pain. So he complains about it to the manager.

Question: If you were the manager, what would you do?

Case 2

Situation: A local guide has arranged a tour to the most popular acupuncture site for a tour group from the United States. But just before setting off, one of the tourists refuses to go and prefers to stay in the hotel because she thinks putting needles in one's body is a sort of **witchcraft** (巫术).

Question: Suppose you were the guide, what would you do then?

Answers for Reference

Module V
Outbound Travel Service

Unit 13　Major Attractions and Leisure Activities in Western Countries

Unit 13　Major Attractions and Leisure Activities in Western Countries

Warm-up

1. What do you know about some famous tourist attractions in the world? Can you name the tourist attractions in the following pictures?

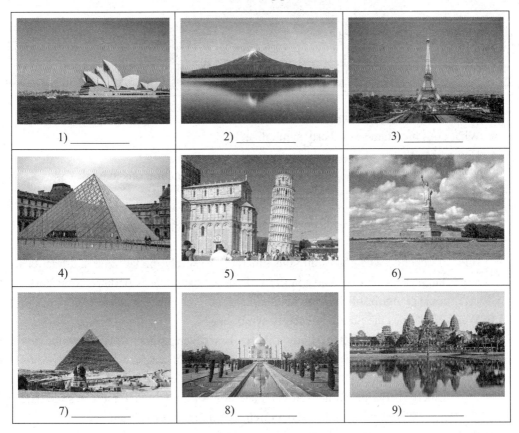

1) _____

2) _____

3) _____

4) _____

5) _____

6) _____

7) _____

8) _____

9) _____

2. What foreign country would you like to travel to the most? Why?
3. Can you name some leisure activities in Western countries? Have you ever tried any of them?
4. What do you think are proper manners when traveling abroad? Why?

Part A   Major Tourist Attractions in Western Countries

Dialogue: New York

Situation: *Liu Wei, an interested tourist, is sitting with Tom in the lobby of a hotel. Tom, a local guide of an American travel agency, is introducing the major tourist attractions in New York mentioned in a hotel booklet.*

Questions for comprehension and discussion:

★ What does the Statue of Liberty symbolize?

★ How tall is it?

★ Where do people usually gather for New Year's Eve celebrations in New York?

★ When was the Empire State Building built?

Liu Wei: Could you share with me the best places to visit in **Manhattan** (曼哈顿), New York?

Tom: It depends. The places on your itinerary are surely the key tourist attractions. The famous Statue of Liberty built in 1876, for example, is perhaps New York City's most recognizable historic landmark.

Liu Wei: What does the Statue of Liberty symbolize?

Tom: The **crown** (王冠) of Lady Liberty has seven **spikes** (尖芒), symbolizing the Seven Seas and Seven Continents of the world across which liberty should be spread. Others say the spikes represent the rays of the sun and show that the lady Liberty is divine. In her left hand she holds a tablet which indicates the date, July 4, 1776 and in her right hand a torch, symbolizing Enlightenment.

Liu Wei: Sounds interesting. How tall is the statue?

Tom: It depends on how you measure it. The copper statue is 46.5 meters tall and together with the pedestal it reaches a height of 93 meters.

Liu Wei: How do we reach the top?

Tom: You can take the staircase inside the statue and walk 354 steps all the way up to the crown where you'll have a nice view of New York City.

Liu Wei: Oh, I see. And that's **Times Square** (时代广场), isn't it?

Tom: That's right. It's often referred to as the heart of the entertainment area. It's known for many Broadway theatres, cinemas and electronic billboards. On every New Year's Eve, thousands of New Yorkers and visitors celebrate the New Year here.

Liu Wei: And what's that tall building?

Tom: That's the **Empire State Building** (帝国大厦). It was built in 1931. It's about 381 meters high. And you can take an elevator to the top.

Liu Wei: Great!

Tom: New York's top attractions also include the **Metropolitan Museum of Art** (大都会艺术博物馆), **Brooklyn Bridge** (布鲁克林大桥), **Ellis Island** (埃利斯岛).

Liu Wei: What a magnificent city! It's no wonder that New York never stops fascinating tourists from all over the world.

Monologue 1: Westminster Abbey

Situation: *An English tour guide is introducing Westminster Abbey to the tourists. It's one of the world's greatest churches and is located in London, England.*

Questions for comprehension and discussion:
★ What are the main functions of Westminster Abbey?
★ What famous names can be found at the Poet's Corner?

Hello, everyone, we'll arrive at Westminster Abbey in a few minutes. Standing in the heart of London opposite the **Houses of Parliament** (议会大厦) and overlooking the Thames River, Westminster Abbey is a Gothic monastery church and is one of the most impressive attractions in Britain. It's the traditional place for **coronations** (加冕礼) and **burial** (葬礼) for English monarchs. Since 1066, every royal coronation, with the exception of a couple of unlucky **Eds** (爱德华家族成员) like the murdered **Edward V** (爱德华五世, 1470–1483) ①or **abdicated** (退位的) **Edward VIII** (爱德华八世, 1894–1972)②, took place in Westminster Abbey. It was also the

venue (场地) of the renowned wedding of Prince William and Kate in 2011. So taking a tour of

---

① 13 岁的爱德华五世即位两个月后就和他唯一的弟弟约克公爵理查一起神秘失踪。他们的叔父摄政王格洛斯特公爵即位，即理查三世。据说，两兄弟是被理查三世秘密关在伦敦塔并毒害致死。

② 爱德华八世在位仅一年，是唯一一位自愿退位的英国君主。1936 年 12 月退位后，其头衔转为爱德华王子，并被其弟乔治六世封为温莎公爵。

Westminster Abbey is like leafing through Britain's family photo album; famous names from the nation's royal, political and cultural past are commemorated here. On the Westminster Abbey website, the Abbey describes itself as a "must-see living **pageant** (盛会) of British History". That's a quite accurate description, considering the incredible amount of history in and around this building.

Here's Westminster Abbey. It's considered one of the world's most famous examples of **Gothic** (哥特式) architecture. The present building dates mainly from the reign of King **Henry III** (亨利三世, 1207–1272). The architect was remarkably influenced by the new cathedrals at **Reims** (兰斯), **Amiens** (亚眠) and **Chartres** (沙特尔), borrowing the ideas of an **apse** (教堂半圆形的后殿) with radiating chapels and using the characteristic Gothic features of pointed arches, **ribbed vaulting** (肋架拱顶), rose windows and **flying buttresses** (飞拱). The design is based on the continental system of geometrical proportion, but its English features include single rather than double aisles and a long **nave** (教堂正厅) with wide projecting **transepts** (教堂的十字形翼部). The Abbey has the highest **Gothic vault** (哥特式穹顶) in England, about 102 feet. And it was made to appear higher by making the aisles narrow.

This is the famous **Coronation Chair** (加冕椅). It was first used at the coronation of King **Edward II** (爱德华二世, 1284–1327) in 1308, and since then it has been used for the coronations of all but three of our Kings and Queens. The Coronation Chair may look modest, but it's probably the oldest piece of furniture in Britain that is still used for the purpose for which it was made. Can you guess what the purpose is? Actually, it was made for King **Edward I** (爱德华一世, 1239–1307) to enclose the famous **Stone of Scone** (加冕石), which he brought from Scotland to the Abbey in 1296. Edward I was one of this country's great warrior kings who **reigned** (统治) from 1272 to 1307. During his reign Edward was determined to bring the Crown of Scotland under English control. In order to achieve this goal, he fought a long and constant battle to conquer the Scots. In 1296, Edward managed to take possession of the Scottish Crown's **regalia** (王权). He also captured and brought to England the **Scottish Stone of Destiny** (苏格兰命运石), also known as the Stone of Scone, over which Scotland's Kings had been crowned for many centuries. You may ask where the Stone of Scone is. The stone beneath the seat was returned to **Edinburgh** (爱丁堡) in 1996. So the Coronation Chair stands empty now after 700 years.

Here we're in the famous **Henry VII Chapel** (亨利七世礼拜堂). The construction began in 1503 at the expense of Henry VII (亨利七世, 1457–1509). It's the last great masterpiece of English medieval architecture. It's separated from the rest of the Abbey by brass gates and a flight of stairs. The Henry VII Chapel is best known for its **fan vault** (扇形拱顶). That's truly **breathtaking** (非凡的). Around the walls are 95 statues of saints. This is the largest surviving collection of figure sculptures from early **Tudor England** (英国都铎王朝). Behind the altar is the tomb of Henry VII and

his queen **Elizabeth of York (约克的伊丽莎白)**.

Well, here's **Poets' Corner** (诗人之角), a place which literature lovers would never miss. Over 100 poets and writers are buried or have memorials here. Many like William Shakespeare, Geoffrey Chaucer, Jane Austen, the Bronte sisters and Charles Dickens are famous worldwide. Actually, it was not originally designated as the burial place of writers, playwrights and poets. The first poet

Geoffrey Chaucer (1343–1400) was laid to rest in Westminster Abbey because he had been **Clerk of Works** (工程监督) to the Palace of Westminster, not because he had written *the Canterbury Tales* (《坎特伯雷故事集》). Over 150 years later, during the flowering of English literature in the 16th century, a more magnificent tomb was erected for Chaucer and in 1599, **Edmund Spenser** (埃德蒙·斯宾塞, 1552–1599) was laid to rest nearby. These two tombs created a tradition which developed over the following centuries. Please take a look around…

Monologue 2: The Louvre

Situation: *A tour guide is introducing the Louvre to the tourists. Located in Paris, the Louvre is a national museum of France and the world's most visited museum.*

Questions for comprehension and discussion:
★ What are three priceless masterpieces in Louvre?
★ Why is the *Mona Lisa* so well-known?

Hello, everyone, we're now on the way to the Louvre. The Louvre, originally a royal palace but now the world renown museum, is a must-see for anyone with some interest in art. Located on the right (north) bank of the **Seine** (塞纳河), the Louvre is unquestionably one of the greatest museums in the world and is home to thousands of classic and modern masterpieces. Nearly 35,000 objects created from the 6th BC to the 19th century are exhibited over an area of 60,600 square meters. No visitor should miss the three treasures: the *Mona Lisa* (《蒙娜丽莎》), the *Venus de Milo* (《米洛的维纳斯》), and the *Winged Victory of Samothrace* (《萨莫

色雷斯的胜利女神》).

However, the Louvre has gone through several different phases throughout the history. It began as a fortress built in the late 12th century under **Philip II** (菲利普二世，1165–1223). In 1546, **Francis I** (弗朗西斯一世，1494–1547) had the whole site renovated into the French Renaissance style one can see today. In 1682, the palace was **vacated** (腾空) by **Louis XIV**(路易十四，1638–1715) who decided to move to the **Versailles Palace** (凡尔赛宫), and in the succeeding century it was converted into a museum. It was opened to the public in 1793 with an exhibition of 537 paintings. Hence the modern Louvre we can see now.

Here we're at the entrance of the Louvre Museum. Please take a look at the magnificent glass pyramid. It's not only the most recent addition to the Louvre but also another main feature of the Louvre. It was built in 1989 by the noted Chinese-born American architect **Ieoh Ming Pei** (贝聿铭). The modern addition originally received mixed reviews, as it contrasts sharply with the classical design of the surrounding buildings. But today it's generally accepted as a clever solution as it creates a new entrance to the Louvre without blocking the view of the main buildings thanks to its glass structure.

The Louvre is comprised of three wings — the **Richelieu** (黎塞留馆), the **Sully** (叙利馆), and the **Denon** (德农馆) — arranged like a horseshoe, with the Pyramid nestled outside in the middle. Each of these three wings has three floors above ground and one underground level. Since the Denon Wing is the most crowded of the three wings with the *Mona Lisa* being the biggest **crowd puller** (引人瞩目的), I'll first show you around the Denon Wing, and then you'll have free time for about two hours. And after that, we'll meet at the exit right in front of the Pyramid. Now we'll go to the first floor[①] to see the *Mona Lisa*. Well, this way, please.

Ladies and gentlemen, the painting in front of us is the renowned *Mona Lisa*. It's a 16th century portrait painted in oil by **Leonardo Da Vinci** (达·芬奇) during the **Renaissance** (文艺复兴) in Italy. And it's arguably the most famous painting in the world. It's probably also the best known example of **sfumato** (渲染法), a painting technique partly responsible for her **enigmatic** (迷人的) smile. The universal popularity of the *Mona Lisa* is undoubtedly due to her smile. Often described as enigmatic, her half-smile has puzzled people from **Sigmund Freud** (西格蒙德·弗洛伊德, 1856–1939) and **Harvard** (哈佛) professors to countless observers. But who was Mona Lisa? There has been much **speculation** (猜想) about it. The painting is thought to be a portrait of Lisa Gherardini, wife of a **Florentine** (佛罗伦萨的) cloth merchant. It's also been suggested the reason for her smile was that she was **pregnant** (怀孕的). But theories that the woman in the image could have been da Vinci's mother, lover or even a disguised self-portrait, have only added to the Mona Lisa's legend.

---

① 二楼，美国英语 second floor。

Now, here's the *Winged Victory of Samothrace*, another treasure in the museum. Also called the *Nike of Samothrace*, it's a 2nd century BC marble sculpture of the Greek goddess of Victory (Nike). As you can see, the *Winged Victory of Samothrace* shows a female figure standing on a base **resembling** (像) a ship. Standing over 18 feet high, it's made of a heavy block of **Parian marble** (帕罗斯岛产的白色大理石) and was excavated in 1863. Over time, the arms and head were lost or damaged, yet one hand has been recovered in pieces and partially reconstructed. Based on the position of that hand and what's known of the position of the arms, it's assumed that her right hand was raised to her mouth in a shout of victory. The head was never found.

Now we'll head to the Sully Wing for the charming Venus. This way, please…

Part B　Leisure Activities in Western Countries

Dialogue 1　Musical

Situation: *Linda is showing her Chinese friend Chen Rong around Broadway in Manhattan and they are going to see one of the most popular musicals.*

The Lion King | Girl From the North Country | The Phantom of the Opera | Come From Away

Moulin Rouge! The Musical | Tina: The Tina Turner Musical | Wicked | Hadestown

Questions for Comprehension and discussion:
★　What is the longest-running show in Broadway history?
★　Who is the phantom in *The Phantom of Opera*?
★　Why is the show romantic and scary?
★　What seat does Chen Rong choose?

> **Linda:** Broadway boasts many featured shows, it would be a pity for anyone interested in dramas to miss a classic musical experience when visiting Manhattan.
>
> **Chen Rong:** Bingo, that's what I'm thinking about. Since I have only one night left here in

Manhattan, which one do you recommend?

Linda: Well, it depends. Dozens of featured musicals are on in various theatres here every day such as **The Lion King, The Phantom of Opera** (《歌剧魅影》), **Moulin Rouge** (《红磨坊》), **Chicago** (《芝加哥》), **Wicked** (《恶毒》), **Hamilton** (《汉密尔顿》), etc. Personally, I love *The Phantom of Opera*. If this is the first time for you to see a Broadway musical, you shouldn't miss this **Broadway blockbuster** (百老汇火爆剧). It's the longest-running show in Broadway history since 1988 and is noted for its gorgeous music, romantic story and onstage talent.

Chen Rong: Really? I've heard of it before but have never imagined that I could see the show on Broadway. The name sounds quite horrible. It must take place in an opera house, right?

Linda: Yes, it's based on the 1910 horror novel by Gaston Leroux, and has been adapted into countless films. A deformed composer haunts the grand Paris Opera House. Sheltered from the outside world in an underground cavern, the lonely, romantic man tutors and composes operas for Christine who is a gorgeous young **soprano star-to-be** (即将成名的女高音).

Chen Rong: Well, the deformed composer must be the phantom of opera.

Linda: Exactly. He falls in love with Christine. However, Christine has a handsome **suitor** (追求者) from her past which makes the Phantom grow mad, so he terrorized the opera house owners and company with his murderous ways. Still, Christine finds herself drawn to the mystery man.

Chen Rong: Quite **intriguing** (引人入胜) and romantic, though a bit thrilling.

Linda: Yes, both romantic and scary, *The Phantom of the Opera* is definitely a thrilling night of theater with grand emotions. By the way, the show is also well-known for its beloved **signature song** (标志性歌曲) *The Music of the Night* as well as *Think of Me*.

Chen Rong: Ah, yes, I love *Think of Me*, it's very popular in China. Wow, I can't wait to see it. What time is it on?

Linda: Well, let's check it online right now.

Chen Rong: Ok. It's nearly 5:00 pm, I'd like sometime later than 7:00 pm so that I can have something to eat before seeing the play.

Linda: I see. Here's the Broadway's website. Let's find *The Phantom of Opera*. Ah, here it is. It's 8:00 pm. Does it suit you?

Chen Rong: Perfect. What's the price?

Linda: The cheapest price is $29, but all the seats for that price are already sold out. Now there are only few left. The price ranges from $70 in the **rear mezzanine** (夹层楼后排) to $249 in the **premium orchestra** (正厅前排居中座位). Which one do you prefer?

Chen Rong: I'm afraid the rear mezzanine is too far away from the stage, and it's not easy to see the show clearly.

Linda: How about the **front mezzanine** (夹层楼前排)? There are only two seats, one is $169 in C101 and the other is $125 in E18. I'm afraid you have to make a quick decision, otherwise they will sell very quickly.

Chen Rong: Well, then I'll take the $125 seat.

Linda: Ok, but just to remind you that you have to pay additional $47.50 for service and handling. I'm sorry it's a must. It's $172 altogether.

Chen Rong: That's alright. Can I pay by VISA?

Linda: Sure. By the way, you can choose the Box Office Pickup which means you can pick up the ticket at the venue box office 30 minutes before the show starts.

Chen Rong: Good. By the way, where is the theatre?

Linda: It's Majestic Theatre on 245 W 44th St, just two blocks from here. It was opened in 1927, the largest theatre of its day. Its interior and exterior were designated as a New York City landmark in 1987.

Chen Rong: Perfect. Well, let me buy the ticket online myself.

Linda: Ok, here's the website.

Chen Rong: Thank you very much.

Linda: My pleasure. Please enjoy yourself.

Chen Rong: Thank you, I will.

Dialogue 2   Golf

Situation: *The tour leader Li Fei is calling an American golf club to make a golf reservation for his group members.*

Questions for comprehension and discussion:

★ What's the name of the golf club?

★ How many days in advance can Li Fei make a reservation at this club?

★ What's the tea time reserved for Li Fei?

★ What are the costs of hiring shoes and clubs?

Clerk: Good morning. This is LPI International Golf Club. How may I help you?

Li Fei: Yes, please. I'd like to make a golf reservation.

Clerk: When would you like to play?

Li Fei: This Monday, if possible.

Clerk: I'm sorry. The reservation needs to be made at least four days in advance. So you can only make a reservation after Tuesday.

Li Fei: Well, how about 8 o'clock on Wednesday morning?

Clerk: I'm sorry. It has been reserved already.

Li Fei: What other time is available on Wednesday morning then?

Clerk: Will 11:00 am be okay for you?

Li Fei: Yes, that'll be fine.

Clerk: How many people do you have, please?

Li Fei: Five in all.

Clerk: May I have your membership number, please?

Li Fei: The number is 555587.

Clerk: All right. It's done now. Your **tee time** (开球时间) is 11:00 am on Wednesday.

Li Fei: Thank you. By the way, we need **clubs** (高尔夫棒) and ten pairs of **plimsolls** (胶底帆布鞋). Could you please tell me where to get them?

Clerk: Shoes can be rented in the changing room for 16 dollars per pair, including a new pair of socks. And clubs can be rented from the **caddy master** (球童管理员) for $7 per round or $10 per day.

Li Fei: I see. And do you have any **caddies** (球童) who can speak Chinese?

Clerk: Yes, I think so. There's a Chinese caddy.

Li Fei: Great. Thanks a lot.

Part C　Tips on Being a Responsible Tourist

Questions for comprehension and discussion:

★ Brainstorm any tips on how to be a responsible tourist.

★ Why is it important to be a responsible tourist?

★ Do you know anything about tourists' bad behavior abroad?

Traveling to a foreign country can broaden our horizon and enrich our life experiences. When we do sightseeing, it's natural to expect our holidays to be memorable and be in line with ideas of ecotourism. However, some tourists have been criticized for their improper behavior. Although it has been reported that tourists have improved their manners in the past five years in the foreign countries, bad behavior including spitting, littering, cutting in line, talking loudly can still be seen somewhere.

Therefore, it's still necessary for us to know some tips on how to behave well in the tourist destinations or simply in the public.

☆ Don't litter in the public places. It's definitely ill-mannered to drop litter everywhere. Nowadays garbage classification has been strongly advocated throughout China as well as other countries, and people are getting used to classifying their garbage. However, we should always keep in mind that we should throw our wastes into the **appropriate** (恰当的) trash bins wherever we are.

☆ Don't spit in public. Spitting is very disgusting. The casual spraying of **saliva** (口水) can spread **germs or bacteria** (细菌) to people around you. If you really need to spit, do it into a handkerchief or a tissue, then throw into the trash bin nearby.

☆ Don't cut in line. It's very rude to jump queue and it's frustrating to anyone else waiting in line. Whether at an airport check-in counter, in a line at a box office, or in a restaurant, you should always remember to queue up.

☆ Don't talk too loud. Talking loudly and making noise are considered annoying and disturbing in public places in western countries. However, in China, people tend to speak with increased volume when they want to make a point or simply show friendship. Therefore, many tourists or guests are often seen talking in a loud voice either in a restaurant, hotel or office, yet they may not be aware that they are making noise which may bother other people around. So when traveling abroad, you'd better keep your voice low when talking to someone else and don't make so much noise that you disturb others.

☆ Don't smoke in non-smoking areas. Smoking is widely banned by law in non-smoking areas in public places such as shopping malls, airports, train stations, hospitals, schools as well as all other workplaces. If you really want to smoke, try to find a **designated** (指定的) area.

☆ **Observe** (遵守) the "Ladies First" rule. Ladies enjoy **priority** over gentlemen in the West. For example, a gentleman is supposed to open the door for a lady, and then walk after the lady, but he has to choose the table and help the lady sit down. While in China, the senior person or the guest receives more respect. So, when in Rome, do as the Romans.

☆ Don't remove shoes and socks in public. Some tourists often take off their shoes and socks in the tourist areas for a good rest after a long walk or to cool themselves off in hot weather. However, such behavior in public is regarded as inappropriate in the west. So please keep your shoes on whenever you travel, even if you feel exhausted after a long walk.

☆ Don't blow your nose in public. Blowing one's nose in public is considered rather **offensive** (无礼的). If you have **a sniffle** (鼻塞), it's better excusing yourself and blowing your nose in a rest room.

☆ Don't take pictures when it's not allowed. You can see a sign with a **pictogram** (象形图) of a camera with a red line across it when visiting a library, museum, a church, or other premises, it means "No Photography". So when you see this sign, just stop taking pictures. If in doubt, please ask for **clarification** (说明). What's more, try to avoid taking pictures of other people without asking for permission.

☆ Don't wear pajamas (睡衣裤) in public. In China, some people can be seen in pajamas while walking in the neighborhood or even in the street. However, it's quite embarrassing and **disconcerting** (令人尴尬) to see people wearing such clothes in public places. Such clothing is only to be worn in private. Remember to dress properly when leaving home or hotel.

☆ Flush the toilet after use. Avoid messing the toilet seat and clean it properly after use.

This is simply a courtesy for the next guest after you.

☆ Don't polish your shoes with the **bed sheet** (床单) or a bath towel in a hotel room. Take care of hotel property as if it were your own. If hotel property is damaged, the guest may well have to pay for the damage.

☆ Don't take the commodities from a hotel room. The only things you can take away are the complimentary bottles of water as well as the "**disposables** (一次性用品) " offered to make your stay more convenient, such as shampoo, soap, sometimes bath slippers. But you're not supposed to help yourself to the other things such as hotel towels, ash tray, bath robes and so on. If you really want these items, call the hotel reception and make a request to purchase them.

☆ Eat quietly at a restaurant. **Slurping** (发出声响) the soup and **burping** (打饱嗝) after eating are considered disgusting in the west. Remember to avoid such actions when having dinner in a restaurant abroad.

☆ Don't waste your food at a **buffet** (自助餐). Take a moderate amount of food for a normal serving so that food is not wasted. If you want to eat more, you are welcome to make a second, or a third round to the buffet. You can go as often as you wish. Returning to the buffet often is considered to be very polite, as opposed to piling up your plate on the first round.

Part D   Language Checklist

A. Tourist Attractions

Tourist Attractions	中 文 名	国　　家
Niagara Falls	尼亚加拉大瀑布	美国
Yellowstone National Park	黄石国家公园	美国
Statue of Liberty	自由女神像	美国
Times Square	时代广场	美国
World Trade Center	世界贸易中心	美国
Metropolitan Museum of Art	大都会艺术博物馆	美国
Big Ben	大本钟	英国
Buckingham Palace	白金汉宫	英国
Hyde Park	海德公园	英国
London Tower Bridge	伦敦塔桥	英国
Westminster Abbey	威斯敏斯特大教堂	英国
Cologne Cathedral (Kölner Dom)	科隆大教堂	德国
Notre Dame de Paris	巴黎圣母院	法国
Eiffel Tower	埃菲尔铁塔	法国
Arch of Triumph	凯旋门	法国
The Louvre	卢浮宫	法国

续表

Tourist Attractions	中 文 名	国　　家
Leaning Tower of Pisa	比萨斜塔	意大利
Colosseum	罗马圆形剧场	意大利
Sydney Opera House	悉尼歌剧院	澳大利亚
Great Barrier Reef	大堡礁	澳大利亚
Pyramids	金字塔	埃及
Angkor Wat	吴哥窟	柬埔寨
Taj Mahal	泰姬陵	印度
Mount Fuji	富士山	日本

B. Vocabulary

Times Square 时代广场 Empire State Building 帝国大厦 Manhattan 曼哈顿	Statue of Liberty 自由女神 crown 王冠 spike 尖状物 Brooklyn Bridge 布鲁克林大桥	coronation 加冕礼 Coronation Chair 加冕椅 Scottish Stone of Destiny 苏格兰命运石 Stone of Scone 加冕石
Houses of Parliament 议会大厦 Henry VII Chapel 亨利七世礼拜堂 Gothic architecture 哥特式建筑 ribbed vault 肋架拱顶 Gothic vault 哥特式穹顶	Edward II 爱德华二世，1284-1327 Edward I 爱德华一世，1239-1307 Henry III 亨利三世，1207-1272 Edward V 爱德华五世，1470-1483 Henry VII 亨利七世，1457-1509 Edward VIII 爱德华八世，1894-1972 Tudor England 英国都铎王朝	Poet's Corner 诗人之角 Geoffrey Chaucer 杰弗里·乔叟 William Shakespeare 威廉·莎士比亚 Charles Dickens 查尔斯·狄更斯 Edmund Spenser 埃德蒙·斯宾塞 The Canterbury Tales《坎特伯雷故事》
the Richelieu Wing 黎塞留馆 the Sully Wing 叙利馆 the Denon Wing 德农馆	Philip II 菲利普二世，1165-1223 Francis I 弗朗西斯一世，1494-1547 Louis XIV 路易十四，1638-1715	Mona Lisa《蒙娜丽莎》 Venus de Milo《米洛的维纳斯》 Winged Victory of Samothrace《萨莫色雷斯的胜利女神》 sfumato 渲染层次
orchestra/stalls 正厅 premium orchestra 正厅前排居中 mezzanine 最低夹层楼 balcony 楼座	The Phantom of Opera《歌剧魅影》 Moulin Rouge《红磨坊》 Chicago《芝加哥》 Wicked《恶毒》 Hamilton《汉密尔顿》	musical 音乐剧 Broadway blockbuster 百老汇火爆剧 soprano star-to-be 即将成名的女高音
clubs 球杆 caddy 球童 caddy master 球童主管 tee time 开球时间	litter 扔垃圾 spit 吐痰 burp 打饱嗝 slurp 出声 cut in line 插队	pajamas 睡衣裤 disposables 一次性用品 offensive 无礼的 disgusting 令人恶心的

C. Key Patterns

Check-in and Customs at the Airport 登机手续和机场海关	• Where is the check-in counter for British Airways? 请问英国航空公司的办理登机手续柜台在哪里？ • I'd like to check in. 我要办理登机手续。 • I'd like to have a window/aisle seat. 我想要一个靠窗/过道的座位。 • Will you assign us two seats together in a non-smoking section? 能给我们安排两个邻近的非吸烟区座位吗？ • Alcoholic drinks cannot be checked in. 酒类不能托运。 • Is my luggage overweight? 我的行李超重了吗？ • What's the weight allowed for each passenger? 每位乘客的行李重量限制是多少？ • How much does it cost for overweight luggage? 超重行李的费用是多少？ • I'd like to apply for/claim a tax refund. 我要办理退税。 • Here's the tax refund form, my ticket and boarding pass. 这是我的退税单、机票和登机牌。 • How long does it take to get the tax refund? 请问多久能够收到退税呢？
Cultural Landscape 人文景观	• The Louvre comprises three wings — the Richelieu (黎塞留馆), the Sully (叙利馆), and the Denon (德农馆) — arranged like a horseshoe, with the Pyramid nestled outside in the middle. • It's probably also the best known example of sfumato (渲染法), a painting technique partly responsible for her enigmatic (迷人的) smile. 这也许是用渲染法绘画的一个最为著名的例子，达·芬奇就是用这种绘画技巧展示她的迷人微笑。 • The Louvre is unquestionably one of the greatest museums in the world and is home to thousands of classic and modern masterpieces. 毫无疑问，卢浮宫是世界上最伟大的博物馆之一，拥有成千上万件经典作品和现代杰作。 • Nearly 35,000 objects created from the 6th BC to the 19th century are exhibited over an area of 60,600 square meters. 从公元前 6 世纪到 19 世纪以来搜集的近 35,000 件艺术品陈列在 60,600 平方米的展区里。 • *The Winged Victory of Samothrace* shows a female figure standing on a base resembling (像) a ship. 《萨莫色雷斯的胜利女神》展示了一位站立在像一艘船头上的女性。 • The British Museum is a museum of human history and culture in London. Its collections, more than seven million objects, are amongst the largest and most comprehensive in the world and originate from all continents, illustrating and documenting the story of human culture from its beginnings to the present. 大英博物馆位于伦敦，是人类历史和文化的宝库。该馆拥有来自世界各大洲的七百多万件文物，是世界上规模最大、藏品最丰富的博物馆之一，也是一部阐明和记载由始至今的人类文化的简史。 • Highlights include the Rosetta Stone (罗塞塔石碑), the Parthenon sculptures (帕特农神庙石雕), and the mummies in the Ancient Egypt collection. • Opened in 1973, Sydney Opera House is situated in Sydney Harbor at Bennelong Point. 悉尼歌剧院于 1973 年开放，地处悉尼港的本纳隆角。 • The Sydney Opera House is one of the most famous buildings in the world. It's considered to be one of the most recognizable images of the modern world although the building has been open for only about 30 years. The Sydney Opera House is as representative of Australia as the pyramids are of Egypt. 悉尼歌剧院是世界上最著名的建筑之一。虽然这项建筑只开放了三十年，但是它被公认为世界上最与众不同的现代建筑。悉尼歌剧院是澳大利亚的象征，就像金字塔是埃及的象征一样。 • The Louvre is now the largest museum in Paris and possesses one of the richest and most impressive art collections in the world. • The Louvre possesses a huge collection of 455,000 works of art, 35,000 of which are on display to the public, ranging from the Middle Ages to 1848.

Natural Landscape 自然景观	• The Great Lakes are the greatest wonder of Middle America. It is the largest group of lakes in the world and the biggest body of fresh water. 五大湖是美国中部最伟大的自然奇观，是世界上最大的湖群，也是世界上最大的淡水水系。 • Located in Arizona, Grand Canyon National Park encompasses 277 miles (446km) of the Colorado River adjacent uplands. • The Niagara Falls (尼亚加拉瀑布) is 180 feet high and 2,500 feet wide. The depth of the Niagara Falls is 180 feet. Water rushing over the Niagara Falls comes from four of the five Great Lakes.
Leisure activities 休闲活动	• Broadway boasts many shows. 百老汇有很多表演。 • Dozens of featured musicals are on in various theatres here every day such as *The Lion King, The Phantom of Opera* (《歌剧魅影》), *Moulin Rouge* (《红磨坊》), *Chicago* (《芝加哥》), *Wicked* (《恶毒》), *Hamilton* (《汉密尔顿》), etc. • It's been the longest-running show in Broadway history since 1988. • It's based on the 1910 horror novel by Gaston Leroux (加斯东·勒鲁), and has been adapted into countless films. • The price ranges from $70 in the rear mezzanine (夹层楼后排) to $249 in the premium orchestra (正厅前排居中座位). • You can choose the Box Office Pickup which means you can pick up the ticket at the venue box office 30 minutes ahead of the start of the show. • Your tee time (开球时间) is 11·00 on Wednesday. • The goal of golf is to get the ball into the hole with as few hits as possible. 打高尔夫球的目的是尽量用最少的杆数把球打进洞。
Dos and Don'ts in Traveling 旅游中的行为准则	• Don't litter in public places. • Don't spit in public places. • Don't talk loudly. • Don't smoke in non-smoking areas. • Don't remove shoes and socks in public. • Don't blow your nose in public. • Don't take pictures when a sign says "No Photography." • Don't polish your shoes with bed linen (床单) or hotel towel. • Don't wear pajamas on the street. • Observe (遵守) the "ladies first" rule. • Don't cut in line. • Don't waste food at a buffet.

Part E　English in Use

I. Reading Comprehension

Task 1: Choose the best answer to complete each sentence below.

1. At the Poet's Corner, you can see graves and memorials to Geoffrey Chaucer, William Shakespeare and _____.

   A. Charles Dickens　　B. Mark Twain　　　C. Francis Bacon　　　D. Alexandre Dumas

2. New York continues to be one of the top tourist _____ in the world.

   A. destinations　　　B. constitutions　　　C. conservations　　　D. information

3. The Eiffel Tower is _____ close to the Seine River in Paris.

    A. situates   B. situated   C. be situated   D. lies

4. In 1078, King William began to build a large stone building _____ the north bank of the Thames River and named it the Tower of London.

    A. on   B. in   C. at   D. down

5. The British Museum is home to some of the world's finest and broadest _____.

    A. places   B. structures   C. materials   D. collections

6. The Louvre Museum is located on the right bank of the _____.

    A. Danube   B. Rhine   C. Seine   D. Volga

7. The three most popular pieces here are *Mona Lisa*, the *Venus de Milo* and _____.

    A. *Winged Victory of Samothrace*   B. *Rosetta Stone*

    C. *Elgin Marbles*   D. *Night Watch*

8. The Louvre was opened to the public in _____ with an exhibition of 537 paintings.

    A. 1791   B. 1792   C. 1793   D. 1794

9. Established in 1949, this museum holds a variety of articles _____ from pre-historic era to modern works of art.

    A. ranging   B. moving   C. changing   D. falling

10. *Mona Lisa* is in _____ Wing in the Louvre Museum.

    A. Sully   B. Chartres   C. Richelieu   D. Denon

Task 2: Answer the following questions concerning the passage in Part A and Part B.

1. What's the purpose of making the Coronation Chair?
2. Why is the glass pyramid generally accepted as a clever solution today?
3. What are three treasures in the Louvre Museum?
4. What painting technique is used in illustrating *Mona Lisa*?
5. What's the *Winged Victory of Samothrace* also called?

Task 3: Decide whether each of the following statements is True or False according to the passage in Part C.

1. Many Chinese are said to be the world's worst tourists now. (   )
2. It is advisable for a person to spit into a handkerchief when he really needs to spit. (   )
3. You can take pictures without asking for permission. (   )
4. If you really need the ash tray in the hotel room, you can take it away with you without informing the hotel. (   )
5. It's not proper to talk loudly and disturb others in a restaurant. (   )

II. Translation

Task 4: Translate the following sentences into English.

1. 请问法国航空公司（Air France）的办理登机手续柜台在哪里？
2. 我的行李超重了吗？
3. 我想要一个靠窗的座位。
4. 这是我的退税单、机票和登机牌。

5. 价格从夹层楼后排座位价 49 美元到正厅前排正中座位价 259 美元不等。

6. 威斯敏斯特教堂是全伦敦最古老的建筑之一。它是传统上英国君主举办加冕礼和丧葬的地方。

7. 毫无疑问，卢浮宫是世界上最伟大的博物馆之一，拥有成千上万件经典作品和现代杰作。

8. 你可以选择到售票处取票，这样你就可以在戏开演前三十分到定点售票处拿到座位票。

9. 《歌剧魅影》是自 1988 年以来在百老汇上演历史最长的一出戏。

10. 周二上午还有哪个时间段可以预约？

Task 5: Translate the following sentences into Chinese.

1. The Louvre Museum possesses a huge collection of 455,000 works of art, 35,000 of which are on display to the public, ranging from the Middle Ages to 1848.

2. The Louvre Museum is now the largest museum in Paris and possesses one of the richest and most impressive art collections in the world.

3. The crown of Lady Liberty has seven spikes, symbolizing the Seven Seas and Seven Continents of the world across which liberty should be spread.

4. Most people think Big Ben is the huge clock tower at the House of Parliament but actually it refers to the bell hung inside the clock tower.

5. This is the famous Coronation Chair. It was first used at the coronation of King Edward II in 1308, and since then it has been used for the coronations of all but three of our Kings and Queens.

6. Here's Poets' Corner, a place which literature lovers would never miss.

7. Standing in the heart of London opposite the Houses of Parliament and overlooking the Thames River, Westminster Abbey is a Gothic monastery church and is one of the most prolific attractions in Britain.

8. The Denon Wing is the most crowded of the three wings with the *Mona Lisa* being the biggest crowd puller.

9. *The Phantom of the Opera* is based on the 1910 horror novel by Gaston Leroux (加斯东·勒鲁), and has been adapted into countless films.

10. Standing over 18 feet high, the *Winged Victory of Samothrace* is made of a heavy block of Parian marble (帕罗斯岛的白色大理石) and was excavated in 1863.

III. Role Play

Task 6: Play a role in any of the following situations with your partner(s).

Situation 1: You're a tour leader for a group of elderly Chinese people who are visiting New York. On behalf of your group members, have a discussion with your local American guide as to what you want to visit and tell the guide any of your interests and requirement.

Situation 2: You're a new outbound tour leader. You're taking a group of Chinese tourists to France. Now you and your group are visiting the Louvre. Show your interests and make a dialogue with the local guide who is introducing the museum by asking some questions.

Situation 3: You and your family are visiting Westminster Abbey in London. Make a dialogue with your local English guide and ask any questions while walking around the Abbey.

Situation 4: You work as a tour leader for a group of Chinese tourists. Now you and your Chinese group are going to see a musical play in London. Your local English guide is introducing the play to you. Make a dialogue with the guide by asking any questions you want to know.

Situation 5: Your business partner in any of the foreign countries in the world is showing you around the local scenic spots. Show your interests and make a dialogue with him or her by asking any questions you don't know.

IV. Problem-solving

Task 7: Make an analysis of the following cases, and answer the questions as required.

Case 1

Situation: You work for a China Travel Service as a tour leader. Now you and your Chinese group are in London. You're going to visit Cambridge University tomorrow, but all your group members want to visit Oxford University too which is unfortunately not included in the itinerary.

Question: What would you do then?

Case 2

Situation: Li Xia, an outbound tour leader, is leading her tour members to travel in England. One day, she takes them to a local restaurant. They really enjoy their time there and start to talk and laugh quite loudly. Then the manager of this restaurant comes to tell her that other guests are complaining about the noise.

Question: Suppose you were Li Xia, what would you do then?

Reference

[1] Acupuncture [EB/OL]. Traditional Chinese Medicine Information Page [2012-06-12]. http://www.tcmpage.com/acupuncture.html.

[2] Ancient City of Pingyao [EB/OL]. UNESCO [2012-05-20]. http://whc.unesco.org/en/list/812.

[3] Bilbow, Grahame T. & Sutton, John. 朗文现代酒店业英语 [M]. 管燕红，译. 北京：外语教学与研究出版社，2005.

[4] Chinese Opera [EB/OL].Travel China Guide [2011-10-20]. http://www.travelchinaguide.com/intro/arts/chinese-opera.htm.

[5] Chinese Painting and Calligraphy [EB/OL]. Top China Travel [2013-07-05]. http://www.topchinatravel. com/china-guide/chinese calligraphy-painting/.

[6] Classical Gardens of Suzhou [EB/OL]. UNESCO [2012-08-22]. http://whc.unesco.org/en/list/813.

[7] Donald Bedford, Deh-Ta Hsiung, Christopher Knowles. Eyewitness Travel Guides: China [M]. London: Dorling Kindersley Limited, 2005.

[8] Doug Kennedy. Train Your Hospitality Team To Say "YES!" To Guest Complaints [EB/OL]. Hotel, Travel & Hospitality News, (2010-06-03) [2020-05-15]. https://www.hospitalitynet.org/opinion/4046848.html.

[9] Erika Strum. Top 10 Unspoken Rules of Restaurant Service Etiquette [EB/OL]. The Wine Enthusiast, (2010-02-20) [2020-05-10]. https://www.linkedin.com/pulse/top-10-unspoken-rules-restaurant-service-etiquette-mir-niaz-morshed.

[10] Imperial Palaces of the Ming and Qing Dynasties in Beijing and Shenyang [EB/OL]. UNESCO [2013-09-23]. http://whc.unesco.org/en/list/439.

[11] Letitia Baldrige. Letitia Bladrige's New Manners for New Times [M]. New York: Scribner, 2003.

[12] Masterpieces, Accessible Visitor Trail [EB/OL]. Louvre. http://www.louvre.fr/en/routes/master pieces-0.

[13] Mausoleum of the First Qin Emperor [EB/OL]. UNESCO [2013-07-13]. http://whc.unesco.org/en/list/441.

[14] Mogao Caves [EB/OL]. UNESCO [2012-11-12]. http://whc.unesco.org/en/list/440.

[15] Monique Van Dijk, Alexandra Moss. Hangzhou [M]. Beijing: Atomic Energy Press, 2006.

[16] Palace of Westminster and Westminster Abbey including Saint Margaret's Church [EB/OL]. UNESCO [2013-05-12]. http://whc.unesco.org/en/list/426.

[17] Peggy Post. Entertaining-A Classic Guide to Adding Elegance and Ease to Any Festive Occasion [M]. New York: Harper Collins Publishers Inc., 1998.

[18] Summer Palace, an Imperial Garden in Beijing [EB/OL]. UNESCO [2012-10-18].

http://whc. unesco.org/en/list/880.

[19] Temple and Cemetery of Confucius and the Kong Family Mansion in Qufu [EB/OL]. UNESCO [2013-06-21]. http://whc.unesco.org/en/list/704.

[20] The Palace Museum [EB/OL]. http://www.dpm.org.cn.

[21] West Lake Cultural Landscape of Hangzhou [EB/OL]. UNESCO [2012-05-13]. http:// whc. unesco. org/en/list/1334.

[22] World Heritage List [EB/OL]. UNESCO [2012-05-12]. http://whc.unesco.org/en/list/.

[23] 北京市人民政府外事办公室，北京市民讲外语活动组委会办公室. 美食译苑：中文菜单英文译法 [M]. 北京：世界知识出版社，2011.

[24] 陈刚. Greater Hangzhou A New Travel Guide（大杭州旅游新指南）[M]. 杭州：浙江摄影出版社，2001.

[25] 中华人民共和国国家旅游局. 走遍中国：中国优秀导游词精选（综合篇）[M]. 第 2 版. 北京：中国旅游出版社，1998.

[26] 李虹，诸葛锦花，龚勤芳. 杭州之旅 [M]. 杭州：杭州出版社，2009.